Malcolm X
VISITS ABROAD

Malcolm X VISITS ABROAD
APRIL 1964 – FEBRUARY 1965

Marika Sherwood

Malcolm X: Visits Abroad (April 1964 – February 1965)
Copyright © 2011 by Marika Sherwood. All rights reserved.

Apart from any fair dealing for the purpose of private study, research, criticism or review, as permitted under the Copyright Act, no part of this publication may be reproduced in any form, stored in a retrieval system or transmitted in any form by any means—electronic, mechanical, photocopy, recording or otherwise—without the prior permission of the publisher. Enquiries should be sent to the undermentioned address.

Tsehai books may be purchased for educational, business, or sales promotional use. For more information, please contact our special sales department.

Tsehai Publishers
P. O. Box: 1881
Hollywood, CA 90078

www.tsehaipublishers.com
info@tsehaipublishers.com

ISBN: 978-1-59907-050-6

First Edition in the United States: May 2011

Publisher: Elias Wondimu
Typesetting: Tessa Smith and Yoseph Gezahegne
Cover Design: Endrias Zewde (www.endriasdesign.com)

Library of Congress Catalog Card Number
A catalog record for this book is available from the Library of Congress.

British Library Cataloguing in Publication Data
A catalogue record for this book is available from the British Library.

10 9 8 7 6 5 4 3 2 1

Printed in the United States of America

for
André Elizée
who died suddenly and unexpectedly in January 2010
with my thanks for his invaluable help over many years
of research at the Schomburg Center

CONTENTS

Introduction 1
Timeline 5
Preface 7

1. Mecca, Beirut and Cairo, April — May 1964 15
2. Nigeria and Ghana, May 1964 (stop-overs in Monrovia, Dakar, Morocco, Algiers, May 17 — 21) 25
3. New York, The founding of the OAAU (May — June 1964) 65
4. London, Cairo and Further East (July — September 1964) 69
5. Kenya, Tanganyika, Zanzibar, Addis Ababa (October 1964) 97
6. Nigeria, Ghana, Liberia, Guinea, Algiers, Geneva and Paris (October — November 1964) 121
7. London and Paris, 22 — 24 November 1964 139
8. New York, 24 — 30 November 1964 147
9. England, 1 — 6 December 1964 149
10. USA, December 1964 — February 1965 173
11. Britain and Paris, February 1965 183
12. The Return 207
13. The post-mortems 209

Conclusion 227
Bibliography 229
Acknowledgements 233
Index 235

INTRODUCTION

Malcolm Little was born in 1925 in Nebraska; his mother was of part-Scottish heritage from Grenada; his father was African-American. Both parents were followers of Marcus Garvey and his father was an outspoken Baptist Minister. The family had to move many times because of threats by local Klansmen and other racists. In 1931 Mr Little died – or as many claim – was murdered by White supremacists in Lansing, Michigan where the family then lived. Mrs Little could not cope with his death and ongoing threats: she was moved to a mental hospital and the children were sent to separate foster homes or orphanages.

Though a good student, Malcolm also 'deteriorated', becoming a petty criminal, gambler and drug-pusher. He was arrested and imprisoned in 1946. While in prison he read voraciously and joined the Nation of Islam (NOI). He decided to stop using his father's name, as one bequeathed by slave-owners; not knowing his ancestral African name, he replaced it with 'X'.

On his release from prison in 1952 he became a preacher for the Nation and attained fame for his ability to attract converts and for his growing eloquence as a speaker. He was soon put in charge of mosques – his magnetism drew in many converts. It could probably be safely argued that it was through Malcolm that the NOI became a nationwide mass movement. By 1957 Malcolm was the National Representative of Elijah Muhammad, the founder of the NOI.[1] He was soon speaking from many pulpits, giving lectures at universities and appearing on radio and television programs, espousing the Nation's belief that the only solution to the racial 'problems' in the USA was the total separation of the races. After all, in America 'Negroes' were living in the hell created by the 'white devils' who had enslaved them. A very intelligent, quick-witted debater

---

1 There are innumerable books on the NOI. One of the earliest is C. Eric Lincoln, *The Black Muslims in America*, Boston: Beacon Press, 1961; a later one is Karl Evanzz, *The Messenger: the rise and fall off Elijah Muhammad*, New York: Pantheon Books, 1999; and most recent: Herbert Berg, *Elijah Muhammad and Islam*, NYU Press, 2009

and very articulate interviewee, Malcolm was always very careful to state that he was but a mere follower of Elijah Muhammad. He did not want to be seen as a rival.

Discusses the Koran at Semiramis Hotel

Malcolm continued his voracious reading, becoming better and better educated. He was now also meeting other Muslims, not NOI followers. When he began to doubt Elijah Muhammad's interpretation of the Koran he does not reveal in his *Autobiography*. However, his disappointment at his inability to persuade the NOI to engage in political action is well documented. We also know that his discovery of Muhammad's hidden mistresses and illegitimate children disturbed him deeply. Did Muhammad seize on his rival's statements[2] at the assassination of President Kennedy in 1963, to punish Malcolm? Muhammad 'silenced' Malcolm for 90 days.

But Malcolm did not wait out the 90 days. On 8 March 1964 he announced that he had broken with the Nation of Islam. Four days later he held a formal press conference to announce that he had formed the Muslim Mosque Incorporated, which, according to the *New York Times* (13/3/1964, p.20), was 'a broadly based politically oriented black nationalist movement for Negroes only, financed by voluntary contributions.'[3] The *National Guardian*, a New York weekly, reported that at the press conference Malcolm did not 'rule out acceptance of possible communist support'. (21/3/1964, p.4) Malcolm called for all civil rights groups to band together to fight police brutality. His Mosque would have a 'religious base broad enough to allow for whatever action is necessary to solve the problems of our people, mentally, economically, politically, etc.'

Malcolm then assembled what Peter Goldman calls a 'brain trust of writers, academics, politicians, students, celebrities, professional people, Old Muslims and budding revolutionaries and put them to work devising a [political] organisation and a program'.[4] The result was the Organisation

---

2 Malcolm described the assassination as a case of 'chickens coming home to roost...The Muslim leader cited the murders of Patrice Lumumba, Congo leader, of Medgar Evers, civil rights leader, and of the Negro girls bombed earlier this year in a Birmingham church.' (*New York Times*, 2/12/63, p. 21) The NOI had sent condolences to the Kennedy family.

3 The text of his statement is available in Breitman (1966), pp.18-22.

4 Goldman (1982), pp.189-190. This is the most 'definitive' biography of Malcolm. *The*

of Afro-American Unity (OAAU), chaired by Malcolm; the OAAU's Basic Aims and Objectives and its Program were made public on 28 June 1964.[5]

Interestingly, on 8 April Malcolm had given his first address to the socialist Militant Labor Forum.

But before embarking on putting policies into practice, Malcolm wanted to go on pilgrimage to Mecca. With money borrowed from his sister, on 13 April 1964 he set out to perform the *Hajj*. He expected to be away for three weeks, but did not return until 21 May. Was it the contacts he had made while on the *Hajj* that resulted in his first trip to Africa south of the Sahara, or could some prior arrangements have been made before he left the USA?

It seems to me that Malcolm realised that he had much to learn in Africa, and perhaps even in Britain and France. He began to question the generally accepted American perspectives, philosophies and politics. Tragically this highly gifted, truly exceptional man was assassinated before he could fully formulate his own philosophies and begin to put them into practice. He was – he is – a great loss to us all. We have much to learn from his new analyses. Much of what he said in those brief, hectic months is relevant to the world we inhabit today.

Autobiography of Malcolm X was edited by Alex Haley and published in 1964.
5 Breitman (1968), pp.105-124.

TIMELINE

1925 Malcolm Little was born in 1925 in Nebraska; his mother was of part-Scottish heritage from Grenada; his father was African-American. Both parents were followers of Marcus Garvey and his father was an outspoken Baptist Minister. The family had to move many times because of threats by local Klansmen and other racists.

1931 Mr Little died – or as many claim – was murdered by White supremacists in Lansing, Michigan where the family then lived.

1939 After suffering a nervous breakdown, Mrs. Little is committed to the State Mental Hospital; the children are sent to separate foster homes or orphanages.

1940 When Malcolm tells his teacher he wants to be a lawyer, she responds by telling him being a carpenter was more suitable for a 'nigger' – Malcolm leaves school.

1941 Moves to live with his half-sister Ella Collins in Boston, moves from one unskilled job to another.

1943 Moves to New York; becomes involved in various petty criminal activities.

1945 Imprisoned; reads voraciously; becomes a follower of Elijah Muhammad's version of Islam.

1952 Released early; goes to live in Detroit with Elijah Muhammad and joins his Nation of Islam (NOI). The NOI then has four temples and c. 400 members. He drops the 'slave name' of Little and adopts 'X'.

1953 In less than a year Malcolm's recruiting drive triples the membership of the NOI. He is appointed Assistant Minister in Detroit; then moved to set up a mosque in Boston and others along the North East Coast. He is very successful.

1954 Appointed chief minister in Harlem's Temple #7.

1954-5 Largely due to Malcolm's efforts, the NOI membership grows to 25 – 40,000.

1957	Malcolm's success in calming a vast, angry crowd in Harlem brings him to the attention of the media. (FBI surveillance, which began in 1953, escalates.)
1959	After a 1959 television broadcast in New York City about the Nation of Islam, *The Hate That Hate Produced*, Malcolm's popularity with the media increases.
	First trip to Africa to arrange a tour for Elijah Muhammad.
1960	Malcolm establishes *Muhammad Speaks*, a newspaper to promote the NOI message.
1961	Elijah Muhammad appoints Malcolm the NOI's National Representative. Malcolm's visibility escalates hugely, with innumerable television and radio interviews and lectures at universities.
1963	Malcolm describes President Kennedy's assassination as 'a case of chickens coming home to roost' – this referred to the ongoing lynchings/murders of African-Americans. There is a public outcry against this 'hate-mongering' 'Black supremacist' preacher.
	He confronts Elijah Muhammad about his adulteries and illegitimate children.
1964	Elijah Muhammad removes Malcolm from Mosque #7 and from his post as the NOI's National Representative; he is suspended 'indefinitely' from the NOI.
	He spends many months in Africa; receives instruction in Sunni Islam; speaks at an OAU meeting in Cairo. His pilgrimage to Mecca in April has a profound effect on him. Also visits Europe.
	Malcolm leaves the NOI and forms the Muslim Mosque Incorporated and the Organization of Afro-American Unity.
1965	Another visit to Britain; refused entry to France.
	'I believe we should protect ourselves by any means necessary when we are attacked by racists' stated Malcolm in an interview with the Young Socialist Alliance. (He was challenging the non-violence espoused by some African American leaders and allegations that he was espousing violence.[1])

21 February Malcolm X is murdered.

---

1. George Breitman (ed), *By Any Means Necessary*: speeches, interviews and a letter by Malcolm X, New York: Pathfinder Press 1970, p.160.

PREFACE

For me, Malcolm X was indeed the 'shining prince' described by Ossie Davis at Malcolm's funeral. A man of prodigious intellect, hugely charismatic yet very humble, he was also a man of great political and physical courage. For a man who knows that he is front-page news to announce that he is rethinking his philosophy and that he is not yet sure where he is heading, takes tremendous political courage. For a man whose life was constantly threatened not to renege on what had evoked such murderous intentions, takes both political and physical courage. Malcolm X was the most truthful of men, unafraid to proclaim his ever-evolving religious, political and social understanding of the ever-enlarging world he inhabited.

In the last year of his life Malcolm clearly wanted to establish new programs of political activity. His emerging anti-imperialist, anti-capitalist analyses and the beginnings of his plans of action were a direct challenge to the policies of the United States. These changes always provoked a question in my silent 'conversations' with Malcolm: What made you move away from the accepted American – even African American – vision of the world?

I first met Malcolm on television in the early 1960s, when I was a relatively young, innocent and ignorant young woman. He fascinated me. Entranced me. A marvellous speaker, with great presence, even on a small screen. And a man who was not afraid to articulate that, if the then ongoing civil rights marches did not succeed in bringing about equality, and if Blacks continued to be attacked by Whites, they had the right to employ 'any means necessary' to defend themselves and achieve their aims. 'You are right', I said. 'I agree.' I cried when he was murdered. As soon as it became available in Australia, where I was then living, I bought the *Autobiography* so I could learn more and attempt to understand why Malcolm was killed.

It was not till I moved to England that I found more books on Malcolm. And in my five years in New York, I found many more, and read them eagerly. I showed the film of Malcolm at the Oxford Union debate in the prison in Harlem where I was a volunteer, teaching literacy. After that we talked for many 'literacy' sessions, the prisoners and I, about Malcolm.

By then I had also done much reading about Africa as in London I had had many students from both East and West Africa. I now read much on the history of those of African descent in the USA. But it was only after my first visits to East and West Africa that I began to question the books on Malcolm: why were his trips to Africa so unreported, seemingly so uninteresting? To me, they began to seem absolutely crucial. To a westerner, Africa is mind-blowing. The many peoples, languages, cultures and histories. The courtesy, the measured, questioning welcome. The centuries of the catastrophe of the trade in enslaved women, men and children, followed by the ongoing devastations wrought by colonialism and imperialism. The immense struggle to create new nations, to find ways to combine the many peoples comprising these nations, to find a new politics that espoused equality, and freedom for all. To find a new unity.

Those trying to understand, to interpret the influence on Malcolm of seeing Muslims of all ethnicities making the *Hajj* ignore what I imagined to be equally revolutionary experiences in Africa. One day, I'll try to research that, I promised myself. Then maybe I'll be better able to imagine the many paths he might have chosen to follow. But should I do that? I, a Hungarian woman living in England? I put it aside.

Then came 9/11 and I returned to thinking about the USA and its role in the world. About the racism I had witnessed, or confronted when in the company of African American friends and colleagues while I lived in New York and in the prison in which I worked. And about American attitudes and ignorances, so amply demonstrated in my conversations about the then recent US invasion of Grenada. Almost everyone told me that this was justified, as Grenada was about to invade the US. But the total population of that island was about 85,000, while Manhattan alone had a population of about 1.5 million. Were these New Yorkers serious? Oh yes. I took to carrying a map of that small island around with me with statistics of its size and population.

Was it such attitudes that led to historians of Malcolm not investigating his long sojourns in Africa? Or his numerous visits to England? Surely Malcolm must have met people who interested him even there, or he would not have returned. Who were these people?

I decided that I would try to research Malcolm's travels. I had almost finished doing this when the news came of his daughter intending to sell his travel *Notebooks*, and other materials. Naturally, I postponed the work until I could read these. This proved to be a very moving experience. I kept asking him questions: how did you meet so-and-so? Why did you go to…?

What did you talk about with...? What did you think of...? Why did you not go to...? Did you try to meet...? But – the silence was profound.

This book is an account of Malcolm's travels, of his meetings, of his conversations, with an outline of the political situation in each of the countries he visited. It is an attempt to provide the information which may allow the formation of answers to questions I have been asking Malcolm for many years about the 'destination' he was prevented from reaching. Thus I have selected what seemed to me pertinent from his speeches and writings – these are most often taken from the books about Malcolm. Other sources of information are the voluminous CIA/FBI reports now available on the web, State Department files, newspaper articles and some memoirs.[1] I have quoted most extensively from Malcolm's *Notebooks,* now at the Schomburg Center in Harlem, New York.[2] I also interviewed some people who had known Malcolm during his travels. As I did not receive any funding for this research, it is limited, and I hope others will visit the countries, libraries, archives and contacts that I have not been able to reach.[3]

What I found does not answer the question: 'Malcolm, if you had had time to think it all through, what would your political philosophy have been?' But it does indicate that his experiences were profound, that he could have gone in what some would call very 'un-American' directions.

The US government did not take kindly to being challenged by anyone, most of all by a Black man – especially by one of the most charismatic men of the age. That the USA feared Malcolm and his influence abroad is demonstrated in the CIA/FBI papers. Though not all have been released, it is clear that Malcolm was kept under close surveillance, and that the US government officials in Africa attempted to minimise and counteract the importance of his meetings with Africans. This is demonstrated, for example, by the January 1965 visit of James Farmer of the Congress of Racial Equality to the many African countries visited by Malcolm. The Department of State informed its African embassies that the trip was sponsored by the 'American Negro Leadership Conference (ANLC) on Africa, [and that its] purpose is to attempt to present a "true picture of the progress of civil rights in America and to state the true aspirations of most American Negroes as compared with what has been said in Africa by Malcolm X and Cassius Clay"'. The 'usual courtesies' were to

---

1 There should have been material in the British government files, as Malcolm visited many newly independent ex-colonies and their heads of state; the old 'mother country' must have taken a keen interest in these visits, but no files are available, despite a thorough search and many requests for them.

2 Henceforth cited as *Notebooks.*

3 I should note here that I have been told that there is nothing in the OAU and Addis Ababa archives.

be extended, and Farmer was to be 'facilitated in making contact with government leaders, university students, media representatives and other influential groups'.[4] The ANLC was a subsidiary of the CIA-funded American Society for African Culture. (see chapter 7)

The State of the 1960s World

The early 1960s were turbulent, complex and fraught years. The Cold War between the Western powers (led by the USA) and the USSR was in full swing. Relations between the two major communist powers, China and the USSR, were in turmoil. The United States and the USSR and then China were in conflict over Korea, resulting in a war which ended in 1953, while a similar war for control of Vietnam was escalating. In Africa and the 'Middle East' more and more countries, often created by the occupying Western powers, were becoming independent and were facing many historic problems within their borders. The creation of Israel by Britain, with subsequent support by the USA, added to the tensions and seemingly inevitable wars.[5] The leaders of the new countries had to deal with competing ethnic groups, and with developing new political philosophies and associations. Setting up administrations was difficult, as during the colonial era administration workers (whether in government or private firms) had been prevented from holding any but the lowest clerical jobs. The struggle by the Western and communist powers for access, if not control, of raw materials in the ex-colonies was in full swing and the new leaders had to learn to balance and survive these competing forces.

To judge by Malcolm's statements and actions in 1964–1965 world events had a serious influence on him. Ghana had attained its independence in 1957 and was supporting the independence movements of those Africans still under the European yoke. In December 1963 Kenya became an independent nation after years of armed struggle by the Land and Freedom Army (the so-called Mau-Mau) to rid the country of the British overlords. In March 1962 Algeria, a French 'settler colony' since 1840, gained its independence after a much bloodier war than that in Kenya.

---

4 NARA: SOC 14-1 US: Dept of State 'airgram' 24 December 1964 to African embassies; Nairobi to 'Amembassy Kampala', 30/12/1964. (Please note dates are: day/month/year.)

5 There is an important reason to note the 'Suez Affair' resulting from (then) Colonel Nasser's nationalisation of the Suez Canal in 1956 and the hidden alliance between Israel, France and Britain. According to historian Hugh Thomas (*The Suez Affair* [1966], London: Penguin Books 1970)' 'the biggest mistake was to commit the country to war with what...must be seen as a deliberate deception of the people' (p.178); Parliament was told 'half-truths' (p.225) by 'mendacious' Ministers (171). Clearly one of the many forerunners of the supposed 'Weapons of Mass Destruction' propaganda that was used to justify the invasion of Iraq in 2003.

The Congo had won independence from Belgium in 1960, but, in order to keep the copper-rich province of Katanga under Western 'influence', Patrice Lumumba, the elected leader, was assassinated in 1961. Belgium and the USA were widely suspected of collusion in the murder. Malcolm had met Lumumba on his visit to the US in July 1960.[6]

The Background to Malcolm's Travels

Malcolm met many Africans in the USA, not only students at the various colleges where he lectured, but the ambassadors to the UN and their entourages. His first encounters with such dignitaries might have been at the April 1958 Nation of Islam conference to celebrate the Third Pakistan Republic Day, which was attended by Pakistani officials as well as the head of the Arab Information Center.[7] A few months later there was a conference between American Muslims and Muslim delegates to the UN, attended, for example, by representatives of Algeria's National Liberation Front and the Egyptian attaché to the UN.

Malcolm was a member of the 28th Police Precinct Welcoming Committee, whose function was to welcome foreign dignitaries to the Precinct. Mosque #7 was in this Police Precinct and was thus invited to join the Committee. It welcomed, for example, presidents Kwame Nkrumah of Ghana, Sékou Touré of Guinea and Gamal Abdel Nasser of Egypt, as well as Fidel Castro of Cuba.[8] Malcolm and Nkrumah were the main speakers at a rally attended by thousands in front of the Hotel Theresa in Harlem; Malcolm spoke mainly about the US involvements in the Congo and the imprisonment of Prime Minister Lumumba. Nkrumah introduced Malcolm to Alex Quaison-Sackey, Ghana's representative at the UN.[9]

---

6 See Ludo de Witte, *The Assassination of Lumumba*, London: Verso 2001. It was not until February 2002 that the Belgian government gave a somewhat indefinite apology for its actions.

7 Abdullah Abdur-Razzaq, who had worked with Malcolm both before and after the NOI years, believes that Malcolm would not have attended such gatherings — or certainly not as a representative of the Nation of Islam, which 'avoided such political affairs...There was a Pakistani...who taught Arabic at Mosque #7 and generally acted as a foreign aide'. (Letter from Mr Abdur-Razzaq, 30 October 2006. My most profound thanks to Mr Abdur-Razzaq for his comments and critiques and the hospitality he extended to me when I visited him.)

8 Castro was in New York to attend a United Nations meeting in September 1960. Hotels in downtown New York refused him accommodation so Malcolm arranged for rooms at the Hotel Theresa in Harlem. 'During the course of their conversation, Cuba's Castro and Harlem's Malcolm covered much political and philosophical ground. *The Militant*, vol.59 no.41, 6/11/1995. (www.themilitant.com/1995/5941/5941_20.html).

9 Some of the best accounts I have found on these meetings, with excellent references are in Karl Evanzz, *The Judas Factor* (1992). Oxford-educated Alex Quaison-Sackey, then First Secretary of the Ghana Embassy in London, had helped with the organisation of the Conference of Independent African States held in Ghana in 1958.

According to Kojo Amoo-Gottfried, who was to become Ghana's Ambassador to Cuba, Malcolm met many Africans at the UN. 'Many had an interest in him. He was an important, a charismatic figure. They learned from each other, exchanged ideas.'[10] According to biographer Peter Goldman, Malcolm 'had become a regular visitor [to the UN], teetotaling at the delegate parties and gossiping in the delegate lounge'. (p.156)

Among the diplomats Malcolm might have met this way was Dr. Mahmoud Youssef Shawarbi of Yemen, who was to play such an important role in Malcolm's re-education into the Muslim faith and his performing the pilgrimage to Mecca, the *Hajj*. Yemen had joined the UAR – the United Arab Republic – formed by President Nasser. Shawarbi, a scholar from the University of Cairo, had been sent to New York not only to represent his country at the UN but to set up an Islamic Center in the city.

It is possible that Malcolm also met Diallo Telli, the representative of Guinea to the UN since independence in 1958, whom Malcolm often mentions in his travel *Notebooks*. William Sales in his *From Civil Rights to Black Liberation* (1994, p.104) quotes from FBI reports on Malcolm's friendship with Quaison-Sackey and with Mahmoud Boutiba, the representative of Algerian President Ahmed Ben Bella at the UN, who was 'a personal adviser to Malcolm X of long standing'. It is very likely that Boutiba introduced Malcolm to Algeria's principal representative to the UN, Tewfik Boutorra. Another colleague, or mentor, was Tahseen Bashir from Egypt, educated at Princeton, spokesman in President Nasser's delegation to the UN from 1956 until 1959, who 'was comfortable in Harlem'. Bashir had been 'intrigued' by the 'obscure pseudo-Islamic group in Harlem and sought out its articulate young leader...Their relationship became a key factor in Malcolm X's travels abroad in 1959 and 1964, and his early exposure to and later embrace of traditional Islam.'[11]

It must have been quite a relief for many of the African representatives to the UN to make contacts with African Americans. They clearly did not have an easy time in New York: in 1964 the Afro-Asian sub-committee of the UN met with Secretary General U Thant to discuss the possibility of moving the UN's headquarters from New York because of the 'incessant attacks and molestations' their members suffered.[12] These were, after all, the years of the Civil Rights struggle in the USA – an era of police violence, riots and the murders of numerous activists, both Black and White.

---

10 Evanzz, (1992), pp.185-6, 190-193, 221. Interview with Kojo Amoo-Gottfried, East Legon, Ghana 7 & 12 February 2003.

11 Email (dated 17/1/2003) from 'Sunni', kindly forwarded to me by Paul Lee, 28/11/2006.

12 *West Africa* 26/9/1964, p.1098.

To judge by the list of his reading materials, now preserved at the Schomburg Center, Malcolm supplemented what he was learning from those he met in New York by reading widely.[13] In Africa Malcolm met critics and critiques of capitalism and imperialism and could observe the ongoing struggles in many of the newly independent countries. In Africa, the UK and Paris he met not only expatriate African Americans, but also Black and White anti-imperialist thinkers and activists. He found people whose ways of thinking were different from those currently (with fairly rare exceptions) in the USA.

In December 1964 Malcolm spoke of

> a change I've undergone and am still undergoing...I don't intend to let anybody make my mind become so set on anything that I can't change it according to the circumstances and conditions...[In my five months of travel] I learned a great deal. Because in each country that I visited I spoke with people at all levels. I had an open mind...My travels have broadened my scope...I can get along with white people who can get along with me. In whatever I did or do, even if I make mistakes, they were made in sincerity. I'd rather... respect a person for their sincerity than anything else. Especially when you're living in a world that's so hypocritical. This is an era of hypocrisy.[14]

---

13 See lists in folder 1, reel 15.
14 'Getting it on the record with Claude Lewis', in David Gallen (1992), pp.167-8;177.

CHAPTER 1

Mecca, Beirut and Cairo
April – May 1964

Malcolm's First Visit to Egypt, July 1959

In 1959 Elijah Muhammad's interest – and support – for Muslim diplomats in the USA resulted in an invitation by President Nasser of Egypt to visit his country. The leader of the Nation of Islam also wanted to go on *Hajj*, and despatched Malcolm to make the arrangements.[1] However, when the FBI learned of Elijah Muhammad's intentions, the Department of State withheld his passport.

Abdullah Abdur-Razzaq,[2] who had worked closely with Malcolm and the OAAU, wrote me that Malcolm had departed

> with the primary objective of preparing a way for Mr Muhammad to make Hajj. Brother Malcolm was welcomed to Egypt where he saw but did not meet Nasser. He told me he met the Vice President, Anwar Sadat...He did, however, after his passport was released, make umra. This leads one to believe that Malcolm was successful

---

1 Louis A. de Caro, *On the Side of My People*, New York: NY University Press 1996, p.138.

2 Abdullah Abdur-Razzaq had been a member of Malcolm's Mosque #7 during his NOI years, and became a lieutenant in the FOI (Fruit of Islam, the NOI's military wing) and the Circulation Manager of the NOI's *Muhammad Speaks* newspaper. 'After the schism, Brother Malcolm appointed me as Captain of the men in the Muslim Mosque Inc, of which brother Malcolm and Earl Grant and myself were trustees', Mr Abdur-Razzaq wrote me on 8 March 2007. As Malcolm had such little time in New York, Mr Abdur-Razzaq 'was often forced to act on his behalf'.

in obtaining recognition...as an authentic Muslim.

His itinerary took him as far as Jedda as one of my notes read: 'His Holiness Sheikh Muhammad Harkan with whom I had tea in 1959 (in Jedda)'.

According to Malcolm he did not reach Mecca. Reasons for not reaching Mecca are either sickness or reluctance to precede Mr Muhammad.

When Malcolm did meet Nasser, their relationship was such that Malcolm named one of his daughters Gamela after Gamel Nasser.[3]

The FBI report, kindly sent me by Mr Abdur-Razzaq, relates that at a meeting 'at the S.Nicholas Arena on 26 July, Malcolm stated that he had just returned from the Far East. He stated he did not speak with Nasser but saw him. He stated that he was well entertained and squired around due to the fact that he was a Muslim...he became very ill and as a result was not able to go to Mecca. (Was it the FBI informant who designated Egypt as being in the 'Far East'?)

In his *Autobiography* Malcolm barely mentions the visit, simply saying that 'on a three week trip to Africa...as Mr Muhammad's emissary, I went to Egypt, Arabia, to the Sudan, to Nigeria, and Ghana'.(p.273) I have not been able to find any information on Malcolm's visits to Nigeria and Ghana.

1964

Malcolm, according to his biographer Peter Goldman, on leaving the Nation of Islam 'remained a religious man, a true believer cut loose from one system of faith and looking for another...He sought it in true Islam.'[4] Omar Osman, a Sudanese college student, who had given Malcolm literature published by the Islamic Centre in Geneva, advised him to approach Dr Mahmoud Shawarbi for tuition. The director of the Islamic Foundation in New York, Dr Shawarbi, a professor at the University of Cairo and the author of many books, now also served as a delegate at the United Nations. He was 'impressed by his [Malcolm's] desire to learn about Islam' and agreed to tutor him.[5] After some months, he encouraged

---

3 Letter, 30 October 2006.

4 Goldman (1979), p.163.

5 Dr Shawarbi was also the Director of the Islamic Federation of the United States and Canada. See Ama F. Shabazz, 'The Legacy of Malik Shabazz', www.icna.org/tm/shabazz2.htm. Mahmoud Yousef Shawarbi's books in English include *Islam* and *Islam Versus Communism* and *Mutual Understanding between Islam and Christianity*, all published by Cairo University Press.

Malcolm to make the *Hajj*. Malcolm's sister Ella provided the funds.

Abdullah Abdur-Razzaq, wrote me that
> Whereas the first trip was to authenticate Mr Muhammad...This trip in April 1964 was in order to obtain a distinction higher than that of Mr Muhammad.
>
> Additionally: whereas Malcolm had established the Muslim Mosque before embarking for Hajj, he told me before he left 'When I return from this trip I want an organization formed. Its name is to be the Organization of Afro-American Unity.' He named the individuals who were to form this organization. He also made it clear that he held me responsible for its formation.
>
> It is easy to see that even before he left for Hajj, Malcolm planned to establish political ties with the African continent through the OAAU with the OAU, as he planned, through the Muslim Mosque Inc., to establish religious ties with the Muslims of Africa and the Middle East.
>
> Malcolm had nearly three months in which to determine what paths to follow as an independent, unfettered individual. His viewpoints, aims, goals and modus operandi would have been, and from my viewpoint were, completely different [from that of the NOI].

The Hajj, April 1964

(As Malcolm gives a very full description in his *Autobiography* of his experiences in Cairo, Mecca and Jedda what follows is a brief summary.)

Malcolm travelled to Mecca via Frankfurt and Cairo. In Frankfurt on 13 April Malcolm and a 'Cairo-bound [Muslim] brother' went sightseeing and were 'struck by the cordial hospitality of the people' in the shops they visited.

Malcolm found Cairo crowded with
> throngs of people, obviously Muslims from everywhere, bound on pilgrimage, hugging and embracing. They were of all complexions, the whole atmosphere was of warmth and friendliness. The feeling hit me that there really wasn't any color problem here. The effect was as though I had just stepped out of prison...I spent two happy days sightseeing in Cairo...before continuing to Jedda.[6]

Dr Shawarbi had prepared the letter of recommendation for a visa, required by the Saudi Embassy for all converts. Having presented him with The *Eternal Message of Muhammad*, a book by 'Abd al-Rahman Azzam,

---
6 *Autobiography*, pp.369-370.

Malcolm X with Prince Al-Faisal, Saudi Arabia

Dr. Shawarbi gave Malcolm an introduction to the author, who was the Secretary General of the Arab League in Saudi Arabia.[7] Azzam Pasha was a 'scholar, statesman and recognised author on international affairs'; he was, in the 1960s, a close advisor to Prince Faisal of Saudi Arabia. Dr. Shawarbi also gave Malcolm the telephone numbers of his own son in Cairo and that of Omar Azzam, Dr Azzam's son in Jedda. Through these contacts Malcolm was mentioned to Crown Prince Faisal, who granted him an interview and announced that he was 'an honoured guest of the government'. Malcolm was also introduced to visiting African politicians and senior government officials.[8]

---

[7] *The Eternal Message of Muhammad* has been reprinted many times; it is not so much a book of theology, as an examination of the Muslim state: its economy, society, law and justice as expressed in the Qur'an. 'Abd al-Rahman Azzam (1893-1976) was one of the founders, and the secretary-general of the Arab League from 1945 till 1952; he had been a member of the Egyptian Wafd from 1923 until the early 1930s; and was Egypt's Minister Plenipotentiary to Iraq and Iran in 1936. The League's secretariat is in Cairo; it works though committees on eg economic, education, law, trade and foreign policy issues. The quotation is taken from the introduction to his *Causes of World Unrest: imperialism, the barrier to world peace*, #1 in a series of Arab League pamphlets on International Relations published in 1947 by the Government Press in Cairo. In this, after describing earlier forms of imperialism, Azzam defines 'modern imperialism [as] the possession of so-called colonies and dependencies, and their exploitation in the widest sense of the term, at the expense and to the utter bewilderment and disgust of their wretched inhabitants...It was the main cause of most wars in the past 200 years...this modern evil will continue to be a barrier to world peace...Islamic doctrines do not permit the claim to superiority of a nation over another nation, or a race over another race...' (pp. 9, 11, 14, 16)

[8] *Autobiography*, Chapter 17.

Mecca and the Muslims he met on his trip led Malcolm to rethink his attitudes. He now realised that

> "White man", as commonly used, means complexion only secondarily; primarily it described attitudes and actions...[I]n the Muslim world, I had seen that men with white complexions were more genuinely brotherly than anyone else had ever been...The *color-blindness* of the Muslim world's religious society and the *color-blindness* of the Muslim world's human society: these two influences had each day been making a greater impact, and an increasing persuasion against my previous way of thinking.[9]

Malcolm arranged for wide publicity in the USA for his radically altered views.[10] His letters recounting his experiences were published and in these he admitted that 'You may be shocked by these words coming from me, but I have always been a man who tries to face facts, and to accept the reality of life as new experiences and knowledge unfold.' These words, together with other excerpts, reached not only the Black press, but were also quoted in the Socialist Workers' Party newspaper, *The Militant*, on 25 May 1964.

Meeting many Africans on the Hajj also led Malcolm to realise that 'the single worst mistake of the American black organisations, and their leaders, is that they have failed to establish direct brotherhood lines of communication between the independent nations of Africa and the American black people'.

Beirut, 30 April

Lebanon had been part of Syria under the Ottoman Empire. Britain and France intervened in the civil war of 1860 and pressured the Turks into establishing a new Christian-dominated administration for Lebanon. After World War I, Lebanon became a French mandate. During the 1920s the French redefined Lebanon's borders, combining the largely Muslim-inhabited coastal plain with the Christian-dominated mountains to create the Republic of Lebanon, which became fully independent in 1943.

Relations between Christians and Muslims were complicated by the Arab-Israeli conflict as Palestinian refugees fled to Lebanon; this evoked attacks by Israel. In 1958 a Muslim rebellion ended when American marines landed in Beirut. The USA was (and is) a powerful supporter of Israel.

---

9 *Autobiography*, pp.383, 389. Throughout, I have kept the spelling and formatting in the original documents.

10 See letter from Jedda, 20/4/64 in Breitman (1966), p.59-60.

In his *Autobiography*, Malcolm relates that 'some friends I had made in the Holy Land had urged and insisted that I make some stops en route [to West Africa] and I had agreed. For example, it had been arranged that I would first stop and address the faculty and the students at the American University in Beirut (AUB).'[11] However, elsewhere Malcolm wrote that, on learning of his presence, the 'African students at the American University arranged for me to lecture at the Sudanese Cultural Center'. Is it possible that the University refused to have Malcolm speak on its premises? This is quite possible as Samar Mikati Kaissi, Archives and Special Collections Librarian at AUB, in correspondence in 2008 emphasised that Malcolm spoke 'outside the AUB to AUB students; no AUB publication mentioned his visit'.[12]

'The overflow audience received the lecture warmly and gave me a glimpse of the interest, sympathy and support our case has among the people abroad once they fully understand our deplorable plight here in America', Malcolm reported. 'The Sudanese and Lebanese Muslim students kept me up until 3 a.m...trying learn how they themselves could help the Afro-American in his struggle for freedom and human dignity.'[13] There were 'American white students' in the audience; Malcolm 'felt the subjective and defensive reactions – but gradually their hostillity lessened...But the students of African heritage – well, I'll *never* get over how the African displays his emotions.'[14]

The Beirut Daily Star reported Malcolm's 'stirring talk' on page 1 of the May 1 issue. There was

> a large audience, mainly of University students, at the Sudanese Cultural Center...The renowned American Muslim Negro leader... unequivocally stressed that there was a new generation of Negroes in the United States in 1964 who had lost their patience and are on the verge of bursting forth into a violent explosion...there were no practical gains made in 1963 toward achieving civil rights...Non-violent Negro leaders like Martin Luther King Jr...had achieved very little if anything toward solving the racial question in the United States...If I sound pessimistic, you have to know that if you have waited for 200 years to get what you want and you still don't have it, you're bound to be a bit pessimistic...To give back the American Negro his self-confidence, to make him love the color of

---

11 *Autobiography*, p.400.

12 *Autobiography*, pp.383, 389. Throughout, I have kept the spelling and formatting in the original documents.

13 Malcolm X, 'We Are All Blood Brothers', *Liberator*, July 1964, pp.4 - 6.

14 *Autobiography*, p.401. There is no more information on his time in Beirut in his *Notebooks*.

his skin, to make him proud of his cultural heritage, to reverse the dehumanising process through which the Negro has gone, [is] the great task ahead. In this manner, the American Negro could regain his sense of dignity as a human being...When the constitution of the United States was written we were not even regarded as humans; and being second class citizens today is still nothing but a form of 20th century slavery.[15]

The article concludes by describing the 'lively discussion' following Malcolm's talk, which 'centered on whether he really did represent what was going on in the United States in regard to the racial problem there and whether he represent[ed] a true expression of what the vast majority of Negroes in America felt'.

The *New York Times* (2/5/1964, p.56) reported that Malcolm had 'charged' that American Negroes were living in 'modern slavery'. Martin Luther King was too moderate and had not addressed this issue. 'The United States had made no practical gains towards achieving civil rights', Malcolm concluded. 'Only a minority of Negroes believe in non-violence.'

Malcolm himself recalled that he had spoken about
the truth of the American black man's condition...As I spoke I felt the subjective and defensive reactions of the American white students present– but gradually their hostilities lessened...the African students all but besieged me for autographs; some of them even hugged me...Later, with astonishment, I heard that the American press carried stories that my Beirut speech caused a "riot". What kind of riot?[16]

(Now, over forty years later, we have to question why the newspapers would mis-report this event in such a fashion. Had they begun to see Malcolm X's travels and audiences abroad as a danger?)

What else did Malcolm do in Beirut? Searching the web, I found that there was a lecture, 'Encounter with Malcolm X in 1964', given by Graham Leonard as a 'Black History Month Bonus' at the Warren-Wilson College in North Carolina. The advertisement for the lecture stated that
Malcolm X made his first Pilgrimage to Mecca in 1964 and was profoundly moved and challenged by the experience. Arriving in Beirut, he asked a friend there to speak with an English-speaking expert on Islam. He was brought to a Quaker named Graham Leonard, then at the UN Relief Agency for Palestine Refugees in

---

15 My profound thanks to Samar Mikati Kaissi for sending me a copy of this article.
16 *Autobiography*, p.401.

Beirut. Malcolm X questioned him and others for a week about Islam, and also spoke to Palestinian students about the political, racial, and economic realities of the USA.[17]

Initially I could not find Mr Leonard, but I did find Professor Ben Feinberg at the College. He wrote me that 'Graham Leonard's talk was many years ago, so my memory is not strong. I do remember that he felt that this leg of Malcolm's trip was extremely influential for him. He may have even interviewed Malcolm in Beirut, where he (Leonard) was living at the time. I do not recall many details of the talk.'[18]

Cairo, Alexandria, May 1-4

Egypt is home to the oldest civilisation in the world. Its people are a conglomeration of 'Black' Africans, Arabs, and the mixtures resulting from empire-building, conquest and cross-Mediterranean trade. It was incorporated in the Ottoman Empire in 1517; Britain occupied it in 1882. In 1914 Britain deposed the Khedive and declared Egypt a 'protectorate' under the nominal rule of King Farouk. Nationalists succeeded in gaining independence in 1936, but Britain retained the right to maintain troops there in order to 'protect' the Suez Canal, through which about half of the Middle East's oil was shipped.

In 1952 anti-British riots in Cairo escalated into a seizure of power by the military, under the leadership of Colonel Abdel Nasser. He assumed the prime ministership in 1954 under the presidency of General Mohamed Neguib, but replaced him when Egypt was declared a republic. In 1957 Nasser organised the Asian-African Peoples Solidarity Conference, which attracted about 500 delegates. Determinedly non-aligned, the Conference passed many anti-colonial and anti-Western resolutions. This was a blow to the Western powers during this Cold War era. An African-Asian Solidarity Council was set up, which planned annual meetings. A permanent secretariat was established, housed in Cairo and under an Egyptian Secretary-General.

The creation of Israel in 1948 and usurpation of Palestinian lands led to much conflict. In 1956, when Britain and the USA withdrew their offer of financial support for the building of the Aswan Dam, Egypt nationalised the Suez Canal. Israel, Britain and France invaded, only to be

---

17 After serving in WWII Leonard worked with UNESCO's Volunteers for International Development in Egypt. He was appointed dean of students and an associate professor at American University of Beirut from 1960 to 1963, and then assistant to the Director of Education at the UN Relief and Works Agency for Palestine Refugees till 1965.
(http://www.usatoday.com/news/politicselections/index.aspx?sp=TN&oi=H) I did contact Dr Leonard in Kingsport, Tenn., but could not elicit more information on Malcolm's visit.

18 Email from Prof. Feinberg, 18/4/2008.

ordered to withdraw by the United Nations with the support of the USSR. The Soviet Union then took over financing the dam. In 1958 Egypt and Syria joined to form the United Arab Republic (UAR), but Syria left after a couple of years.

This was the virtual beginning of Soviet involvement in the 'Middle East' and North Africa. The USA at this time was arming Turkey, Pakistan and Iraq, which increased the inter-Muslim conflicts. US aid to Egypt increased from $7 million in 1957 to $194 million in 1964; US exports increased from $151 million in 1960 to $268 million in 1964. In 1956 the USSR (mainly Soviet Bloc countries) exports to Egypt amounted to $23 million.[19] By 1964 the USSR had loaned Egypt $44 million for the Aswan Dam, for armaments and for a metallurgical plant, and was also training Egyptian troops. In competition with China for influence and access, USSR President Khrushchev visited Cairo in May 1964.[20]

According to his *Notebook*, Malcolm arrived in Cairo from Beirut at 10am on May 1st and left immediately by train for Alexandria. There he met President Nasser, with whom he had a 'lengthy discussion'. As he explained in a speech at a meeting in Detroit in February 1965, 'I had a chance to speak in Cairo, or rather in Alexandria, with President Nasser for about an hour and a half. He's a very brilliant man. And I can see why they're so afraid of him…they know he can cut off their oil. And actually the only thing power respects is power.'[21] (But here we have to recognise that Nasser had also to negotiate the Cold War.)

Could the report below from the FBI Papers be related to the attempt to poison Malcolm on his next visit to this ancient city? Or just to surveillance? Who was this person referred to as being on the same flight as Malcolm? The informant's name is inked out:

> […] advised that […] had a prior reservation for himself from New York to Cairo…She advised that […] indicated that he and 'M. El Shabazz' would leave together…On April 14, 1964 […] advised that one […] departed on their flight on April 13, 1964, the same flight utilized by 'Shabazz'. In addition the flight manifest reflected that […] and 'Shabazz' were the only passengers on that flight who had connecting reservations at Frankfurt, for Cairo…[22]

---

19 Stewart Smith, *US Neocolonialism in Africa*, Moscow: Progress Publishers, 1974, pp. 79, 93. The author uses data from the *Statistical Abstract of the US*; American Assembly, *The United States and Africa*, Washington: Library of Congress 1958, p.75.

20 *Newsweek*, 18 May and 6 July 1964.

21 Malcolm X (1992), pp.81, 147.

22 FBI Papers, Part 11 of a long memorandum on Malcolm emanating from the New York office. (pp.63-4)

Malcolm was well aware that he was followed by the CIA, even in Africa. He reportedly told his wife Betty that 'It's like staying in a room full of spider webs. If a man is aware of the web, it is visible in that one room – if you go to another country you suppose at first that it's not there, but if you look closely it's still being spun around you.'[23]

On 4 May Malcolm noted that he was back in Cairo; what did he do other than go sightseeing? All Malcolm says in his *Autobiography* is: 'I kept my camera busy during each brief stopover. Finally I took a plane to Nigeria.'

---

23 Eric Norden, 'The Murder of Malcolm X', *The Realist*, #73, February 1967, p.9.

CHAPTER 2

Nigeria and Ghana
(Stop-overs in Monrovia, Dakar, Morocco, Algiers, May 17 – 21)
May 1964

Nigeria 6 - 10 May

The country we know today as Nigeria consists of some of the territories which had been 'allocated' to Britain at the conference held in Berlin in 1885. There the Europeans, who had been contending with each other for control, divided Africa among themselves, ignoring existing historical, social, linguistic and political boundaries. 'Nigeria' was the home of about 56 million people; more than half lived in the mainly Muslim northern region.

During the Cold War era, when the USA and the USSR were vying for control of Africa politically as well as for trade purposes, US direct investment rose from nil in 1957 to $3 million in 1960 and $25 million in 1964. Imports from the US rose from $26 million in 1960 to $64 million in 1964. In 1956 the imports from the 'Soviet Bloc' were $11 million (almost none from the USSR itself).[1]

---
1 Spelling, punctuation and emphases in the original documents have been retained.
Stewart Smith, *US Neocolonialism in Africa*, Moscow: Progress Publishers 1974, pp. 79, 93 (the data is taken from the *Statistical Abstracts of the US*); American Assembly, *The United States*

The situation in Nigeria was fraught when Malcolm arrived. Independence had been granted by Britain in 1960. Nigeria was divided into three regions: the North, mainly Hausa and Fulani Muslims, the West, mainly Yoruba, and the East, mainly Igbo. (But there were c. 500 languages spoken – and hence ethnic groups.) With the struggle for independence and then power, historic ethnic divisions – and nationalism – were flaring. Nnamdi Azikiwe, the Igbo leader, advocated a government of all the main groups within a federal structure, but this did not appeal to Obafeni Awolowo, the Yoruba leader of the Action Group. In 1963 a fourth region was created and Nigeria declared itself a republic. Abubakar Tafawa, a leader of the Northern People's Congress, became the first Prime Minister and Azikiwe the first President of Nigeria. They formed an all-party national unity government, but struggle for control escalated. Constitutional government collapsed in 1966 and the Igbo seceded, leading to what became known as the Biafra War.

On May 6 Malcolm flew from Cairo to Lagos. The plane must have touched down at Kano, as Malcolm noted that 'at Kano took more pictures at airport'. He was met at Lagos airport by M. Shawarbi, the son of his New York tutor. Malcolm did not record what advice he had received from S.O. Adebo, Nigeria's representative at the United Nations, whom he knew well.[2] In Lagos Malcolm checked into the Federal Plaza Hotel.

At Ibadan University

From Cairo he had cabled the time of his arrival to Professor E.U. Essien-Udom, then teaching at the University of Ibadan. (Malcolm had met Professor Essien-Udom while the latter was working on his book, *Black Nationalism* (1962) in the USA.[3]) The Essien-Udoms gave a dinner party in his honour that evening. Among those present were 'Dr. Davis and KM'. Malcolm records that he stayed at 'KM's home'.[4] They appear to have left for Ibadan the next day, where Malcolm was to address the students at the University of Ibadan.

Malcolm's lecture was advertised, probably more widely than the Notice preserved in his *Notebooks*[5].

---

 and Africa, Washington: Library of Congress 1958, p.75.

2 Evanzz (1992), p.161.

3 Most of English-speaking Africa follows the British academic customs; thus a 'professor' is a very senior lecturer, usually in charge of a department.

4 Schomburg Center: Malcolm X Papers: Box 9, *Notebook*, entries for 4, 6, 7 & 8 May 1964. Who 'KM' was I could not discover.

5 Notebook. Afro-American boxer Cassius Clay had just won the world title. A former pupil of Malcolm's, he was a this time a protégé of Elijah Muhammad

6 *Notebook*. Afro-American boxer Cassius Clay had just won the world title. A former pupil of

> Public Lecture
>
> *Mr Malcolm X, a leader of the Black Muslim Movement in the United States of America and an Associate of Cassius Clay will give a public lecture on 'Our Struggle in the Context of African Liberation Movement' in Trenchard Hall, 6pm, 8 May 1964. Malcolm X Committee A rare opportunity to learn about the Black Muslims at first hand.*

The report sent to the State Department by the American consulate in Ibadan, claimed that the students had less than 10 hours' notice of Malcolm's imminent arrival, so 'only' (sic) about 500 came to hear him. The meeting was chaired by Professor J.F. Ajayi, a historian and Dean of the Faculty of Arts.[7] The Consulate noted that the students were 'highly responsive and apparently sympathetic to the case Malcolm X presented in his lecture'. The consul remarked on the timing of his visit: it was the night before the students were to hold a march to solicit 'Anglo-American support for the imposition of economic sanctions on South Africa'. Consul Meagher noted that, 'following the speech and during next day Malcolm X had meetings with several small groups of students. According to competent Nigerian and expatriate faculty members speech most vitriolic and emotional heard on campus in many years. They believe speaker induced large number of those present to agree with his anti-white racist approach.'[8]

Malcolm notes in his *Autobiography* (p.403) that he was made an honorary member of the Nigerian Muslim Students' Society at the reception in his honour. There he was renamed 'Omowale', which in Yoruba means 'the child has come home'. Malcolm wrote Jimmy Booker of the *N.Y. Amsterdam News*. 'So my Nigerian name is El Hajj Omowale Malcolm X'.[9] The Essien-Udoms recalled that the African staff and students were 'impressed by the forcefulness and obvious honesty of his account of the

---

Malcolm's, he was a this time a protégé of Elijah Muhammad.

7 Professor J.F. Ajayi was appointed Vice-Chancellor of the University of Lagos in 1972.

8 NARA: SOC14-1 US: John P. Meagher, Ibadan to State Dept.12 May1964 (Meagher sent two missives on this date, one an 'airgram' the other a telegram.) I must thank Dr Walter Hill for sending me this document and others from the State Dept. files.

9 *N.Y. Amsterdam News*, 27 March 1965, p.11. Though the *News* claims in its introduction to this post-assassination article that 'No one knew Malcolm X better than the Amsterdam News staff', this assertion is not borne out by the reporting of Malcolm.

black man's conditions in America' and noted that Malcolm stated that African Americans should 'develop a working unity within the framework of Pan-Africanism'.[10]

The reports available on Malcolm's speech to the students are from the FBI files (#100-399321, part 14), which contains a long – 150 pages – report on Malcolm, compiled by the Bureau's New York office.[11] This gives the following 'excerpts' from Malcolm's speech:

> Our little chat will be informal. I speak for those Negro Americans who have been oppressed for 400 years and are still oppressed today in 1964. The American propagandists have tried to tell you that American Negroes are not interested in Africa and Africans are not interested in American Negroes...The black man has been so victimised in America that we don't even like each other. We have lost our self-respect...They have killed us morally. They have made drunkards out of us, they have made drug addicts out of us. Three people are responsible for the Negro loss of identity: the slave trader, the slave master and the slave maker, etc. The government of the United States is a government of white people by white people and for the benefit of white people...Remember, the white man is the greatest hate teacher who ever walked the face of the earth.

Consul John Meagher ensured that he would be kept informed: he had sent 'both the Branch Public Affairs Officer and his deputy' to attend the lecture.[12] Most interestingly, the State Department report, compiled by the US Information Service and the consulate, which the FBI must have used for its report, includes more of the speech. (Or did the FBI have its own agents in Nigeria?) For example, where Malcolm speaks of Negroes being made into drunkards, the 'reporter' adds: 'They put bars in our neighbourhoods to get us drunk. They don't show us how to set up factories. They show us how to set up breweries.' Before going on to talk about who is responsible for the loss of identity, Malcolm said:

> The white man brought us there [to the USA] to exploit us as merchandise, and we made them the richest people in the world. They got all that wealth from the sweat of our brow. We're also

---

10 Ruby M and E.U Essien-Udom, 'Malcolm X: An International Man', in Clarke (1969), pp.235-267.

11 Malcolm was also under wide FBI surveillance: the US officials in Accra sent a telegram to the Department of State beginning 'FBIS report', which presumably indicates that the FBI's local agents were watching Malcolm. The telegram summarises the radio report of Malcolm's session on campus. NARA, SOC 14-1 US: Telegram from 'AmEmbassy', Accra, #717, 12 May1964.

12 NARA SOC 14-1 US: Meagher to Department of State, 12 May 1964.

economically dead. The Negroes in America have $22 billion in annual income at their disposal. That's more than Canada or Sweden and many other countries, but we cannot buy food, we cannot have our own businesses, we cannot own our homes. In spite of all that money, we are economically dead.

The report states that 'this theme and variations went on for approximately 45 minutes, followed by questions. The first speaker was West Indian O.R. Dathorne, then teaching at the University's English department.[13] He said that much of what he had heard was true, but there was no point in 'going over and over these things. Sheer nonsense is all we have heard in this lecture'. This was greeted with jeers and attempts were made to remove him. After he had left the hall, questions were resumed, and Malcolm reported in his *Autobiography* that he had enjoyed the 'politically sharper questions' asked by the students 'than one hears from most American adults'. That the white man was the greatest hate-teacher, was part of Malcolm's response to a question asking why the US was sending money, technicians and Peace Corps volunteers. 'They have the same things in mind', Malcolm replied. The report notes that this statement proved to be unpopular. However, elsewhere in the report it is noted that 'Malcolm X achieved an affirmative response from his audience' and that 'a number of Nigerian staff agree with Malcolm X'.

In contrast to the consular and FBI reports, according to the Essien-Udoms, Malcolm

> argued that the Afro-American community should cooperate with the world's Pan-Africanists; and that even if they remained in America physically, they should return to Africa philosophically and culturally and develop a working unity within the framework of Pan-Africanism.[14]

Consul Meagher concludes his missive with the note that 'later in the evening Malcolm X appeared for an eight minute interview on WNTV'. And, that 'in an effort to dilute the influence of Malcolm's lecture, USIS mimeographed 500 copies of Ambassador Adlai Stevenson's article, "Human Rights and Complete Justice", and placed them in the foyer of Trenchard Hall'.[15]

---

13 Repeated requests to Professor Dathorne, to recount his encounter with Malcolm X have proved fruitless.

14 Ibid; the quote is from p.247.

15 NARA, SOC 14-1 US: report of Ibadan speech in Meagher, Ibadan to Dept. of State, 12/5/1964. It is interesting that the Consulate estimate of the numbers of students present precisely matches the numbers of copies of this publication that were distributed.

In his *Autobiography* (p.403) Malcolm recalled that he had told the students that it was 'time for all the Afro-Americans to join the world's Pan-Africanists'. In a letter home Malcolm wrote that he 'gave a *true* picture of our plight in America and of the necessity of the independent African nations helping us bring our case before the Unites Nations.'[16] Thus it seems clear that only an extremely truncated/distorted version of what Malcolm had said reached the US government.

In his *Notebook* Malcolm wrote that he had 'later learned that the [Professor driven from the rostrum and the hall] married a white woman... solid support from the students...Nigerian faculty objective'. He also noted that at the 'special affair in Students Union – almost fantastic interest and sympathy – misconception of American Negroes...until midnight'.[17]

There is a very hostile report of this meeting by Abram V. Martin, then teaching at Ibadan. While admitting that Malcolm was a 'superb orator and held his audience spellbound', he accuses Malcolm of 'brimming over with hatred of the white man...Many of the specific factual allegations he made about the racial situation in America were accurate, the overall picture was badly distorted by his overall denial of any positive aspects of the situation.' He quotes Malcolm as saying: 'If a man sticks a knife in my back six inches deep, and then pulls it out 3 inches, I don't call it progress. If he pulls it all the way out I don't call that progress because I still have a hole in my back.'[18]

Making Contacts

In his *Notebook* Malcolm recounts that he 'had private discussions with many government and religious leaders and other persons of prominence in Nigeria. All showed genuine concern for our problems and expressed a sincere desire to help...Nigeria has unlimited natural wealth and beauty... [it] could easily become the 'bread basket of the world.' He goes on to note that the day after he arrived he 'called JW...several reporters came'. Could 'JW' have been Jaja Wachuku? Wachuku had been the Deputy Leader of the National Council of Nigeria and Cameroons, set up by Azikiwe in 1944 to combat British colonialism. Wachuku had been elected to the House of Representatives in 1959; he had served as Nigeria's representative to the UN in 1960-61 and could well have met Malcolm in New York. He was now the Foreign Affairs Minister. Ruby and E.U. Essien-Udom report that 'Malcolm also met with highly placed Nigerian officials who lent a very

---

16 Breitman (1965), p.62, quoting from letter 'Accra 11 May 1964'.
17 *Notebook* entries for 4, 8 May 1964. Malcolm's notes are precisely that – notes, with dashes or simply a space between recollections.
18 Abram V. Martin, 'Apartheid and Malcolm X', *New Leader*, 22 June 1964, vol. 47 no.3, pp.7-9.

sympathetic ear to his ideas. He reports one of them as saying that when black people throughout the Americas and Africa link up their struggle, the political picture of the world would undoubtedly change.'[19]

In his talk with Claude Lewis in Harlem in December 1964, and in a speech in Detroit in 1965, Malcolm mentioned that he had had 'an audience with President Azikiwe', but, as always, we do not know what the two men discussed in their 'long discussion'.[20]

On May 9, Joseph Iffeora of the Ministry of Works and Surveys, was waiting for Malcolm in Lagos. Iffeora took him to see 'JAW' who was 'interested in co-operation between African Americans and Africans'. Then he was taken to the Palace of the Oba (King), who granted him a thirty minute audience. As always, Malcolm did not record the substance of the discussion with the Oba.[21]

Also preserved in Malcolm's papers is a card from Alhaji A.F. Masha, the chair of the Lagos City Council, but whether they met is not known. (I have not recorded all the names and addresses Malcolm wrote in his *Notebooks*.) Clearly Malcolm met many people and presumably discussed issues affecting Africa and African-Americans and the extension of pan-African philosophy to include the African diaspora.

Working the Media

The Nigerian media was also interested in Malcolm. He appeared on Nigerian TV and radio 'explaining the plight of the Afro-American to the Nigerian people.' The Essien-Udoms recall that 'in his television and radio appearances Malcolm stressed the need for African support to bring the violation of Afro-American human rights by the United States before the United Nations.'[22]

The *Daily Express* (11 May 1964, p.6), which was partly British-owned, interviewed Malcolm. Calling him the 'leader of the extremist Black Muslim Group', the paper reported that Malcolm was asking for help 'to bring the problem of black Negroes in the US to the notice of the United Nations'. The US government 'had given the American Negroes the impression that African states were not interested in their problems'. His

---

19 Essien-Udoms in Clarke (1969), p.247.
20 Gallen (1992), p,168; Malcolm X (1992), pp.81, 111.
21 Notebook, entries for 4, 9 and 10 May 1964. I could not decipher the initials of the person who took Malcolm to the Oba possibly 'NS'. Malcolm usually just gives initials, and sometimes just a – (dash) for a person. Whether this indicates that he does not want to even note the initials (perhaps because of scrutiny by the CIA), or that he was unsure of the person's name I cannot guess.
22 Essien-Udoms in Clarke (1969), p.247.

movement's immediate task was 'to change the image of Negroes in the US to a positive one with a view to restoring our cultural identity and build up communications and understanding between black Muslims in the US and African countries.' He wanted to establish a black Peace Corps which would carry black civilisation to all African countries. 'No', Malcolm said, 'the Peace Corps now in Nigeria are not spies, but are the missionaries of old who are paving the way for neo-colonialism.'

Malcolm was also questioned by Ben Orubu for Azikiwe's *West African Pilot* (8 May 1964, p.1), a paper known for its 'pugnacious political journalism'.[23] What Orubu reported contradicts the report in the *Daily Express*:

> Peace Corps are spies of the American Government and missionaries of colonialism and neo-colonialism...Every American recruited into the Peace Corps had a special assignment to perform. They are all agents of espionage...The Negroes in the Corps were being used by the American government to place a wedge between the American Negro and the African with a view to thwarting the concept of Africanisation of the Negroes. The Peace Corps have been instructed to present a repugnant image of the American Negro.

Malcolm stated that he was making films of the life of the people for the civil rights campaign in the US to 'belie Senator Douglas' propaganda in America that Africans are not interested in American Negroes. He explained the aims of his new organisation as being the achievement of equality.[24]

Bola Ige of the *Sunday Express* also interviewed Malcolm. The 'airgram' from the US Embassy in Lagos notes that Ige was the publicity secretary of the Action Group, a Yoruba political organisation and 'an *Express* columnist and a frequent critic of the United States'. Consul Bennett wrote that the 'article describes some of the activities of the Black Muslims and terms Malcolm X as the "epitome of the extremists of the Black Muslims".' 'The story begins by mis-describing Malcolm as a Black Muslim, then notes the "tumultuous applause" of the students for Malcolm, and reports that Malcolm X is "very impatient with all Negro resistance movements, particularly those lauded and participated in by white liberals". Concluding, the article states

---

23 Fred I.A. Omu, *Press and Politics in Nigeria 1880 – 1937*, New Jersey: Humanities Press 1978,p.240. The paper had been founded in 1937 by Dr Nnamdi Azikiwe, who had received his education in the USA. See his *My Odyssey*, London: C. Hurst & Co. 1970.

24 The US Embassy in Lagos transcribed much of the article and sent it to the Secretary of State in Washington and to the embassies in Accra, and Conakry on 8 May. My thanks to the librarian at the Lyndon B. Johnson Library and Museum for a copy of this.

> Malcolm X can be said to be haunted by the souls of black millions: the millions who died in raids, the millions who died in slave ships across the Atlantic, the millions who died on American plantations. He is haunted by the soul of people like Emmett Till, Mark Parker and Medgar Evers whom Americans murdered. He is haunted by the lynchings and the roasted black bodies he has seen...Malcolm X admits you cannot defeat your enemy unless you thoroughly hate him.[25]

Malcolm's arrival was noted by American journalists in Lagos: John Williams of *Newsweek* magazine telephoned Malcolm at the hotel, asking for an interview.

Malcolm's Reactions to His Visit

From Lagos Malcolm wrote to the OAAU that

> In the Muslim world they loved me once they learned I was an American *Muslim*, and here in Africa they love me as soon as they learn that I am Malcolm X the militant American Muslim; Africans in general and Muslims in particular love militancy...The Koran compels the Muslim World to take a stand on the side of those whose human rights are being violated, no matter what the religious persuasions of the victims are...In Africa, the 22 million American blacks are looked upon as the long-lost brothers of Africa. Our people here are interested in every aspect of our plight and they study our struggle for freedom from every angle...Despite Western propaganda to the contrary, our African Brothers and Sisters love us, and are happy to learn that we also are awakening from our long 'sleep' and are developing strong love for them.[26]

Malcolm was clearly impressed by Nigeria. He wrote in one of his letters that

> The natural beauty and wealth of Nigeria and its people are indescribable. The people of Nigeria are strongly concerned with the problems of their African brothers in America, but the US information agencies in Africa create the impression that progress is being made and the problem is being solved. Upon close study,

---

25 NARA: SOC 14-1 US: Josiah W. Bennett, Lagos embassy to State Department, 14/5/1964. By 'Black Muslim' Bennett meant the NOI. Unfortunately I do not have access to the *Sunday Express*. It would be interesting to check whether Ige calls Malcolm a Black Muslim. Were Nigerian reporters innocent of the difference between Islam and the Black Muslims of the USA?

26 *The Militant* 25 May 1964; the full texts of Malcolm's letters from Lagos 10/5/1064 and Accra 11/5/1964 can be found in George Breitman (1966), pp. 61-63.

one can easily see a gigantic design to keep Africans here and the African-Americans from getting together...Unity between the Africans of the West and the Africans of the fatherland will well change the course of history...It is time for all African-Americans to become an integral part of the world's Pan-Africanists...even though we might remain in America physically...we must 'return' to African philosophically and culturally...[27]

Ghana, 10 – 17 May

Almost the whole of what the British called the Gold Coast came under their dominion once they had managed to defeat the Asante Kingdom (grown rich on the export of gold and slaves) in their third war in 1874. This was recognised at the Berlin Conference in 1885; the new borders created there put some people historically hostile to each other under the one flag and divided some others between different European 'possessions'. Almost a hundred languages are spoken by the diverse ethnic groups living within the Berlin-imposed borders of this British colony.

The Gold Coast's struggle for independence culminated in 1957: Kwame Nkrumah, the leader of the Convention People's Party, which had been demanding immediate self-government since 1950, had to be released from prison and won the elections in 1957.[28] Prime Minister Nkrumah changed the country's name to Ghana, made it into a republic and soon declared that it was a non-aligned state. President Nkrumah was a Pan-Africanist, and was generally considered a socialist. What form of socialism the country should adopt led to much discussion and rancour.

In 1960 the population of Ghana was about 7 million. The Central Bureau of Statistics reported in 1967 that 82% of the rural and 60% of the urban population were illiterate. The main exports were cocoa butter, logs and timber, industrial diamonds and gold. Britain, anxious for markets for its manufactures, had forbidden industrialisation/ manufacturing in its colonies.

Ghana became host to many of the African liberation groups struggling to take their countries out of the clutches of the imperialists. It was one of the many African countries embroiled in the Cold War, with both the USSR and the USA contending and vying for power and access to raw materials. For example, US exports had increased from $17 million

---

27 Breitman (1966), p.62.

28 On Nkrumah's years as a student in the USA and Britain see Marika Sherwood, *Kwame Nkrumah: the years abroad*, Legon: Freedom Publications 1996.

Malcolm surrounded by African American friends: (left to right) Maya Angelou, Frank Robertson, Alice Windom, Accra, May 1964

in 1960 to $25 million in 1964, while US imports rose from $52 million to $74 million in the same period. In 1956 the 'Soviet Bloc' exported $5 million worth of goods and imported $5.7 million.[29] In April 1964 Ghana signed a 'cultural exchange protocol' with the USSR, and signed a fishing deal the following month.[30]

The situation in Ghana was tense in the months before Malcolm's arrival. The USA was accused of possible involvement in the attempted assassination of President Nkrumah. In February there had been demonstrations outside the Embassy denouncing US imperialism.[31] The papers carried articles excoriating the racial situation in the US. The government was in a difficult situation, as it had signed a deal with Kaiser, an American company, for the building of an electricity-producing dam on the Volta River.[32] The US government advised Ghana that this would

---

29 Smith (1974), p.93; American Assembly (1958), p.75.

30 *West Africa*, 25 April 1964, p.468 & 16 May 1964, p.555.

31 *West Africa* reported that T.D. Baffoe, the editor of the *Ghana Times* had said over a loudspeaker at one of these demonstrations that 'we are fed up with your imperialist American dollars. We will massacre you as you massacred the people in Korea, in Cuba and Panama.' (2 February 1964, p.159) Ambassador Mahoney protested to Ghana's Foreign Minister, Kojo Botsio. But the US clearly needed Ghana on its side during the Cold War as a US Trade Mission began touring Ghana in April. (*West Africa*, 9 May 1964, p.529)

32 Kaiser was to be given a large proportion of the electricity generated at a discount price to process imported, not local aluminium. About 75% of the funding for the aluminium

be terminated if the attacks on the Embassy continued: 'Ambassador Mahoney maintained diplomatic pressure on Nkrumah', according to historian Kevin Gaines.[33] This clearly worked as *West Africa* reported on 9 May 1964 that there had been no attacks on the Embassy for the past three months and that a US trade mission was touring Ghana.

The American government was less than happy with the growing numbers of radical African-American expatriates living in Ghana.

Prior to his departure, Malcolm sought advice. Among those who helped was 'Kwabena', who, according to biographer Peter Goldman, was a relation of President Nkrumah. (p.172) Kwabena gave Malcolm the names of government officials in both Nigeria and Ghana. Nigerians, Kwabena advised, were 'servants of American businessmen'. Malcolm should concentrate on the Northern, Muslim city of Kano, he advised. In Ghana, 'political awakening comes first; religion is always secondary'. Malcolm should avoid journalists, but should remember that Ghana 'is the most powerful UN African voice'.[34] Malcolm appears not to have followed many of Kwabena's suggestions, but undoubtedly welcomed the historical summaries.

It has not been possible to determine whether Malcolm followed the advice of Mr. Omayad, Chief of the Ghana Director of Overseas Information in New York, to get in touch with the Chief of Ghana Information Services on his arrival in Ghana. However, clearly Mr. Omayad had alerted his counterparts in Accra of Malcolm's planned visit, as he told Malcolm that 'Mr Victor Wood, the Director, will acquaint you with the arrangements made for you to see as much of the country as possible'.[35]

Malcolm flew to Accra, the capital city of Ghana on May 10. He saw Ghana as 'the fountainhead of Pan-Africanism', and expected these 'last days of my tour should be intensely interesting and enlightening'.[36] According to the *New York Times* (17 May 1964, p.17) at the press conference on the morning after his arrival from Nigeria he said

> that African nations should not restrict themselves to pointing a finger at South Africa in the United Nations, but should take up American racial segregation in the world organization. What is going on in the United States is worse than what is going on in South Africa. The American system perpetuates the enslavement

---

smelter was a loan from the US government. (*West Africa*, 16 May 1964, p.553)
33 Kevin Gaines (2006), p.190.
34 Schomburg Center: Malcolm X Papers, Reel 15, folder 14, file 2: Advice from Kwabena.
35 Malcolm X Papers, Reel 1, folder 5: Mr Omayad to 'Dear Brother', 10 April 1964.
36 Breitman (1966), p.62

of the Negro. The essence of his trip to Africa is to establish good relations and communication between the Africans at home and the Africans in America.

Was it Mr Wood who had alerted the African American community of Malcolm's imminent visit? Certainly the community organised itself and Malcolm seems to have spent more time with the expatriates than with Ghanaians. Ghana was the (temporary) home to about two hundred African Americans who had begun to emigrate there in 1957. They were not there, according to Leslie Lacy, 'because they loved Mother Africa, but rather, because they hated Father America...They were indeed a strange breed of political expatriates. Unable or unwilling to deal with racist and imperialist America from within, these black Americans had come to Ghana to help other black people achieve their revolution.'[37] Malcolm reported that some of the 'Afro-Americans' 'refer to themselves as expatriates, others as exiles'.[38] Lacy himself, described by Maya Angelou as 'an expert on Marxism and Garveyism', was teaching at the University of Ghana at Legon.[39]

Malcolm arrived with high hopes, as evidenced by his letter to Jimmy Booker dated 10 May 1964, but not printed in the *N.Y. Amsterdam News* till 27 March 1965:

> Thus, having just arrived here in Ghana, the progressive nation that is looked upon by an increasing number of Africans today as the 'Fountainhead of Pan-Africanism', the remaining days of my African tour should be even more interesting, enlightening and fruitful.
>
> We can learn much from the strategy used by the American Jews. They have never migrated physically to Israel, yet their cultural, philosophical and psychological ties to Israel have enhanced their political and economical and social position right there in America. Pan-Africanism will do for people of African descent all over the world, the same that Zionism has done for Jews all over the world. If we too return to Africa, not physically, but philosophically, culturally and psychologically, it will benefit us right there in America, politically, economically and socially. Just as Jews all over the world help Israel and Israel in turn helps Jews all over the world, people of African descent all over this earth must help Africa to

---

[37] Leslie Lacy, 'African Responses to Malcolm X', in L. Jones & L. Neal, *Black Fire*, New York: William Morrow & Co 1968, pp.19-38 (the quotation is from 24-25). See also Kevin Gaines (2006).

[38] Malcolm X, 'We Are All Blood Brothers', *Liberator* July 1964, p.5.

[39] Angelou (1987), p.18.

become free and strong, and Africa in turn must obligate itself to help people of African descent all over this earth.

The intellectuals and professionals among the 22 million Africans in America should unite now among themselves to form a nucleus around which the rest of us can really to make this vital dream a living reality.

The Busiest of Days

Malcolm's days in Ghana were so crowded, and so much has been recorded, that it is best to detail his activities day by day.

Sunday, May 10

According to Alice Windom, then living in Accra, Malcolm had rested on his first night in town. He was staying at the Ambassador Hotel.

Monday, May 11

In his *Notebook* Malcolm wrote that 'J[ulian] M[ayfield] came by...Alice Windom...went back to JM's...about 15 Afro-Americans came by...showed eager desire for news about the struggle in America'. In his *Autobiography*, Malcolm says he telephoned 'the author Julian Mayfield, who seemed to be the leader of Ghana's little colony of Afro-American expatriates'. (p.405) According to Alice Windom, many of the Afro-Americans rushed over to Malcolm's hotel and then those who could take time off work lunched at the Mayfields' home to the music of Bessie Smith and Miles Davis.[40] (Julian Mayfield was then the editor of the *African Review*.) 'He talked of his pilgrimage and his trip through the Middle East, of Ibadan, and of the break with the Nation of Islam. He said that he "intends to lend his talents to the building of unity among the various rights groups in America", and told us that, in his view, no useful purpose could be served by exposing all the roots of dissension. He dealt with the question in terms of the disagreement on political direction and involvement in the extra-religious struggle for human rights in America.'[41]

---

40 Lacy (1970), chapter 13.

41 Schomburg Centre: Clarke Papers, 24/33: Alice Windom in Accra to 'Christine' (nd), forwarded to 'Dear Friend', 29 May 1965. Unless stated otherwise, much of this report on Accra is from this long letter. Alice Windom was working at various odd jobs, according to Angelou (1987), p.30; in 1967 she was part of the Economic Mission for Africa based in Addis Ababa. A copy of this letter is in the FBI's Papers on the OAAU! (Schomburg Center: SC Micro R-7081) Did the FBI have access to all mail from Ghana, or was it watching 'Christine' and John Henrik Clarke? See also Malcolm's letters from Lagos 10/5/1964 and Accra 11/5/1964 in Breitman (1966), pp. 61-63.

Julian Mayfield, actor, author, playwright, journalist, ex-Communist Party member, Castro-supporter and a critic of the non-violent strategy espoused by the Civil Rights leaders, was working closely with President Nkrumah as a writer and editor. He was the founder and

(Malcolm lists the following people in his *Notebook*: Maya [Angelou] Maké; Alice Windom, Helen Darden, Victoria Nye, Dr. Robert Lee and Preston King.) In the evening some 40 Afro-Americans congregated in the Mayfield home for broad-ranging discussions with Malcolm.

Tuesday, May 12

On Tuesday morning Malcolm noted that he went to see the 'new building where the offices of his [Julian Mayfield's] new magazine are located...Drove to the Cuban Embassy and met their Ambassador... who immediately offered to give a party in my honour (diplomatic).' According to Carlos Moore, the 'Ambassador, Entralgo Gonzales, offered Cuban support, and that of the communist bloc, at the United Nations, should Malcolm succeed in getting sponsorship for his petition. If he did not succeed, Gonzales told Malcolm that Cuba would be willing to act as sponsor and also raise the issue of Puerto Rican independence...Malcolm was impressed by these offers, but remained as "leery" of "progressives" as he had been in 1960 when he had talked with Castro at the Hotel Theresa in Harlem. Nevertheless Malcolm accepted the offer but said that "Africans will have to erect safeguards against the eventual co-optation of their struggles". He hoped that Cuban involvement with Africa would help Cuban Blacks.'[42]

But is Moore correct in his assessment of Malcolm's exchange and feelings towards the Cuban Ambassador? Malcolm reported that the Ambassador was an 'expert on African affairs. I proudly visited his embassy and accepted an invitation to his home where I met his beautiful wife and children. They made me feel like one of the family. He was so down-to-earth and unassuming, it was difficult to remember that he was actually His Excellency Armando Entralgo. He also gave a dinner in my honour to which he invited the entire diplomatic community.'[43] Malcolm was by now certainly not 'leery' of 'progressives': he would give his first talk on the Socialist Workers Party platform on his return to New York.

Presumably it was after visiting the Ambassador that Malcolm 'went to Maya's...Helen...Alice...'.[44]

---

editor of *African Review*, a magazine of political and economic affairs.

42 Carlos Moore, *Castro, the Blacks and Africa*, Los Angeles: UCLA 1988, p.187. Castro was in New York to speak at the UN conference on the situation in the Congo; the UN was attacked by Castro and many African members for not having defended Patrice Lumumba and prevented the Katanga secession. See *The NY Courier*, 1 October 1960 and the *N.Y. Amsterdam News* 24 September 1960, p.1 for reports of Castro's visit. These reports do not indicate any hostility between Castro and Malcolm.

43 Malcolm X, 'We are All Blood Brothers', *Liberator*, July 1964, pp.4-6.

44 *Notebook 4*, 12 May 1964.

By that morning so many invitations had come pouring in that Malcolm was unable to accept them all. A hastily organised Malcolm X Committee of African Americans helped to make the arrangements.

According to Cameron Duodu, the Ghana Press Club was the centre of some of the debates about the political directions in which the country should be heading.

> Malcolm X was brought there by an African-American writer and very good friend of mine, Julian Mayfield, with the intention of getting him to address us; there was immediate murmuring against the idea…At that time, there was quite a large colony of African-Americans in Ghana and some were sitting with us as this debate occurred. This embarrassed me, for Ghanaians are known for their hospitality and it seemed to me odd that we should seem to be refusing a hearing to one of our brothers from the US, who was a guest in our country. So I intervened…That killed the murmuring stone dead and, within short time, Malcolm was talking to us.
>
> The man was impressive, both as regards physical presence and oratorical prowess. Physically, he was tall and handsome and his skin colour showed that he had inherited the best of both the black and white worlds. No one could accuse him of mindless racism, for he indisputably belonged to both the black and the white races – if they exist. But striking though his physique was, it was when he opened his mouth that his personality shone through. He had a deep voice, and through preaching at mosques, he had acquired a modulation of tone that was absolutely musical.
>
> We sat mesmerized as he sketched out in detail for us the struggles that African-Americans faced in the US, and warned us to be wary of the US government, which condoned the maltreatment of our brothers in the US, yet came down to us in Africa, grinning at us as if it was our greatest friend.[45]

At a press conference held at the Club later that day, Malcolm recorded that 'Mr Anim & Mr Kofi Batsa' were there.[46] G.T. Anim was the managing director of the Ghana News Agency and Kofi Batsa was the editor of *The Spark* and Secretary General of the Pan-African Union of Journalists. Two other attendees, mentioned in the *Autobiography* are T.D.

---

45 My grateful thanks to Cameron Duodu, who sent me his article from which this is taken. 'Malcolm X when he came to Ghana', *New African*, May 2005. Mr Duodo was then also the editor of the monthly *Drum*.

46 Malcolm X Papers, Box 9, *Notebook 4*, 12 May 1964.

Baffoe, the Editor of the *Ghanaian Times* and Cameron Duodu, writing for the *New African*.[47] It was 'jam-packed'; Malcolm wrote,

> I stressed...the need for mutual communication and support between Africans and Afro-Americans whose struggles were interlocked...I said that the 22 million Afro-Americans could become for Africa a great positive force – while, in turn, the African nations could and should exert positive force at diplomatic levels against America's racial discrimination...All Africa is united in opposition to apartheid in South Africa and oppression in the Portuguese territories. But you waste your time if you do not realise that Verwoerd and Salazar, Britain and France, could never last a day if it weren't for the US support. So until you really expose the man in Washington, you haven't accomplished anything.[48]

The *Daily Graphic's* story was headlined 'Help US Negroes – Malcolm X' and related that Malcolm had asked for support to take the case of the struggle 'by Negroes for civil rights' to the UN. The US was a 'master of imperialism'. He praised 'Osagyefo the President and said as a result of his able, sincere and dedicated leadership, America feared Ghana...[H]e tries to unite the people of the continent [so] they label him as a dictator in order to discredit him.'[49]

According to the *Ghanaian Times* (13 May 1964, p.3) the 'Afro-American Muslim leader [was] acquainting himself with the mounting wave of nationalism in Africa'. The 22 million Afro-Americans were being humiliated in the USA, and needed the support of Africans in their struggle for racial equality. Their position had not changed from 1864 to 1964. Good relations between Africans and Afro-Americans was 'bound to have far-reaching results for the common good. Malcolm explained that his new movement intended to raise racial dignity and build black nationalism and social and economic advancement.'

Malcolm noted that he spent some time with Maya Angelou, Vicki Nye, then went to visit Julia Wright (daughter of African American novelist Richard Wright) and met Preston King and his wife at her house. In the evening, 'Maya, Vicki and Helen stopped at my hotel and we talked for about two hours'.

---

47 In his *Notebook* Malcolm notes for Saturday, 16 May 'Cameron – McCartie: strong desire to understand.' I have not been able to trace 'McCartie'.

48 *Autobiography*, p. 407.

49 Lacy (1970), p.215.

Wednesday, May 13

The day began, Malcolm noted, with 'wonderful talk with the Afro-Americans and then with CA...KB[50] came by and brought me up to date on the States...He and Julian took me to Accra Union for the lecture. Tremendously receptive audience. [see below] Another social affair for me at the Press Club – many of the Afro-American community present.' This was a soirée given by the Association of Ghanaian Journalists and Writers. 'All night Malcolm was surrounded by eager listeners and questioners, and he had his first chance to watch Ghanaians dance the high-life, which he thoroughly enjoyed. He made a short speech, again emphasizing the need for unity between Africans and Afro-Americans.' According to the *Corriere della Somalia* he 'insisted that the African people should not allow themselves to be deceived by the flattery of the United States, which claims to be a friend of the Africans'.[51]

'KB' was probably Kofi Batsa, mentioned above. I have been unable to discover the identity of 'CA'.

The Marxist Study Forum at the University of Ghana at Legon had arranged for Malcolm to address the students on Wednesday. Leslie Lacy, its organiser, noted that 'the university officials tried to sabotage our efforts, but we out-manoeuvred them'.[52] Though the University and its students were, according to Lacy, a bastion of conservatism, an estimated 500 students attended the session which was chaired by African American Preston King. The title of his address, Britz told the Department of State, was 'Will Africa Ignite America's Racial Powder Keg?'. Demonstrating the close co-operation between the US embassies, the telegram sent by the Embassy to the Department of State stated that 'Malcolm appeared repeat speech given Ibadan May 8. Impact on audience considerably lessened by anti-Christian bias, belittling remarks on President Kennedy and civil rights movement.'[53] The report in the *Ghanaian Times* bears out the Embassy's assertion that the speech was mainly a repetition. But it adds a new aspect of Malcolm's thinking: 'While South Africa preaches and practises segregation, the US preaches integration and practises segregation...As in Angola, South Africa and other colonial countries, the

---

50 I don't know who these initials stand for. I presume 'KB' was from the USA, if he brought Malcolm 'up-to-date' on the USA. Or could Malcolm have meant American activities in Ghana? In that case this could have been Kofi Batsa, or even Kojo Botsio?

51 *Corriere della Somalia*, 19/5/1964.

52 Lacy (1968), p.215

53 NARA: TRV-Malcolm X Accra 935, Telegram dated 15/5/1964. There is a version of Malcolm's speech in Smith, 1967, pp.211-220; other excerpts are in Lacy (1970), pp.216-7.

price of liberty in the United States is the willingness to die.' Kevin Gaines emphasises that Malcolm

> targeted specific acts of white supremacist brutality inflicted on black demonstrators in the South. He condemned the American media's paternalistic notion of 'responsible' black leadership, and the press's condemnation of Nkrumah and other nonaligned leaders critical of American hegemony...[He] spoke of the hypocrisy of American diplomacy in Africa that pursued cordial diplomatic exchanges while seeking tighter economic control over African resources. Malcolm rejected the US government's injunction that black American official visitors to Africa privilege their American identities over expressions of black solidarity.[54]

According to La Ray Denzer, 'at least half, perhaps even two-thirds of the audience was expatriate. Of that number one-half was white (both European and American) and the other half was Afro-American. The rest was Ghanaian...The European whites didn't like the factual misrepresentation, but they were impressed by the delivery. The American whites didn't like either the speech or the delivery, but agreed that he was an impressive and persuasive speaker. The Afro-Americans for the most part reacted as they would at a revival meeting...to the extent that they gave Malcolm X a standing ovation...The Ghanaians enjoyed the speech, although they did not accept everything he said as gospel.'[55]

Thus at least some of the students had a different opinion from that of the US Embassy of their experience of Malcolm. The 'spellbound' students at Legon reported in an article entitled 'The Plight of the Afro-American' that Malcolm had given 'one of the most brilliant expositions ever heard in this University...Mr. Malcolm X...sought philosophical and spiritual links between the North of America and Africa.' Malcolm did then give his usual description of the plight and situation of African Americans, and went on to say it was difficult for him 'to understand how whites can sit and laugh with Negroes here. Back home they have two faces when they look at the Negro...The Negro in America demands human dignity *now*'. In response to a question Malcolm said that 'he who is not ready to die for freedom is not fit to mention that word', and paid tribute to Nkrumah

---

54 Gaines (2006), pp.192-3. In his *Notebook 5* Malcolm lists the topics he intended to address: e.g not visitor but at home; hospitality, brotherhood, paradise; Ghana – one of the most progressive; progressive leadership – president; Yardstick – good African leaders; Nkrumah, Ben Bella, etc.; controlled education? Colonial mentality; neo-colonialisms –USA; USA...

55 Schomburg Center: St.Clair Drake Papers, Box 67: Historian La Ray Denzer to Untermeyer, 1/7/1964. Denzer also notes that Malcolm was 'pleased to see the modern buildings of Accra and so forth because the white man had never told him about them; they had only told him that there were jungles, lions and naked people here in Africa'.

for 'teaching human dignity to Ghanaians and all Negroes'. After the two-hour long meeting, which was 'never tiresome', a group of students met with Malcolm and 'christened' him 'Ababio'.[56]

Journalist Cameron Duodu reports that

> Malcolm developed his arguments for us in full in a speech he gave at the Great Hall of the University of Ghana. The place was packed and he skillfully elucidated every aspect of the life that blacks were constrained to live in the US and explained why, when we met them in Africa, they sometimes surprised us with their actions.
>
> We should not blame African-Americans if they did not rise to our expectations because, he said: 'We have no roots – we are the only people who do not have a language of our own. Our slave master took out our tongue when he took us away from you. So we speak with our slave master's voice. How can someone looking just like you but speaking with another person's tongue make sense to you?'
>
> Malcolm continued: 'The 'American Negro' is the only American who brings America first when he wants to denominate or name himself. We have Polish Americans, Italian Americans, Irish Americans. They all put their ancestry first before America. Only the 'American Negro' mentions America first. That shows you that he has no sense of identity. And you in Africa have to understand that and help him get his identity back.
>
> 'The strange thing is that although the "American Negro" puts America first, America always puts him last. They send us to World War II, and we're the best soldiers they've got. They send us to Korea and we're the best soldiers they've got. They send us to Vietnam and we're still the best soldiers they've got. But when we come back home after fighting their wars, they tell us we're not fit to ride with them on the same side of the bus; we must sit at the back of the bus! We are fit to die for America but not fit to sit with America in the same bus.'
>
> And then he added: 'Mind you, I have not come here to condemn America. But if what I say condemns America, then America stands condemned!'
>
> There were wild cheers!
>
> Malcolm also talked about the emphasis that the world press constantly placed on the Holocaust in Germany, in which six

---

56 *Sputnik*, the Akuafo Hall Bulletin, 22 May 1964. Akuafo Hall is one of the halls for students on the Legon campus.

million Jews were killed. Why wasn't a similar fuss made about the 20 million Africans who had died on the high seas after being seized as slaves in Africa and put in horrible ships bound for North America and the Caribbean?

'I am sometimes asked why I don't talk about the Holocaust but only about Africans who were killed during the slave trade,' Malcolm said. 'If I don't talk about the Holocaust, it's because, after I've wept for the 20 million Africans, I have no tears left.'

Malcolm stressed that it was important that Africans should get together with their '22 million black brothers in America. We should not allow the white man to use us against each other. The white man would send African-Americans to Africa and give them assignments that would hurt Africa, but because they had a black skin, we wouldn't realise they were dangerous.

'Similarly, the white man could send Africans to America who would carry the message that Africans have no memory of their brothers who were carted off as slaves, and that the Africans and the American blacks therefore had nothing in common. But we're one people, divided by the effects of the white man's wickedness towards us – slavery and colonialism.'[57]

The *Daily Graphic* (15 May 1964, p.7) printed a photo of Malcolm and of the crowded hall. The paper noted that, after describing the situation of Afro-Americans, and asking for the aid of African states, Malcolm had said that 'African leaders like Osagyefo the President, President Nasser and President Ben Bella are very much disliked by the colonial powers because of their unyielding attitude towards neo-colonialism, imperialism and racial discrimination. They are always branded as dictators because they are revolutionary.'

Clearly, the Embassy assertion regarding the audience's reaction to Malcolm was somewhat less than accurate. Ms. Windom wrote that Malcolm was 'accorded a standing ovation'; Lacy recalls that the students 'cheered and they chanted. They shouted at the top of their voices songs of praise in different Ghanaian languages'. Maya Angelou, whose son was a student at Legon, noted that Malcolm's 'oratorical skill captured the audience…The Africans relished Malcolm's use of proverbs…Black Americans led the applause and soon the entire audience was standing,

---

[57] From Cameron Duodu, 'Malcolm X when he came to Ghana', *New African*, May 2005. Some of Malcolm's speech is reproduced in *Malcolm X Talks to Young People* (1965), pp.12-21.

clapping and laughing its approval...A group of students began to chant the football cheer, *Asante Kotoko*.'[58]

According to Lacy, Malcolm's final words were:

> Brother, you think your life is so sweet that you would live at any price? Does mere existence balance with the weight of your great sacrifice? Or can it be you fear the grave enough to live and die a slave? Oh brother! Let it be said that when you're dead and tears are shed that your life was a stepping stone, which your children crossed upon; look each foeman in the eye – lest you die in vain.

'These were addressed to a hostile young American-trained Ghanaian geologist who had accused Malcolm X, at the end of an emotional and lively question period, of bringing to Africa 'the gospel of racial violence'.'[59] A student in the audience demanded that the speaker should be thrown out. He was. The students now 'cheered and chanted' their approval of Malcolm. The following morning Lacy breakfasted with the students at the Mensah Sarbah Hall, and found them still enthusiastic about Malcolm. Even those who had opposed the Marxist Forum came to speak to him: 'Malcolm was, they said, militant, dynamic; but they all said, "He is so honest".'[60]

These accounts flatly contradict the Embassy's report. 'University lecturers', Ms. Windom adds, 'and others said later that they never before saw the students respond with such enthusiasm to any speaker. The University, unfortunately, has been noted for the students' conservative, reactionary political views – a colonial heritage...'

After Malcolm left, ten students formed a Malcolm X Society. A folk singer created a song in his honour, which included the lines,

> Malcolm Man, Malcolm Man
> You speak your tale of woe
> The red in our face lime our
> Blood in the land
> You speak your tale of woe
> Malcolm Man, Malcolm Man
> The anger that you feel
> Will one day unite our people

---

58 Lacy (1970), p.217; Angelou (1987), pp.136-138.

59 Lacy (1968), p.19.

60 Lacy (1968), p.28.

And make us all so real
Malcolm Man, Malcolm Man.[61]

Thursday, May 14

In his *Notebook* Malcolm records that 'Maya took me to the Nigerian Ambassador – once lived in DC...to the Mali Ambassador...Kwabena took me to see Boaten [Kwaku Boaten, Minister of Education] spoke to him for an hour...Went to JM...then to Kofi Baako Minister of Defence several other ministers and influential Ghanaians were there...drinks, music, then dinner. (African food)...Baako a remarkable, down to earth man, very quick minded, alert.'

Was it perhaps on this day that Malcolm had lunch with Cameron Duodu at his house? After discussing the influence of seeing White Muslims on the *Hajj*, Malcolm told the young journalist that

> when he got back to America, he would start a new organisation to be called the Organisation of Afro-American Unity (OAAU), which would work closely with its near-namesake, the Organisation of African Unity (OAU). Just as the OAU contained both white and Arab Africans as well as black Africans, the OAAU would seek coalitions with all areas of the world where the people, irrespective of their colour, were opposed to racial discrimination and imperialist domination.
>
> The OAAU would establish fraternal relations with the Arab League and with the Afro-Asian People's Solidarity Organisation. The African-Americans would keep these organisations informed of what the American government was doing, or not doing, about racial discrimination in the US, and in that way, the US government would not be able to lie to the rest of the world that it wanted friendly relations with all peoples, irrespective of colour – the message the US State Department sought to convey to the world.
>
> In the immediate future, the OAAU would seek the assistance of its friends in the UN to lay a complaint against the US for its violation of the human rights of African-Americans.
>
> I could see immediately that, with his charismatic personality, Malcolm X could bring this off. Such a magical coalition of forces around the globe could embarrass the US tremendously, and I was convinced that he would never be allowed by the US government to put his plan into action. So I said to him: 'Brother Malcolm, they will kill you!' He didn't answer, but I was sure the thought had

---
61 Lacy (1970), pp.225-6; Lacy (1969), p.223.

crossed his mind. His silence meant that he was prepared to pay the price for his beliefs.⁶²

Friday, May 15

'Had breakfast with Dr. Makonnen (Br. Guiana) need for Pan-African militancy', notes Malcolm. According to Leslie Lacy the two had met previously at one of the evening functions.⁶³ The British Guiana-born activist, now settled in Ghana, had been one of the organisers of the 1945 Pan-African Conference held in Manchester, UK, and had been involved in the politics of liberation in the UK since the 1930s. At the 1945 Congress it had been decided to send resolutions to the United Nations seeking representation on that body for Africans, and justice in South Africa.⁶⁴ In his *Autobiography*, Mak (as he was usually called in the UK) stated that he 'had to take Malcolm X to task: 'What is all this Muslim business? We are fighting a hell of a rear-guard action here in Ghana against them. Because these Muslim fellows are all over the place, and Nasser may be using them against the Party at a certain point...Because of the need to have a single, strong one-party state, we felt we couldn't allow these fellows to belong to the party and at the same time be working with Nasser's UAR ambassador...Malcolm admitted that he had been learning a lot on this African trip. His views on this were not static.'⁶⁵

Later Malcolm listed Makonnen among the 'Afro-Americans and West Indians who have migrated to Ghana [and] have played a prominent role in the very progressive intellectual atmosphere that prevails throughout the country. Some of the more famous names involved are the late Dr. W.E.B. Du Bois...his wife...George Padmore, Miss Cecil McHardy, Dr. T.R. Makonnen, and many others Cairo-based Muslim Brotherhood.'Malcolm

---

62 From Cameron Duodu, 'Malcolm X when he came to Ghana', *New African*, May 2005. Mr Duodu also records that 'Although he had very little time on his hands, he managed to write a postcard to me (from Switzerland). In red ink, he had written: "Mr Cameron Duodu, Your Brothers in Harlem remember you."'

63 Lacy (1968), p.30. Unfortunately we do not know whether Malcolm also met with I.T.A. Wallace-Johnson of Sierra Leone, who was in Ghana giving a series of lectures at the Institute of African Studies. Wallace-Johnson had been a close colleague of Makonnen's and George Padmore's in the UK in the 1930s. One of Wallace-Johnson's lectures at the Institute of African Studies at Legon is noted in the *Evening News*, 7/5/1964, p.7.

64 Hakim Adi & Marika Sherwood, *The 1945 Manchester Pan-African Congress Revisited*, London: New Beacon Books 1995, pp. 57-9, 111-112.

65 Ras Makonnen (edited by Kenneth King), *Pan Africanism from Within*, Nairobi: OUP 1973, pp.76-7; When Makonnen was jailed after the overthrow of Nkrumah, Julian Mayfield was among those who pleaded for his release. Is it from Makonnen that Malcolm had learned about Padmore? I have not been able to trace Cecil McHardy.

recorded that 'we discussed the need for the type of Pan-African unity that would also include Afro-Americans'.[66]

Malcolm also visited Dr. Robert Lee, an ex-patriate African-American dentist, who had, by 1964, lived in Ghana for some time, and still lives there. Dr. Lee remembers that Malcolm was 'everywhere – at Legon, in Parliament, everywhere. He spoke mainly of race – could have given his talk with his eyes closed. When he was at my house, the African-American women just took over; they would have held his hands if they could. (Here Dr. Lee demonstrated to me how Malcolm tried to hide his hands.) The men were excluded!'[67]

The *Notebook* states, 'Audience with Nkrumah (for an hour)[68] well-informed, concerned about Afro-Americans' plight – Unity of Africa and people of African descent (Pan-Africanism) is key to the problem – religion?' In his *Autobiography* Malcolm described Dr. Nkrumah as wearing

> ordinary dress, his hand was extended and a smile was on his sensitive face. I pumped his hand. We sat on a couch and talked. I knew he was particularly well-informed on the Afro-American's plight, as for years he had lived and studied in America. We discussed the unity of Africans and peoples of African descent. We agreed that Pan-Africanism was the key also to the problems of those of African heritage, I could feel the warm, likeable and very down-to-earth qualities of Dr. Nkrumah. My time with him was up all too soon, I promised faithfully that, when I returned to the Unites States, I would relay to Afro-Americans his warm personal regards.[69]

According to Maya Angelou, it was Shirley Graham Du Bois who had arranged for Malcolm to be received by President Nkrumah, to whom she was 'close'.[70] But Malcolm had met Nkrumah previously in the USA, so why did Mrs. Du Bois have to intervene? Kevin Gaines explains that, given the political situation, 'Nkrumah probably judged it prudent to keep his distance from Malcolm. With a massive aid package under consideration by the US government, Nkrumah was loathe to further jeopardise relations with the US'.[71]

---

66 *Autobiography*, p.408. Malcolm X (1964), p.5.

67 Interview with Dr Lee, Accra, Ghana, 11 February 2003.

68 Can we presume that whoever had reported to the FBI that Malcolm 'did not have an interview with President Nkrumah' was regurgitating information from the Ambassador's office? FBI 1000-399321: NY 105-8999, Part VIII Foreign Travel, p.94.

69 *Autobiography* (1964) p.410. Malcolm recounts his experiences in Ghana at some length.

70 Angelou (1987), pp.138-142. Gaines adds that Mayfield also helped to secure this audience for Malcolm. (P.310)

71 Gaines (2006), p.190

Alice Windom informed her correspondents, 'We waited at Julian's house for what seemed an interminable time before Malcolm returned. Although we could not ask what transpired between them, it was apparent that Malcolm was moved and gratified by the experience.' Leslie Lacy, also awaiting Malcolm's return, recalled that 'Malcolm was very elated. His visit was complete, for he had seen one of the most progressive black men on the planet. And his face had changed again – he was so happy. Malcolm then said: "Nkrumah, that man understands. He is a real believer in change...He said a lot, but one thing he said which I will never forget is 'Brother, it is now or never the hour of the knife, the break with the past, the major operation".'[72] In his article in the *Liberator* (July1964, p.6) Malcolm reported that the audience with President Nkrumah was an hour long, and that Nkrumah had 'made it clear that he would not consider Ghana free until all Africa and all people of African descent were free'. He goes on to describe the President's philosophy of Pan-Africanism as 'the most advanced political doctrine being voiced on the African Continent today, and for this reason President Nkrumah is both feared and hated by the White Western Powers who are still trying to maintain a neo-colonialist foothold'. According to Carlos Moore, Nkrumah 'had approved the recruitment of highly trained black Americans to serve in Africa in various capacities'. But while Nkrumah was interested in technicians, Malcolm was more interested in supporting freedom fighters.[73]

Malcolm's next appointment was with the Ghana Parliament. But he arrived at Parliament House just after the session was adjourned, 'delayed by other arrangements...But the members of Parliament were still in the building and Mr. Baako (Minister of Defence and also the Leader of the National Assembly) drew Malcolm into the Members' Room.' (Is it possible that Malcolm was delayed because of his lengthy talk with President Nkrumah?) The *Ghanaian Times* reported that 'Members of Parliament yesterday granted audience to Mr Malcolm X...at a lounge of Parliament House, Accra. Mr. X spoke of the degrading status of Afro-Americans in the United States. A lively discussion followed his address, during which the MPs asked questions of topical interest.'[74]

---

72 Lacy (1968), pp.31-2. Norden (1967, p.8) claims that 'Nkrumah had entrusted [Malcolm] with a letter of commission to arrange upon his return for the purchase and installation of a nuclear reactor on Accra'. I have not seen this claim elsewhere nor have I been able to verify it.

73 Moore (1988), p.187. In his footnotes Moore only refers to 'conversations in Paris'. Not only the politics but the veracity of this book have been questioned. See www.afrocubaweb.com/lettertocarlos/htm. Given this, and as Moore gives the year of Malcolm's visit to Africa incorrectly, I have ignored some of Moore's recollections. However, Richard Gibson, one of those who questions Moore, has himself been much doubted.

74 *Ghanaian Times*, 18/5/1964. This issue also carried a photograph of 'Malcolm X at the home of a young Ghanaian friend...a group of Ghanaian intellectuals had gathered for lunch.' Who

Leslie Lacy notes that, before entering the Parliament building, Malcolm stood on the steps and said, 'If I had grown up in a country where black men made the justice, who knows what my life would have been like'. The two of them were then taken inside. 'Malcolm spoke "on the degrading status of the Afro-Americans in the United States", repeating and reemphasizing some of the issues he had raised at the university. He described the United States as the "master of imperialism without whose support France, South Africa, Britain and Portugal could not exist". Malcolm appealed for support from all Africans...He said, "The struggle for civil rights in the United States should be switched to a struggle for human rights to enable Africans to raise the matter at the United Nations". He praised their President and said that as a result of his able, sincere and dedicated leadership, America feared Ghana...He attacked the American press and explained how it was used to divide "people who should be united for a common cause"...He warned the Ministers that they should be suspicious of every American touring Ghana...He explained his name, 'X', saying that Afro-Americans bear white names – the names of their slave master – "and as such had lost their language, cultural and social backgrounds". Although he was not cheered as enthusiastically as he had been at Legon, his very moving address was followed by a lively discussion.'[75]

The *Ghanaian Times* printed a photograph of Malcolm addressing the 200 students at the Winneba Ideological Institute, his next appointment. The Institute had been set up by Nkrumah as a forum for students to work out their own theories and practise for social change. Others describe it as a training institution for African activists and revolutionaries.[76] 'As usual, he was brilliant,' wrote Ms Windom, 'and communicated with [the students] at their own high level of political awareness'. Malcolm made brief notes in *Notebook 5* of his talk:

> you will be called upon soon to help great leaders like President Nkrumah, lead the oppressed people of the world out of darkness into light, out from under the shackles of ignorance that was created by slavery, colonialism and imperialism – into the light of a new world that is now being created by freedom, justice and equality...
> 1. Your success is our success

were the unnamed 'intellectuals'?

75 Lacy (1968), pp.29-30.

76 In 1964 Mr Kodwo Addison, the Institute's director, stated that there were plans to expand the students intake to 500 per annum. He described Winneba as 'home of progressive activists who come to drink deep from the foundation of ideological orientations and to be armed with the greatest weapons for intellectual revolution of our times, philosophical consciencism'. (*West Africa*, 24/10/1964, p.1202. Addison was referring to Kwame Nkrumah's book *Consciencism* (1964), on the philosophy and ideology of decolonisation.

2. We are all the same people
3. We must *unite* against the enemy
4. Can't stop South Africa and Portugal unless you stop the USA
The question: Africanization or Americanization?

Malcolm had to deal with a question by an Afro-American in the audience, who turned out to be a teacher placed in a 'local secondary school by the African-American Institute' in New York. 'After the meeting the students cornered the fellow, and yelled "are you a victim of Rockefeller?", "stop corrupting our children", "stooge", "CIA and American Agent" and "come to this Institute for some orientation". At the close of the meeting Malcolm was presented with a set of President Nkrumah's books.'

The *Corriere della Somalia* of 19 May reported the meeting on page 1. Again Malcolm had spoken of the 'problem American negroes face, the reconquest of their dignity and self-respect and the recognition of their human rights. He asked the assistance of African leaders to American negroes in their fight for racial equality. Malcolm also denounced the USA for the use which is made of American negroes for its false propaganda in Africa.' This article had been sent by the American Embassy at Mogadiscio to the Department of State. Interestingly, the Chargé D'Affaires, Francis N. Magliozzi, hand-corrected the small 'n' into a capital 'N' for 'Negroes'.[77] The US government's interest in Malcolm's visit was clearly widespread.

That evening Malcolm had dinner 'at the Chinese Embassy: met Mrs. W.E.B. Du Bois – Albanian, Cuban', he wrote in his *Notebook*. He found 'the Chinese Ambassador, Mr Huang Ha, a most perceptive, and also most militant man, focused upon the efforts of the West to divide Africans from the peoples of African heritage elsewhere. The guests included the Cuban and the Algerian Ambassadors.'[78]

Afterwards, according to his *Notebook* entry on 15 May, Malcolm he attended a: 'Soirree at Press Club – Nigerian Ambassador encouraged me to speak: dance, sing, but remember Mandela, Sobukane, Lumumba, Angola'. Unfortunately he does not state who organised this gathering.

Saturday, May 16

There was a luncheon for Malcolm given by Alhaji Isa Wali, the Nigerian High Commissioner, at which, according to Ms. Windom, 'The wife of the Pakistani High Commissioner talked to Malcolm for a long time, [and I overheard her saying] "If you come to Pakistan you would get such a welcome you would feel perfectly at home with the people".

---

77 NARA: SOC 14-1 US, Embassy in Mogadiscio (sic) to Department of State 19/5/1964.
78 *Autobiography*, pp.408, 411.

Malcolm wears a turban and a robe and carries the Koran given to him by Alhaji Isa Wali, Nigerian High Commissioner to Ghana (right), Accra, May 1964

In his address to his guests Alhaji Isa Wali spoke of his experiences of racial discrimination while he had been in Washington for two years. He emphasised the existing ties between Africans and Afro-Americans by saying that "the only difference is that one was born in America and the other in Africa". To reinforce this belief, he gave Malcolm a two-volume translation of the Koran and a beautiful blue robe and a striking orange turban. Malcolm bent so that the High Commissioner could arrange the turban properly and when he straightened, he looked so grand that the Pakistani High Commissioner's wife dubbed him "An African prince".

Afterwards, Mrs. Shirley Graham Du Bois, Director of Television, showed Malcolm around her home so he could see where W.E.B. Du Bois had spent his last days. Afterwards they visited the Castle, which Malcolm did not have time to 'really see' when he had had his audience with President Nkrumah there. That evening, Malcolm's last in Ghana, 'the Cuban Ambassador gave a lovely party for him to which the African Ambassadors and the press were invited...Malcolm was perhaps most impressed with the Algerian ambassador, Taher Kaid, with whom he had a critical discussion about the relevance of race and revolutionary potential.' Malcolm reported that the Ambassador had 'a razor-sharp mind, and was well-versed in the principles of revolution. His image of militant sincerity is strongly pictured in my mind'. In his Autobiography Malcolm

Malcolm with Mrs. Shirley, Graham Du Bois, Accra, May 1964

described the Ambassador as 'a man who was dedicated totally to militancy, and to world revolution, as the way to solve the problems of the world's oppressed masses. His perspective was attuned not just to Algerians, but to include the Afro-Americans and all others anywhere who were oppressed'.79 (p.408)

Malcolm spoke about the effect his conversation with Mr. Kaid had on him to the interviewer from the *Young Socialist* on January 18, 1965:

When I told him (Mr. Kaid) that my political, social and economic philosophy was black nationalism, he asked me very frankly, well, where did that leave him? Because he was white. He was an African, but he was Algerian, and to all appearances he was a white man. And he said if I define my objective as the victory of black nationalism, where does that leave him? Where does that leave revolutionaries in Morocco, Egypt, Iraq, Mauritania? So he showed me where I was alienating people who were true revolutionaries, dedicated to overthrowing the system of exploitation that exists on this earth by any means necessary.

So I had to do a lot of thinking and reappraising of my definition of black nationalism...But I still would be hard pressed to give a specific definition of the over-all philosophy which I think is necessary for the liberation of black people in this country.[80]

In his *Notebook* Malcolm wrote that there were 'representatives of African, Arab, Asian and Latin American countries' at this 'cocktail party'.

---

79 Windom, and Sales (1994), p.102; Malcolm X (1964), p.6. *Autobiography*, p.408. On the meeting with Taher Kaid, see also Goldman (1979), pp.179-180.

80 Breitman (1968), p.65.

Malcolm also met with the representatives of the liberation organisations who were receiving Ghanaian support; he was particularly impressed with the representatives of the two South African groups, the African National Congress and the Pan-Africanist Congress of Azania.[81] One night, perhaps after Malcolm had given an extensive interview to the New China News Agency, the Chinese Ambassador gave a state dinner in his honour. Malcolm had told the Agency that 'China's nuclear test helped not only the cause of Afro-Americans, but also that of all people of the world fighting against imperialists and he praised the Chinese Government's proposal for a world summit conference to discuss the complete prohibition and destruction of nuclear weapons...He termed the recent President's election a farce [as] there is no difference between Johnson and Goldwater, for both serve the interests of United States monopoly capital.'[82] Malcolm found that the Ambassador was a 'very impressive, intelligent man and well-informed on the plight of the Afro-American. He very politely reminded me that Mao Tze-Tung was the first head of state to declare the open support of his government and its 800 million people behind the Afro-American struggle for freedom and human dignity in America.'[83]

Despite this frantic activity, Malcolm had time to think about what he wanted to achieve at home and how he was to do this. According to George Breitman, he decided that he needed to form a non-religious organisation: 'he and Afro-Americans living in Ghana founded the first chapter of the new organization before he left that country.'[84] Malcolm set up what the letterhead states was the 'Information Bureau of the OAAU', with a Post Office Box address in Accra. From there he issued a press release, 'Afro-American Troops for Congo – Malcolm X'. This commenced with the assurance that 'thousands of black Americans are ready to fight and die for the genuine independence and freedom of the Congo'. This is emphasised by quotations from his letter to Diallo Telli, the Secretary General of the OAU. The release then explains that the OAAU 'has been lobbying in Africa in an attempt to strengthen the bonds between Africans and people of African descent in the western hemisphere'.[85] (I have not been able to find more information on this branch of the OAAU.)

81 Sales (1994), p.104. 'Azania' = South Africa.
82 FBI report on Malcolm X, #100-399321, memo from SAC, New York, 15/1/1965.
83 Malcolm X (1964), p.6.
84 Breitman (1970), p.34. Malcolm's speeches at the founding rally in New York can be found in this book.
85 Schomburg Center: John Henrik Clarke papers, Box C., file 614. As the OAAU was not formally established till June, and as the press release is undated, it is possible that it was issued after Malcolm's departure, perhaps in order to keep his spirit – and the OAAU - before Ghanaians.

Sunday, May 17

On Sunday morning the Afro-Americans went to Malcolm's hotel to collect him to take him to the airport. They found that the Press Club had paid his hotel expenses. Many came to wish him farewell. 'Underneath our light conversation ran a current of concern for his safety upon his return to the US. We talked with him about it. He, of course, is not prepared to be guided by any such fears.' Maya Angelou records that diplomats from the Nigerian, Chinese, Guinea, Yugoslav, Mali, Cuban, Algerian and Egyptian Embassies accompanied Malcolm to the airport.[86] In his *Autobiography*, Malcolm wrote, 'a small motorcade of *five Ambassadors* arrived – to see me off! I no longer had any words.' (p.413) In his *Notebook* the entry is 'VIP send off at airport...Cameron late'.

In his *Notebook* for this day he summarised his thoughts and feelings about Ghana:

> The Ghanaians are by far the most progressive and independent minded. Even their laughter is tinged always with an ominous note of seriousness - they laugh and joke with each other almost constantly, but it is not the same type of laughter (or jokes) found among other Africans – but all Africa is seething with serious awareness of itself, its potential wealth and power and the role it seems destined to play. We must identify with ('migrate' to) Africa culturally, philosophically and psychologically and the 'life' or new spirit will then give us the inspiration to do the things necessary (ourselves) to better our political, economic and social 'life'...in America.

What I take to be an editorial entitled 'Malcolm Asibe', appeared in the *Ghanaian Times* on 16 May. The author wanted Malcolm to take a new name: the Twi name 'Asibe', as someone as devoted and fearless as he must have come from my tribe'; he had 'met very few people who have impressed me with the urgency and absoluteness of a message as has Malcolm X...[Though] he talked mainly of the plight of the black skinned peoples in the US...[don't] imagine that this plight is one limited to America alone.' Alice Windom also assessed Malcolm's trip somewhat differently from the US Embassy's Third Secretary: 'I've only skimmed over the surface of Malcolm's visit' she wrote. 'Much more of great importance went on, and is still going on...I have a feeling that the American press will try to minimize the importance [of Malcolm's visit]. Some of you may not even get this letter if Uncle Sam's censors are overly alert...we are in a battle and since Malcolm is one of our most significant and militant

---

86 Angelou (1987), p.143. It is possible that Ms Angelou mis-remembers, as Malcolm reported that 'five ambassadors accompanied' him. (Malcolm X [1964], p.6)

leaders, efforts will be made to malign and discredit him...Malcolm spoke to us ceaselessly of unity...the united front is particularly important in a struggle against a common enemy because otherwise we waste much time in factional disputes which masquerade as ideological disagreements, and which help the enemy.'

Reactions to Malcolm in Ghana

Following Malcolm's departure there was a dispute, based on Malcolm's speech at the University, in the *Ghanaian Times* (18 May 1964, p.2 & 19 May 1964, p.2) between White South African journalist H.M. Basner, described by Leslie Lacy as a 'professional Marxist and political advisor to President Nkrumah', and Afro-American Julian Mayfield. The former castigated Malcolm for not giving a purely class-based analysis, while the latter, also a Marxist, placed race above class and pointed out that Malcolm had in fact said that he 'did not believe that the black man would ever experience full freedom under the American system...Is not socialism the only alternative to the system?' The Marxist Forum at the University discussed Malcolm's statements and issued a bulletin, 'Reflections on Brother Malcolm'. This stated that 'Malcolm's message is of vital importance...to the progressive movements of the world. Malcolm's philosophy, we believe, reduced to its barest essential, is that Black America should reject *the Capitalist* and *the Marxist* rationalizations of race relations and construct a theory of change which is consistent with its racial experience.' Lacy goes on to note that subsequent to a speech Malcolm had given in Chicago on his return, Basner wrote another piece on him, published on 29 May. In this he analysed Malcolm's speech as revealing that he had 'at last found the key – the class struggle and the struggle of human society – without which all doors to an understanding of political and social phenomena remain permanently shut...What Malcolm X must have seen in Africa...is the political leadership of men like Kwame Nkrumah and Jomo Kenyatta... Africans who...have reached an understanding that it is the lust for profit and not racial differences which make the white man behave in colonial Africa as he does...'[87]

Preston King, then an advisor to President Nkrumah, had introduced Malcolm at the meeting at the University.[88] The US Embassy reported that King had 'introduced him with seeming discomfort'.[89] Seen at that time

---

87 Lacy (1968), pp.32-38.

88 Preston King fled the USA in 1961 following his arrest and conviction for involvement in the Southern Civil Rights Movement. He was at this time teaching at Legon and then moved to Nairobi; he is the author of numerous books.

89 NARA: SOC 14-1 TRV – Malcolm X, Mahoney, Accra to Secretary of State and US Embassies in Lagos and Conarky, 14/5/1964.

by some as the 'dean' of the Afro-Americans in Ghana, Professor King kindly responded to my request for his memories on Malcolm' visit.

> I was very impressed by him – principally [by] what struck me as transparent honesty. He at no time pretended that he knew what he was wading through. He wanted to learn...His posture was that of a water tank with its top off: demanding in a puzzled sort of way, 'fill me up'...I don't mean to say there was anything passive about his intelligence. Not in the least...
>
> There was a warmth in Malcolm, but of a serious sort; there was no repartee or bonhomie...No grandstanding or rhetorical flourishes. Very economical...
>
> He was by nature, bizarrely, an internationalist, and was gently easing himself into this new role, without seeming quite to know where it would take him...He wanted more than ever to make radical use of the UN. The trouble was that (a) he assumed he would continue with a black support base in the States and (b) his new internationalism intensified the enmity of two key actors, Elijah Mohammed and J. Edgar Hoover...He clearly confronted the prospective return to the US with dread.[90]

Malcolm certainly 'made his mark' on Ghanaians, as described by John Lewis and Donald Harris, two representatives of the American Student Nonviolent Coordinating Committee (SNCC) visiting Ghana late in 1964:

> Among the first questions we were continually asked was 'What's your organization's relationship with Malcolm's?' After a day of this we found that we must, immediately on meeting people, state our own position in regard to where we stood on certain issues – Cuba, Vietnam, the Congo, Red China and the UN...We ultimately found that this situation was not peculiar to Ghana, the pattern repeated itself in every country...Malcolm's impact of Africa was just fantastic. In every country he was known and served as the main criteria for categorizing other Afro-Americans and their political views.[91]

---

90 Email from Professor King, then at the University of Lancaster, UK, 18/4/2000. Unfortunately Professor King has been too ill to respond to requests for elucidation of his comments.

91 Breitman (1966), p.85. This is repeated in John Lewis (with Michael D.Orso), *Walking With the Wind: a memoir of a movement*, San Diego: Harvest Books 1998, pp.295. Lewis and his SNCC colleagues had been invited to visit Guinea by Harry Belafonte who requested aid from the president of Guinea, Sékou Touré (whose name is mis-spelled as Seaakou Toureaa - p.293). Lewis found that the African students he met 'were the victims of pro-American propaganda...meant to give the impression that everything was idyllic in America' (p.296). Once the holiday in Guinea was over, Lewis and Don Harris travelled more widely in West

The US Government's Reaction to Malcolm's Visit

According to the 24 May 1964 report to the Department of State from the US Embassy, Malcolm had been due to arrive on April 16, 'but had failed to arrive as planned'. Daniel A. Britz, the Third Secretary, stated that Malcolm had not been 'officially invited to Ghana by the Ghana Government, but came at the invitation of the 'Marxist Forum', a new 'student' organization at the University of Ghana. He did not have an interview with President Nkrumah, nor did the Government hold any official reception for him', the Embassy maintained.[92]

Mr. Britz reports to his masters that the two government-owned/controlled papers carried fairly full stories of Malcolm's visit, but 'the official CPP[93] Newspaper, the *Evening News* mentioned the visit only once... The lack of coverage may be attributed to the fact that Prime Minister Nkrumah was made aware of the controversial nature of Malcolm X before his visit.' US Ambassador Mahoney detailed his conversation and warning to Nkrumah to the Department of State in a telegram dated 18 April 1964: 'Mentioning reports of visit to Ghana of Malcolm X, I asked Nkrumah if he was aware who Malcolm X is. Nkrumah said he was, but listened patiently if somewhat abstractedly while I filled him in on break with Elijah Muhamad and emphasized dangers inherent in his advocacy of racial violence. Concluded by saying it would be unfortunate if able to use Ghana as propaganda platform and would be particularly hard for responsible Negro leadership in the United States to understand. Nkrumah nodded but made no response.' The Ambassador worries about the 'Prime Minister's' critical attitudes towards the USA: 'Nkrumah generally accepts what his propagandists say about USG (US Government)...it is therefore most important that we continue trying build some sort of rapport between Nkrumah and President Johnson.'[94]

Africa, funded by the American Committee on Africa (p.294).

92 FBI Papers, reel 9, Airgram from Daniel A Britz, Third Secretary, Amembassy in Accra to Department of State, 24/5/1964.

93 The Convention People's Party, headed by Kwame Nkrumah, ruled Ghana, which had been turned into a one-party state. The Interest of the USA in the Godl Coast (Ghana from 1957) began shortly after WWII, as evidenced by the volume of information being sent back by the Embassy there. Among those volunteering information, beginning with his 1953 visit there was Richard Wright. NARA: RG59, Box 3582, 745K- 00/9-1553, 'Reprot from Richard Wright', sent from Accra 15/9/1953; 745K- 00/12-1053, Joyce, from Paris 10/12/53,' re Accra despatch 15/9/53: Richard Wright wanted a meeting to report on Goerge Padmore....'

94 NARA: SOC 14-1 US POL 15-1 Ghana, Telegram from Accra to Secretary of State, 18/4/1964. There is a copy of this in the Lyndon B. Johnson Library & Museum, whose helpful archivist, Jennifer Cuddeback, scoured the holding for me for anything on Malcolm X. It is interesting to note that the American Embassy staff should refer to Kwame Nkrumah as 'Prime Minister' and not as 'President'.

It is not difficult to understand why Nkrumah was 'abstracted': he would naturally have had some knowledge of the Black Muslim movement and Malcolm X. Did the Ambassador, on his 'periodic visit' to Nkrumah, not know that the President had spent many years in higher education institutions in the United States? Or that he had been back in the USA in 1958, when he shared a platform with Malcolm, and again in 1960? It is equally difficult not to interpret the Ambassador's lecture as insulting.[95]

Daniel Britz, presumably writing for the Ambassador (so with his approval of the text) noted, as stated previously, that Malcolm had *not* been received by President Nkrumah. He also alleged that Malcolm 'was not accorded an official welcome [which] may have narrowed his impact on the reading public...While the net effect of Malcolm's visit was probably damaging to American interests...all in all, Malcolm X created less of a stir than the Embassy had feared. As his views were hardly new or shocking...Malcolm X showed no interest in socialism.'[96]

Was the Embassy attempting to play down Malcolm's influence on both Africans and the Afro-American contingent in Ghana? Did it get away with the lies it was telling? Why was it so concerned? Malcolm himself gives some answers, in his letter from Accra to Jimmy Booker, mentioned previously, he wrote:

> The people of Nigeria are strongly concerned with the plight of their African-American brothers, but the US Information Agency in Africa very skilfully give the impression that sincere efforts are being made by the American government to solve the problem and that because the American Negro has made so much progress, there is no need for the Africans here to become unnecessarily concerned or alarmed. The true picture of colour plight in America has been skilfully distorted here purposely to minimize the concern and reaction of the Africans. Not only do these agencies attempt to make it appear that at times we ourselves are to blame for our plight, but the American Negro is even made to look foolish and immature in whatever methods he uses in his struggle for freedom.
>
> Studying the situation in these areas very closely one can easily detect a well-designed plan, or gigantic conspiracy, to keep the Africans in Africa from ever getting together with the Africans abroad. As

---

95 NARA: Accra 855, Telegram from Embassy 18 April 1964. On his visits to the USA see Kwame Nkrumah, *I Speak of Freedom*, London: Heinemann 1961; the book is dedicated to Patrice Lumumba, with whose fate Malcolm was much concerned. On Nkrumah's education in the USA, see Marika Sherwood, *Kwame Nkrumah: the Years Abroad 1935-1947*, Legon: Freedom Publications, 1996.

96 NARA: Britz to State Department, op cit (fn.91).

one highly placed African official told me while drinking tea in the privacy of his home: 'when he realizes the number of people of African descent in South and Central America, and includes them with those in North America, the total number of Africans in the Americas could easily number over 80 million, and once this is realized, one can more easily understand the frantic necessity of keeping the Africans from ever uniting, or developing bonds of common interest with their 80 million Afro-American brothers.'

Unity between the Africans of the west and the Africans in our swiftly emerging African fatherland could well change the present course of history.

The FBI was raving. Its 'Airtel' to its New York and Philadelphia bureaux stated that 'Little [ie, Malcolm X] was in contact Mayfield (considerable activity in communist front movement), Cuban and Chinese representatives on African tour...indicates he is associated with the subversive element within the US...will go to any length to further his own selfish aims...to make himself leading civil rights leader...New York and Philadelphia to investigate...if feasible, a counterintelligence program will be initiated to publicly discredit Little.'[97]

The US government's concern about Malcolm's visit is also demonstrated by the apprehensions of the Embassy in Conakry, which had expected Malcolm to visit. 'Graham' from the Embassy telegrammed to the Secretary of State on 13 May that

> Embassy confident that GOG (Government of Guinea), mindful Malcolm X racist views and statement on JFK death, will lend minimum attention his announced visit here. Subject Department approval Embassy proposes rest on this assumption and initiate no discussion Malcolm X with Guineans. Should discussion arise officers would emphasize right U.S. citizens express any views and Guineans listen any but would suggest Malcolm X representative only of unconstructive opinions small minority Negro Americans. Doctrines, rejected by most authorized spokesmen Islam well as U.S. negro community, are identical on Civil Rights with views white extremists. Advise.[98]

---

[97] FBI Papers on the OAAU, roll 1, section 2, Airtel to New York and Philadelphia, #100-44235
[98] NARA: SOC 14-1 US: Graham from Conakry to Secretary of State, 13/5/1964.

Stop-overs in Monrovia, Dakar, Morocco, Algiers, May 17 - 21

Why did Malcolm not visit Sierra Leone? One of the many friends he had made amongst the African representatives at the United Nations had been Francis Karefa-Smart.[99] Was he short of funds?

We have almost no information about these brief stopovers/visits, we can safely presume that all Malcolm did was change planes.

May 17, Monrovia and Dakar

The country known as Liberia was an area settled by African Americans in the 19th century. Nominally independent, it was under the sway of the USA and at times of the UK. Relations between the settlers and the native inhabitants were often 'difficult'.

Dakar is the capital of Senegal. It had obtained its independence from France in 1960, but France retained considerable economic control.

From the entry for Monrovia in the *Notebook* we learn that the 'head of Peace Corp (white) introduces me to wife and secretary (a Negro who rode with me to Dakar)...we debate "problem" for about 10 minutes. On plane she tells me I'm not like the person pictured by the press.'

As the next entry, for Dakar, is on the same day, it would appear that Malcolm did not have much time in the Liberian capital. He notes that 'French head of airport took me around airport. Signed many autographs.'

May 18, Morocco

Much of the North African coast was under Ottoman control until the late 19th century, when it was taken over by French, Italian and British colonisers. Morocco became an official French Protectorate in 1912. France encouraged emigration, so that there was a considerable French population in Morocco and its other 'possessions' in the Maghreb, Algeria, though fewer in Tunisia. Morocco obtained its independence in 1956.

Notebook entry: 'decided to tour Cape Blanca. 7 pm Mr. Mahi and friend...very race conscious, proud of Black Muslim'. His *Autobiography* adds this: 'I spent the day sightseeing. I visited the famous Casbah, the ghetto which had resulted when the ruling white French wouldn't let the dark-skinned natives into certain areas of Casablanca. Thousands upon thousands of the subjugated natives were crowded into the ghetto, in the same way that Harlem, in New York City, became America's Casbah.'

---

99 Evanzz (1992), p.161.

(p.414) Unfortunately Malcolm does not explain who his contacts were in Morocco.

May 19 – 21, Algiers

Because of the numbers of French settlers, Algeria was made constitutionally part of metropolitan France. Revolts, beginning in 1945 were dealt with brutally and escalated into the formation of the Front Libération Nationale (FLN); torture became an instrument of government. White Algerians refused to accept French offers of quasi-independence and also formed terrorist fronts, which the French attempted to put down. In 1959 the Algerians declared a provisional national government with its headquarters in Cairo; fighting continued until independence was agreed in July 1962 when Algeria became a (more or less) socialist republic.[100]

Notebook entry for Tuesday, May 19: 'my birthday – arrived Algiers – called at Ghana Ambassador's home'. The next day's entry begins with 'To Ghana Embassy – Mr Nutako sent me to the Algerian Foreign Ministry – man I was to see was not in'. Malcolm then took 'a taxi ride to see the city' and took photos, something he often mentions doing. Then back to Foreign Ministry where 'I explained "our plight" for two hours into very sympathetic ears...dinner with Mr Nutako. He related many of his experiences in the Congo at the time of Lumumba's death – met three Ghanaians from the Embassy talked until ??? (illegible).'

In his *Autobiography* Malcolm relates that he 'walked around Algiers, hearing rank-and-file expressions of hatred for America for supporting the oppressors of the Algerians. They were true revolutionists, not afraid of death. They had, for so long, faced death.' (p.414) There is also a note: 'Mr Joseph Ifeora – Federal Minister of Works & Highways, Lagos – met me at airport'.[101] Another note states that the Ghanaian Ambassador had left a telephone message for him at his hotel.[102] Did they meet? Obviously many African government officials were interested in Malcolm.

In a recent book Kofi Natambo states that Malcolm 'celebrated his 39th birthday as an official guest of the Algerian government'.[103] While Malcolm and Algerian officials had met many times, and Malcolm was clearly very impressed by the post-independence struggles in Algeria, I have found no evidence to confirm that he had been the government's guest.

---

100 On the struggles in Algeria, see eg, Frantz Fanon, *A Dying Colonialism* (1959), London: Penguin Books 1970 and *Toward the African Revolution*, (1964), New York: Grove Press 1967.

101 Assiduous search has revealed nothing about Mr If(f)eora.

102 Malcolm X Papers, Reel 1, folder 5, note with his Pan-Am Airlines ticket Accra – Dakar – Casablanca – Algiers – Paris – New York, 17 – 21 May.

103 Natambo (2002), p.304.

On Thursday May 21 Malcolm left Africa to return to the USA. He noted that at the airport he was 'detained and questioned for taking pictures (Americans are suspect)'.

Malcolm arrived back in New York on 21 May 1964.

Malcolm's Reaction to His Tour

Malcolm had met journalists, politicians, students (the next generation of the formally educated intelligentsia), parliamentarians, ambassadors, Marxist expatriates and the socialist president of Ghana, the first country south of the Sahara to attain independence from colonial rule. As Professor King observed, he certainly wanted to learn, as well as to gauge whether and how he could enlist support for his project. Did he also want to clarify his ideas? To move from the embrace of the Nation of Islam to true Islam? To critique capitalism and world imperialism were huge intellectual steps. And to move towards a pan-Africanist philosophy which embraced Africa and the Diaspora? Malcolm was clearly thinking about all this while he doubted that he would be allowed to live long enough to think it all through.

A few hours after his return to New York Malcolm addressed a press conference at the Hotel Theresa in Harlem. He told the pressmen that he had been rallying support for bringing charges against the USA at the United Nations. Apart from the propaganda being put out by the USIS, he charged that the 'American government was trying to buy off African leaders with foreign aid and projects like the Peace Corps'. Following the emphasis by African leaders on the need for unity, he told the pressmen that he had been writing to the civil rights leaders in the US while abroad to discuss how to bring this about.[104]

---

104 *The Militant* 1 June 1964, p.8. USIS = United States Information Service.

CHAPTER 3

New York:
The founding of the OAAU
May – June 1964

On his return, Malcolm gave a press conference in Harlem. He said that he had received pledges of support in the African countries he had visited. The *New York Times* (22 May 1964, p.22) reported Malcolm as saying that 'The United States has colonized the Negro people just as the people of Africa and Asia were colonized by the Europeans. He described the American method as neo-colonialism.'

Malcolm's hectic pace continued. Speaking engagements, preparing for his next trip abroad and setting up the OAAU, could not have left much time for his family or for organising his thinking.

At a symposium arranged by the Militant Labor Forum in New York on May 29, Malcolm was asked: 'What political and economic system does Malcolm want?' he replied

> All of the countries that are emerging today from under the shackles of colonialism are turning toward socialism. I don't think it's an accident. Most of the countries that were colonial powers were capitalist countries, and the last bulwark of capitalism today is America. It's impossible for a white person to believe in capitalism and not believe in racism. You can't have capitalism without racism.

Malcolm returns from abroad with a new Muslim name, El-Hajj El-Shabazz, and with one bestowed on him in Nigeria, Alhadji omowale (in Yoruba, "the child has come home"), New York, May 21, 1964

To the question 'Do you think it's possible for an integrated organization working within a country like this to succeed, with Caucasian members conspicuous in the organization?', he replied:

In my recent travels into the African countries and others, the importance of having a working unity among all peoples was impressed upon me. Black as well as white. But the only way this is going to be brought about is that the black ones have to be in unity first...The black man has to be shown how to free himself, and the white one who is sincerely interested has to back whatever that black groups decides upon to do.[1]

At the inaugural public rally of the OAAU on 28 June 1964 Malcolm again spoke of his trip:

[In] the holy city of Mecca where I met many people from all over the world, plus spent many weeks in Africa trying to broaden my own scope and get more of an open mind...I realized that our African brothers have gained their independence faster than you and I here in America have. They've also gained recognition and respect as human beings much faster than you and I...So it was our intention to try and find out what it was our African brothers were doing to get results...[In founding the Organisation of African Unity] they forgot their differences for the sole purpose of bringing benefits to the whole...Once we saw what they were able to do, we determined to try and do the same thing here in America, to bring about the complete independence of people of African descent here in the Western Hemisphere...[2]

An FBI report dated 13 June 1964 begins with an inked out name, we have to conclude – sadly – that it might have been

---

1 Breitman (1966), pp.70-71.
2 Breitman (1970), pp.35-37, 63.

someone at the meeting who had informed the FBI. The report states:

> [...]advised this date that subject (Malcolm X) attended all day meeting with Clarence Jones, Whitney Young, unknown representatives of A. Phillip Randolph and CORE, and negro entertainers Sidney Poitier, Ruby Dee, and Ossie Davis. [...] advised this date above meeting consisted of a discussion of general future of civil rights movement in US. Following the meeting Jones indicated he considered the best idea presented was subject's idea to internationalize the civil rights movement by taking it to the United Nations. Jones felt it may be possible to present it to the General Assembly next September, and to let subject handle foreign arrangements since "he's been there".³

At the OAAU's second rally on 5 July, Malcolm returned to what he had learned in Africa, firstly by recounting his talk with the Ghanaian Minister of Culture, Nana Nketsia:

> He said that as an African his concept of freedom is a situation or a condition in which he, as an African, feels completely free to give vent to his own likes and dislikes and thereby develop his own African personality. Not a condition in which he is copying some European cultural pattern or some European cultural standard, but an atmosphere of complete freedom where he has the right, the leeway, to bring out of himself all of that dormant, hidden talent that has been there for so long.

Malcolm went on to quote Kwame Nkrumah's famous saying: 'Seek ye first the political kingdom, and all other things shall be added unto it'.⁴ To obtain this, he proposed to lay the situation of Afro-Americans before the next meeting of the Organisation of African Unity (OAU) and to ask for support to take it to the United Nations. During the question-and-answer session he was asked whether he still believed that 'the so-called Negro should ultimately return to Africa'. He responded by repeating what he had said at the first rally, that Afro-Americans should return to Africa 'spiritually and culturally'. He went on to explains that

> The first statement that I made, I made before going to Africa myself...[T]he net result of that trip was that if our people go, they're

---

3 FBI Papers, Part 11, FBI New York to FBI director, 13/6/1964.

4 Clearly Nkrumah had not envisaged neo-colonialism, globalisation, the WTO, the IMF or the World Bank.

welcome. But those who are politically mature over there say that we would be wiser to play a role at this time right here...⁵

According to Ossie Davis and Ruby Dee, in about August Malcolm called a meeting attended by themselves and Whitney Young, Lorraine Hansberry, Roy Wilkins, A. Phillip Randolph and Sidney Poitier 'to plan joint action...a Declaration of Human Rights for Black Americans'. Malcolm was to solicit the support of African leaders for placing this before the United Nations.⁶

It is interesting to speculate about the source of Malcolm's determination to petition the United Nations and his apparent faith in this organisation. Did he see it as a final hope? As a way of embarrassing the United States? Or did he really believe that the UN could take some sort of action against the US? Did he know that the 1945 attempt to do this fell on ears deafened at the very foundation of the organisation?⁷ A subsequent attempt in 1951 by the Robesons, Alphaeus Hunton (whom Malcolm might have met in Ghana) and Claudia Jones to charge the USA with the genocide of Negroes was also ignored.

Malcolm's acquaintance with the Socialist Workers Party (SWP) broadened during this time. He had known Clifton DeBerry, ex-communist labour leader, political activist and SWP member at least since 1963. In January 1964 the SWP nominated DeBerry as candidate for president. Once Malcolm had left the Nation of Islam, DeBerry's 'relationship with Malcolm continued to develop'. 'I used to meet with him almost every Saturday when he was in the country', DeBerry told author Nelson Blackstock. 'We would have discussions about politics – often comparing notes and checking up on what each other had been hearing about the developing nationalist response among Blacks.' De Berry was invited to give 'a couple of classes at the Muslim Mosque Inc., which Malcolm headed', and Malcolm praised the SWP paper, *The Militant* calling it 'one of the best I've read. We always encourage those in Harlem to buy it...'.⁸

---

5 Breitman (1970), pp.86-88, 104.

6 Davis and Dee (1998), p.307.

7 See Marika Sherwood, '"There is no new deal for the blackman in San Francisco": African attempts to influence the founding conference of the United Nations April - July 1945', *International Jnl. of African Historical Studies*, 29/1, 1996 and 'The UN: Caribbean and African-American attempts to influence the founding conference in San Francisco, 1945', *Journal of Caribbean History*, 29/1, 1996.

8 Nelson Blackstock, *Cointelpro*, New York: Vintage Books 1976, pp. 73, 75, 112.

CHAPTER 4

London, Cairo, and Further East
July – September 1964

London, En Route to Cairo, 10 July

The *New York Times* reported on 10 July (p.26) that Malcolm left for London the previous night. He was going to Cairo as an 'observer' to the meeting of the Organisation of African Unity (OAU) where he was going to 'devote his time to intense lobbying to mobilise African pressure on the United States government at the United Nations'. It was not until 13 August (p.22) That the *Times* more fully elucidated Malcolm's thinking to its readers: M.S. Handler explained that 'Malcolm told friends in New York that it was his intention to add a new dimension to the civil rights struggle in the United States. This, he said, could be achieved by "internationalizing" the negro question at the united nations in the manner that south african apartheid was transferred into an international program.'

The *Times* reported that Malcolm was going to stop in London to confer with Muslim leaders at the commonwealth conference, and was 'planning another pilgrimage to mecca'. The following day the *Chicago Tribune* reported that at the London airport Malcolm said, 'violence against the negro in the southern United States has reached a point where members of my race will soon react and America will see a bloodbath'.(P.4)

In his notebook, Malcolm records that he had
> arrived at 9:30...met several reporters at airport...Met H.E. Masha (Lagos City Council) in airport dining room – had met him in Mecca and Medina. Commonwealth Ministers Conference. Nancy Tzibo. Friday prayers at Islamic Cultural Center. In lobby of the hotel met several Ghanaians whom I had met previously. They were very friendly. At the press conference. Director – Dr. Awad (from Egypt) introduced me to all the Muslims. In the 'social period' after the prayers I took time to explain the 'plight' of the 22 million African Americans and emphasised that the US Government was violating the United Nations Charter by violating our basic Human Rights. Phone Nancy T – she gives me the phone numbers of several prominent people...but they'd be busy, debating the question of S. Rhodesia.[1]
> Spoke with three reporters in hotel lobby...TV channel 9...some taped interviews.[2]

Ghanaian Nancy Tsiboe had arrived from the USA, where she had been 'to restore enthusiasm' for Nkrumah's political party, the CPP. She argued that 'Ghana could only be served "via Osagyefo" and nobody should stand aside from contributing towards history'.[3]

Whether the reporters at the airport included any from Tanganyika is doubtful (given the costs of travel to London), but the English language Tanganyikan newspapers (*Tanganyika Standard* and the *Nationalist*) reported Malcolm's presence in London, describing him as the leader of the 'Afro-American Unity Group' and explaining his intentions (as had the *Times* and the *Chicago Tribune*) and his analysis of the situation in the US. According to the US Embassy in Dar-es-Salaam, the *Nationalist* article 'contained praise of the scope and significance of the Civil Rights Bill by the Algerian Ambassador, the Mali Ambassador and the Nigerian

---

1 Southern Rhodesia, another British colony, was headed by Ian Smith, who refused to accept the guarantees demanded by Britain for granting independence: majority rule, end to racial discrimination and immediate improvement in Africans' rights. Smith announced a unilateral declaration of independence in November 1965. The country is known today as Zimbabwe.

2 *Notebook 7*, entry for 10 July 1964.

3 Nancy was the widow of John Tsibo, owner of the newspaper *Ashanti Pioneer*. He and his wife were activists in the opposition Party, the NLM (National Liberation Movement); Nancy, a Juvenile Magistrate, stood for election in Kumasi South in 1954, but lost. She served on the National Executive of the NLM and then as Treasurer of the combined opposition parties, the United Party. In the early 1960s she switched her allegiance to Nkrumah. She had also just spoken at a CPP rally in London. (*West Africa*, 18/7/1964, p.797)

Chargé'.[4] If these views reflected the official policies of their countries, Malcolm was not going to have an easy time in Cairo.

The Metropolitan Police reported that Malcolm X arrived in London on July 10 'ostensibly to meet African Prime Ministers at that time in London to attend the Commonwealth Prime Ministers Conference'.[5] Had he arranged during his previous visit to Africa to meet with some of the Prime Ministers while they were in London? Which Prime Ministers or their entourages he managed to meet is not in this police report.[6] At what must have been a press conference, Malcolm stated that 'there was a blood bath on its way in America' and hoped to persuade the African leaders to take the issue of American Negroes to the United Nations, where he wanted to 'have the US charged with the violation of human rights'.[7]

The *Guardian*, then a left-wing paper, reported Malcolm's visit on page 2 of its 11 July issue. Malcolm, described as 'the Black Muslim leader who has broken with the movement's head' was on his way to Cairo. He 'remains unshaken in his belief that the American Negro will never receive treatment as an equal citizen in the US'. Malcolm is reported as having been suggesting, since his return to the USA from Africa, that

> American Negroes must ultimately return to Africa...[but] could not leave the US in a hurry.' He intended to ask the African Heads of State to 'put the same pressure on the United Nations, as they have on South Africa, the Rhodesias, and other countries where there is a violation of the Negroes' human rights. We want the issue of American Negroes lifted from the level of civil rights to human rights...[T]he African States can help in getting it on the floor of the United Nations.

The *Guardian*'s editorial commentary (p.8) quotes Malcolm's attitude to violence: 'My organisation does not advocate violence, but we believe that our people have the right to defend themselves...We do not believe in turning the other cheek.' This reporter actually managed to *hear* at least some of what Malcolm was saying – quite a rarity! He (or she?) goes on

---

4 Johnson Library, 'Airgram' from 'Amembassy', Dar to Department of State, 15 July 1964. I must here express my very grateful thanks to the librarian for this and other documents.

5 Metropolitan Police report 10/12/1964 on 'Malcolm X/Little'. My grateful thanks to Andrew Brown, the Met's Assistant Departmental Record Officer, for unearthing records on Malcolm for me. These are very sparse but indicate that copies of everything were sent to MI5, roughly equivalent to the US's CIA. This ever-secretive organisation refuses to release its materials.

6 Unfortunately the Commonwealth Secretariat has no files on this meeting. Malcolm's trip and intentions were also noted in the Lagos *Sunday Express* (12/7/1964, p.5) but did not mention whether he had met with the African Heads of State in London.

7 Metropolitan Police memorandum 10/12/1964; *The Times*, 11/7/1964, p.7.

to say that if Malcolm talks 'like an anti-colonialist, it is because he sees the United States as a colonial Power'. He was a 'black nationalist leader doomed to be a failure. But there is a rough logic about his pretensions if his point of view is adopted. The United States has a higher "African" population than any country except Nigeria.' The OAU was not expected to do more than give Malcolm a 'polite hearing', especially as African leaders were looking for US support for their campaign against apartheid. 'Yet it will be odd if some of them do not see in Malcolm X a new world counterpart of themselves struggling for much the same things as they have struggled for.' The US Civil Rights Act is, after all, 'a stage on a journey', whose end 'can only be the full integration of Negroes with whites'. Can the Western man answer Malcolm's charge that he has 'oppressed and degraded, just based on the colour of another man's skin' more than anyone else?

The tabloid *Daily Mirror* printed a photo of Malcolm on page 2 of its 11 July issue under the caption 'Malcolm X has declared a truce'. Reporting that he was on his way to Cairo in search of African backing for an appeal to the United Nations, the paper then went on to misreport Malcolm as warning 'that if his movement, the Muslim Mosque Inc. failed, there would be a bloodbath in America over Negro rights'.

Malcolm's interactions with a variety of people continued – as did his attempts to contact the leaders attending the Commonwealth conference. He seized – and created – every opportunity possible to propagate the OAAU's philosophy and proposed action. As he chronicled in his *Notebook*:

> Sheikh Omar Gabin (director, Islamic Center) and a South African student from Oxford went to my room. I gave them literature explaining the aims and objectives of the OAAU. Ibrahim tried to call several of the ministers and other VIPs but all were out...Checked out of hotel...Ghana High Commission where I met (on the run) with some Ghanaian VIPs and left them the OAAU document...Nigerian High Commission...met several young brothers...Explained our 'plight' and making them see America's 'tricks'. They were interested and sympathetic. Son of Nigerian High Commissioner...gave me some names to contact when I got to Cairo.[8]

Malcolm also rushed into Grosvenor Square to tell the US Embassy that he would be a guest of the Supreme Council for Islamic Unity in Cairo.[9] At

---

8 *Notebook 6*, entry for 11 July 1964

9 NARA: POL 13-10 US, American Embassy Jidda (sic) to State Dept. 29/9/1964. Why Malcolm always informed the US Embassies of his travels/presence is a mystery.

the London airport, Malcolm told reporters that, 'during his 24 hour stay', he had 'talks with African and other Muslims' regarding his intentions.[10]

Cairo: The Organisation of African Unity, July 1964

The foundations for what is today the African Union were laid at a meeting of the six independent African states convened by pan-Africanist President Kwame Nkrumah in Accra in 1958. Not everyone agreed on how this unity could be achieved, and the rapidly emerging new heads of independent states split into a group led by Nkrumah, campaigning for a federation of all African countries and another led by Léopold Senghor of Senegal, advocating only economic co-operation.[11] The dispute was eventually resolved when Ethiopian Emperor Haile Selassie I invited the two groups to Addis Ababa, where the OAU and its headquarters were subsequently established. The Charter of the Organisation was signed by the now 32 independent African states aiming to promote unity and development; defend the sovereignty and territorial integrity of members; eradicate all forms of colonialism; promote international cooperation; and co-ordinate members' economic, diplomatic, educational, health, welfare, scientific, and defence policies, and act as a collective voice for the African continent. This July meeting was the second gathering of the heads of independent African states. President Nasser took over the chairmanship from Emperor Haile Selassie, and Diallo Telli of Guinea was elected Secretary General.[12]

> Malcolm reports that on the plane from London to Cairo
>> Muhammad Fattby, Cultural Counsellor to the United Arab Republic Embassy and Director of the Educational Mission...asked me to sit with him. He had read all the papers and spent the entire trip to Rome [there was a stop-over there] congratulating me on my firm stand and advising me on the best approach to use at least in the Arab countries...I shot holes in the JFK image...He warned me of this for that reason – we discussed many other things.[13]

---

10 *New York News* 12/7/1964, quoted in FBI report on Malcolm, reel 14.
11 The Casablanca group comprised Ghana, Algeria, Guinea, Morocco, Egypt, Mali and Libya; the Monrovian bloc comprised Senegal, Liberia, Nigeria, Ethiopia and the other former French colonies.
12 Diallo Telli represented Guinea at the United Nations from its independence in 1957; in 1962 he served as one of the Vice Presidents of the UN General Assembly.
13 *Notebook 6*, entry for 11 July 1964.

Malcolm arrived in Cairo with an introduction from Dr. Shawarbi, the director of the Islamic Center, with whom he had studied in New York.[14] Within a few days of his arrival he moved from his hotel to the 'Isis', a boat on the Nile, which was also the home of 'the various liberation movements from the different parts of the African continent'. (Who arranged this is not known.) This was no accident, Malcolm implied, as 'they were placed there so that they could all be together and discuss the problems they had in common'. 'I was very honoured to be permitted to be housed along with them. Spending so much time with them gave me a real feeling of the pulse of a true revolutionary...gave me an opportunity to study, to listen and study the type of people involved in the struggle – their thinking, their objectives, their aims and their methods. It opened my eyes to many things. And I think I was able to steal a few ideas that they used, and tactics and strategy.' He believed that these 'would be most effective in the freedom struggle' in the USA.[15]

There were also introductions made by Zaki Borai, from Egypt's Ministry of Foreign Affairs, attached to Egypt's UN mission in New York. He often accompanied Tahseen Bashir, one of Egypt's representatives at the UN, on his visits to Malcolm X in Harlem. 'Tahseen assigned Borai to assist Malcolm on his trips to Egypt as an advance man, to make appointments for Malcolm to see important people in Cairo.'[16]

It is probably safe to assume that it was through his contacts with the African representatives at the United Nations headquarters in New York and thus his familiarity with the UN, that Malcolm knew that in 1963 it had passed a Declaration for the Elimination of All Forms of Racial Discrimination.[17] The 1948 Universal Declaration of Human Rights was part of the founding charter of the UN. Sadly, not much was done to implement either Declaration. Nevertheless, their existence provided Malcolm with a tool which he thought he could use.

In the statement which he submitted on behalf of his Organization of Afro-American Unity, after outlining the situation of Afro-Americans, Malcolm argued that

> We strongly believe that African problems are our problems and our problems are African problems...We also believe that as Heads of

---

14 According to Kofi Natambu (*The Life and Work of Malcolm X*, Indianapolis: Alpha Press, 2002, p.235) 'Yousse' Shawarbi had appeared with Malcolm on an NOI radio program and had attended the Afro-Asian Bazaar held in New York in 1960 with him.

15 Breitman (1970), pp.137-141; Breitman (1966), p.81.

16 Email (dated 17/1/2003) from 'Sunni' forwarded to me by Paul Lee, 28/11/2006. As ever, my thanks to Paul.

17 On Africa's relations with the UN, see G.A. Obiozor & A. Ajala (eds), *Africa and The United Nations System: The First Fifty Years*, Lagos: Nigerian Institute of International Affairs, 1998

the Independent African states you are the Shepherd of all African peoples everywhere...The American Government is either unwilling or unable to protect the lives and property of your 22 million Afro-American brothers and sisters. We stand defenceless, at the mercy of American racists who murder us at will for no reason other that we are black and of African descent. Our problem is your problem. It is not a Negro problem, nor an American problem. This is a world problem; a problem for humanity. It is not a problem of civil rights but a problem of human rights...We pray that our African brothers have not freed themselves of European colonialism only to be overcome and held in check now by American dollarism... In the interests of world peace and security, we beseech [you] to recommend an immediate investigation into our problem by the United Nations Commission on Human Rights.[18]

Honoured with permission to address the Assembly, in his speech on 17 July Malcolm emphasised that 'Your problems will never be fully solved until and unless ours are solved'. He warned the Assembly: 'Don't escape from European colonialism only to become even more enslaved by deceitful, "friendly" American dollarism'.[19]

The Heads of State could not fully support the OAAU's plea; nevertheless they passed

Cairo Mosque, August 1964

18 Breitman (1966), pp.73-77; there is a typescript of the statement in the Schomburg Center: Clarke Papers, 24/18; also in Malcolm X Papers, Box 14, file 5. The *New York Times* reported on 18 July (page 2) that Malcolm had argued that the 'deteriorating plight of American Negroes was definitely becoming a threat to world peace. The United States government is morally incapable of protecting the lives and property of 22 million Negroes...' It is interesting that it was on *page 23* of its 14 July issue that this paper reported that Malcolm had arrived in Cairo 'to show...that our situation is as much a violation of the UN Human Rights Charter as the situation in South Africa or Angola...'.

19 *The Militant*, 24/8/1964. There is a copy of the speech in the Schomburg Center: John Henrik Clarke Papers, box 24/18; it is also available on www.oopau.org/2.html.

a resolution which, while noting with satisfaction the passage of the Civil Rights Act in the US, stated that

> Recalling Resolution 1904 (XVIII) of the General Assembly of the United Nations, adopted on 20 November 1963, The Declaration on the Elimination of all Forms of Racial Discrimination...
> *Considering* that one hundred years have passed since the Emancipation Proclamation was signed in the United States of America...
> Deeply disturbed by continuing manifestations of racial bigotry and racial oppression against Negro citizens of the United States of America
> 1. Reaffirms its belief that the existence of discriminatory practices is a matter of deep concern to member States of the Organization of African Unity;
> 2. Urges the Government authorities in the United States of America to intensify their efforts to ensure the total elimination of all forms of discrimination based on race, colour, or ethnic origin.

The African states never asked for an investigation, but Breitman argues that Malcolm's influence was evident in the 'sharp denunciations of American racial policy at home and abroad voiced by several African delegations in the UN debate over the Congo in December 1964.'[20] The Essien-Udoms point out in their memoir that it was an 'extraordinary concession that Malcolm X was admitted to the OAU as it was a heads of state meeting'. He had had to lobby hard, as the 'US government had almost successfully convinced most Africans that the African American did not identify with Africans and that Africans would be foolish to get involved in their problems...Not only did the Summit pass the resolution, but some of the delegates promised officially to assist the OAAU in its plan to give their support during the following session of the United Nations.'[21]

Malcolm attended two days of the Heads' meetings, according to his *Notebook*: '*July 19*: attended my first Summit Conference. Nkrumah made the best (and most all-inclusive) speech – but all the Heads of State seem to avoid mentioning the US and its racism. I can really see the importance of building bridges of communication and understanding and co-operation between Africans and Afro-Americans. *July 20*: didn't like Nyerere's attacks on Nkrumah – it was pleasing only to the West...Also met Mrs. Padmore and Mrs Seidman...Julia.'[22]

---

20 Breitman (1966), p.87. Che Guevara was one of these speakers. (Moore, 1988, p.192) See below.
21 Essien-Udom (1966), pp.254-5.
22 Mrs Padmore was the wife of George Padmore, Nkrumah's Advisor on African Affairs, who remained in Ghana after Padmore premature death in 1959, working for the President and as a journalist. Julia must have been Julia Wright. 'Mrs Seidman' was probably Anne

Not surprisingly, the 'American Embassy in Cairo engaged in delicate behind-the-scenes negotiations to have Malcolm barred from addressing the Conference, but its efforts were coldly snubbed by both the Egyptian Government and the Conference organizers'.[23] Malcolm understood this, as he wrote in his *Notebook* on 15 July that there was 'a great debate going on backstage at this conference as to whether I should be admitted or heard'.

Malcolm and the Egyptian Press

The English-language Egyptian press was not shy of reporting Malcolm; what appeared in the Arab press I do not know.

On 17 August the English language *Egyptian Gazette*, one of whose editors was David Du Bois, published a two page interview with Malcolm, which ranged from his conversion to Islam, the Black Muslims, the OAU meeting, where he hoped to 'encourage the African leaders to lift the struggle from the level of civil rights to the level of human rights at the United Nations'; and the US 'propaganda campaign stressing the civil rights measures (which were a fraud) to making Africans think that the American Negro does not look to Africa'.[24]

On 23 August the *Gazette* published the first part of a long article Malcolm had been working on:

> My pilgrimage broadened my scope, my mind, my outlook and made me more flexible in approaching life's many complexities...I am now trying to live the life of a true Suni Muslim...I must repeat that I am not a racist nor do I subscribe to the tenets of racism...I wish nothing but freedom, justice and equality, life, liberty and the pursuit of happiness for all people. However, the first law of nature is self-preservation, so

Converses with Egyptian man

Seidman, an economist then teaching at the University of Tanzania at Dar-es-Salaam.

23 Norden (1967), p.9.
24 David Du Bois, the step-son of WEB Du Bois, was a lecturer at Cairo University in American Literature and the News Editor of *The Egyptian Gazette*; he also wrote for other newspapers and for Radio Cairo's English language transmissions to North America. He served as North African public relations consultant to President Kwame Nkrumah. See Gamal Nkrumah, 'Through African Eyes', *Al-Ahram Weekly*, 30 March - 5 April 2000 Issue No. 75 (available on www.weekly.ahram.org.eg/2000/475/spec2.htm)

my first concern is with the oppressed group of people to which I belong...It is not necessary for the Afro-American to seek revenge... We need to spend more time removing the scars of slavery from the backs and the minds of our own people, physical and mental scars left by 400 years of inhuman treatment...The key to our success lies in united action...The common goal of 22 million Afro-Americans is respect as a HUMAN BEING...to obtain the HUMAN RIGHTS that America has been denying us...The denial of HUMAN RIGHTS makes it impossible to obtain civil rights...Civil rights are a domestic problem under the jurisdiction of the United States... But once our struggle is lifted from the confining civil rights label to the level of HUMAN RIGHTS, our freedom struggle can then become internationalised...Can the present Federal Government solve this problem? What concrete gains have our people made?... What chance do the Afro-Americans have in the face of political hypocrisy and trickery?...The Black masses of America, especially the young people, have become disenchanted...they now see that the American Dream is nothing but a racist nightmare...The Afro-American demonstrations against the racist white society during the summer and autumn months may cause white retaliations that could easily precipitate a race war, a race war not limited to the American continent!...If the 22 million Afro-Americans don't get sincere allies in America, we must seek allies elsewhere.

On 25 August the *Gazette* printed the second part of this article, spread over three pages, including a photograph. Malcolm again talks of the 'spirit of true brotherhood' at the *Hajj*, of the demand by African Americans for Human Rights, of the racial brutalities perpetrated in the USA. When 'other oppressed people the world over are fighting bloody battles to gain their freedom, do you really think our oppressed people are going to continue waiting patiently for more...hypocritical civil rights legislative effort of the phony politicians?...Only a world body can be instrumental in obtaining those rights...'

A few days previously a letter by Malcolm was published in the *Egyptian Mail* (22 August), headlined 'US support for Tshombe'. In this Malcolm castigates President Johnson for sending troops to the Congo in support of Moise Tshombe, 'a tool of the neo-colonialist, who is recognised by the entire world as the cold-blooded murderer of Patrice Lumumba'.[25]

---

25 Patrice Lumumba was the first Prime Minister of the independent Congo Republic. With the support of the ex-colonial Belgian masters, Moise Tshombe declared the rich Katanga province independent. Then the army, under Joseph Mobutu ousted both Lumumba and Tshombe. The latter was soon restored, while in January 1961 Lumumba was murdered.

The article that might have caused even more concern to the US Embassy and subsequently the US government, appeared in the *Arab Observer* on 24 August 1960 (pp.31-2). The first paragraph of the article, entitled 'Mister X', states:

> The United Arab Republic has for the past four weeks been host to America's most controversial Negro leader, El Hajj Malik El-Shabazz, known to the world as Malcolm X. It has been four weeks of revelation, re-evaluation and decision for the 39-year old Negro militant.

The article summarises Malcolm's early life, his NOI years and quotes much from his letter from Mecca in which he spoke of the influence the many peoples participating in the *Hajj* had had on him. The article then states that his visit to Cairo was two-fold:

> to expose himself to orthodox Islamic teaching as manifest in the Sunni Islam doctrines accepted and practised; [and] to explain to the OAU delegates his views on the growing danger to the world represented in the intensification of racist violence in the USA. Malcolm attended the OAU meetings as an accredited observer, [and used the rest of his time to speak] with religious leaders and teachers...and with numberless persons of all walks of life in Cairo... and the African Freedom Fighters currently in Cairo...Malcolm can count on the whole-hearted support of the UAR, its Government, its people and its leader, Gamal Abdul Nasser...

The final paragraph would also have increased this alarm at the Embassy:

> All Africa looks in wonder and disbelief as repeatedly more frequent and more violent clashes occur throughout America between Afro-Americans and white American supremacists and asks: 'Can America prevent the "imminent disaster" predicted by Malcolm X by ridding itself of the racist carcinoma'?

Malcolm in the British Press

The only report I could find is in the weekly journal *West Africa*, for 1 August (p.858):

> One of the most interesting 'fringe' visitors came from the US...the riots in Harlem certainly gave arguments put forward by Malcolm X added points. 'Your problems will never be solved until and

---

Recently revealed documents suggest that he was killed, as was suggested at the time, by a conspiracy between the US, the UK and Belgium. (*The Guardian Weekly*, 5-11 July, 2001) Some months after this revelation the Belgian government apologised for its role in the assassination (*The Guardian*, 6/2/2002). See Patrice Lumumba, *Congo, my Country*, New York: Frederick A. Praeger, 1962; Ludo de Witte, *The Assassination of Lumumba*, London: Verso 2001.

unless ours are solved. Our problem is your problem', he said. 'It is not an American problem. This is a world problem, a problem for humanity.'

Response by the US Embassy in Cairo

Malcolm recounted in his *Autobiography* that he was under constant surveillance by the government. (p.427) He was well aware of the US government's concern about his presence and presentation to the OAU. As he related to Milton Henry shortly after the OAU meeting:

> At first [my appearing] did create a great deal of controversy...and apprehension of the part of the powers that be in America...When I arrived here, there was a great deal of publicity in all the press...It was historic in a sense because no American Negroes had ever made any effort in the past to try to get their problems placed in the same category as the African problems...It is true that at first there were stumbling blocks placed in my path...But I'd rather not say what happened in specific details...When I arrived here I had to do a great deal of lobbying between the lobby of the Hotel Hilton, the lobby of the Shepeard and even the lobby of the "Isis", the ship where the African liberation movement was housed. Lobbying was necessary because the various agencies that the United States has abroad had successfully convinced most Africans that the American Negro in no way identified with Africa and that the African would be foolish to involve himself in the problems of the American Negroes...[T]his was only the first of a series of steps that the OAAU has in mind to internationalize the black man' problem...and make it a world problem, a problem for humanity.[26]

On 14 July Mr. Boswell of the Cairo Embassy reported that 'source said he assumed conference would again mention US racial situation... and would note favourably on civil rights bill'. Under the heading 'Miscellaneous' he noted that 'Malcolm X reported in Cairo and may have gotten badge to attend conference. (He is not identified there despite press rumour to this effect.)'[27]

Three days later, Mr. Boswell was clearly much more concerned about Malcolm's presence. Had he perhaps been alerted by both the CIA and the Deputy Chief of Mission in Dar-es-Salaam, who had sent to Cairo as well as to the Department of State, summaries of the reports in 'both English

---

26 Breitman (1966), pp.78-84.

27 Lyndon B. Johnson Library: Boswell, Cairo, to 'Secstate 144, priority'. My thanks to Jennifer Cuddeback, the librarian, for sending me copies of these telegrams.

language newspapers in Tanganyika of Malcolm X's travel to Cairo'? The Embassy was positive that Malcolm would not be 'afforded observer status'.[28] This was obviously said in an attempt to counteract the articles from the English language press which had flowed to Washington from the Embassy. The Embassy forwarded to Washington copies of the articles noted above, and also excerpts from the English language newspapers in Tanganyika – which the Embassy there had already sent to Washington.[29]

Later on the same day Mr. Boswell sent another telegram. He presumed that the Secretary of State had received information (from the CIA?), on Malcolm's activities and press interview 'which, as would be expected, violently attacks situation in US and equally enthusiastically endorses Islam, Nasser and the summit conference. While Malcolm X will not be accorded observer status and his statements are viewed with mixture of amusement and incredulity by sophisticated Egyptians, he may well be having somewhat greater impact on some OAU delegates who are ready to believe misinformation about the US.'[30] Clearly Malcolm was under very close observation.

The following day's telegram from Mr Boswell was slightly less antagonistic towards Malcolm. He reported that 'since Foreign Ministers were working in closed session there was a relative absence of specific information'. However, the USIS (United States Information Service) was sending 'excerpts of long calmly argued memorandum which Malcolm X is circulating'. It summarised Malcolm's argument (as outlined above) and noted that 'It is probable Malcolm X fascinating reporters more than delegations, and we still consider it unlikely that he will get either observer status or make any real headway at this conference, especially if the lead is given by Nasser of civil rights is followed. Nevertheless, he is showing clever lobbying tactics, and this memorandum is not ill-conceived.'[31]

On 28 August the Embassy warned the Department of State that the publication of Malcolm's letter regarding Tshombe in the *Gazette* 'is only the latest in a continuing of similar local press coverage of the opinion of Malcolm X...Interviews, press conferences, press statements and notices of his visits around Egypt are daily fare'.[32]

---

28 NARA: State Department files SOC 14-1 US POL 3 OAU, from Cairo to Dept. of State, 17/7/1964
29 NARA: State Department files SOC 14-1 US, 'Airgram' from Robert Gordon, 'Amembassy' Dar-es-Salaam to Dept of State, with copies to Cairo, London, Kampala, Nairobi and Zanzibar, 15/7/1965.
30 Lyndon B. Johnson Library: Cairo Embassy to 'Secstate 203'.
31 Lyndon B. Johnson Library: Cairo Embassy to 'Secstate 220 priority'.
32 Lyndon B. Johnson Library: Airgram dated 28/8/1964 to Department of State; NARA: State Department files SOC 14-1 US POL 13-9 US, Airgram from Donald Bergus, Cairo Embassy

An 'airgram' from Donald Bergus, the 'Counselor of the [Cairo] Embassy for Political Affairs, the dated 7 November 1964 reveals the ongoing concern of the State Department (or the CIA? or both?) with Malcolm's influence:

> Embassy inquiries regarding the activities of Malcolm X revealed that he talked to a number of the delegations to the OAU Summit Conference but was not admitted to see any of the Heads of State. According to journalists he spent a good deal of time [in the various hotels where the delegates stayed]. He remarked to Victor Reisel, visiting National Syndicated Columnist, that he had not yet seen any delegates but expected to be admitted to the closed session of the OAU Summit that evening.

The newspaper arricles sent by the Embassy indicate that Malcolm X received substantial press coverage during his stay which lasted beyond the Summit meeting.[33]

Response in the USA

Concern in the US was voiced by the *New York Times* on 13 August 1964:
> The State Department and the Justice Department have begun to take an interest in Malcolm's campaign to convince African states to raise the question of persecution of American Negroes at the United Nations...Malcolm's 8-page memorandum became available only recently...The officials studying it are reported as stating that if Malcolm succeeded in convincing just one African Government to bring up the charge at the Untied Nations, the United States Government would be faced with a touchy problem. The United States...would find itself in the same category...as South Africa... and other countries whose domestic politics have become debating issues at the United Nations. The issue would be of service to critics of the United States...and contribute to the undermining of the position the United States has asserted for itself as leader of the West in the advocacy of human rights. (p.22)

By now some politicians in the United States decided that it was time to attempt to put a legal stop to Malcolm's activities abroad. Congressman Charles C. Diggs asked the Department of State on 26 August for their comments on Malcolm's reported activities in Cairo, as had Congressman John Bell Williams on an unknown date. The

---

to State, 28/8/1964.
33 Lyndon B. Johnson Library, 'Airgram' and enclosures, 7/11/1964.

House of Representatives began an investigation and asked the Attorney General if Malcolm could be charged with violation of the Logan Act.[34] The Department of Justice responded on 2 September: 'in view of the seriousness of the allegation, we [are] conducting further inquiries to determine what evidence might be developed'. The Assistant Attorney General now asked the Department of State to request the embassies in the African countries Malcolm was visiting 'to furnish any information which they may have or which they may be able to obtain concerning contacts or meetings, as well as any communications by Malcolm X with respective heads of these foreign governments or their representatives... full reports of his meetings and contacts'.[35]

Most interestingly, the Department of State's response to Congressman Diggs is an outright lie. Did the Department not read the newspapers reporting on Malcolm in Cairo, which presumably congressmen read? The Department wrote to him on 9 September that Malcolm

> had made an unsuccessful attempt to be admitted to the Conference as an observer. He also made extreme statements to the press... However, the petition was not taken up by the Conference, nor was it given recognition or support...It is extremely doubtful that Malcolm X convinced any of the African leaders that his extreme charges were true...

But the Department had to admit that 'However, despite Malcolm's lack of diplomatic success, there is no denying that the propaganda which was generated by his extreme statements may have caused some damage to the United States image.' Given the Cold War and the need to enhance the USA's influence and reduce that of the USSR with African states, the government must have increased surveillance on Malcolm. Whether it tried to poison him remains unproven.[36]

The State Department decided to make public its interest 'in Malcolm X's campaign' to raise the issue of the position of African Americans. M.S. Handler in the *New York Times* on 13 August (p.22) reported that the 'State Department have begun to take an interest in Malcolm X's campaign to convince African states to raise the question of persecution of American Negroes at the United Nations'. On August 17 the *Times* reported that

---

34 The Logan Act forbids unauthorized citizens from negotiating with foreign governments; violation of the Act is punishable under federal law with imprisonment of up to three years.

35 NARA, SOC 14-1 US, Charles Diggs to F.G. Dutton 26/5/1964; J. Walter Yeagley, Asst. Attorney General to Dean Rusk, Secretary of State, 2/9/1964; Robert E. Lee to Congressman Diggs, 9/9/1964; Dept. of State to Embassies in Jidda (sic) Cairo, Beirut, Algiers and Rabat, 10/9/1964; Cairo Embassy to Dept of State, 7/11/1964. Some of this correspondence is also in the FBI papers, part 12; and in the Johnson Library.

36 See below for the possibility of such attempts.

'the issue, officials say, would be of service to critics of the United States, Communist and non-Communist, and contribute to the undermining of the position the United States has asserted for itself as the leader of the West in the advocacy of human rights'. (p.22)

Six days later the *New York Times* reported that Malcolm X had 'accused the United States of practising "a worse form of organized racism than South Africa"'. Malcolm had attended 'the recent African summit conference as an observer'. That Malcolm had presented a Memorandum to the conference, or the OAU's response to it, were not reported. I find it interesting that it should have taken the *New York Times* a month to publish this somewhat curtailed account. Was it printed on *page 86* as it clearly corrected the previous misreporting by the government? Had the government perhaps persuaded the newspaper to relegate this to the back of the paper?

And, did the government only rejoice, or had it in fact suggested to the *Los Angeles Times* (7 August 1964, p.5) that 'Malcolm was not at any of the conference sessions', and that he was mixing with virtually nobody but communists?[37] And why would the *Pittsburgh Courier* (29 August 1964, p.10), if it had not been 'leant on', refute Malcolm's charges against the US government by saying that 'there is no country on earth where an ethnic minority is better off than is the Negro in the United States'?

The *Chicago Defender* had reported on Malcolm's presence in London on 13 July (p.7) in an article headed 'Malcolm X seeks UN Aid against US bias' in which he is reported as saying that 'We want the US charged with violation of human rights'. The next day the paper carried a UPI report in which Malcolm is quoted as saying that 'racism in America is a government policy the same as it is in South Africa. The only difference is that the American government is deceitful and hypocritical about it.' On July 27 the *Defender* (p.6) printed the UPI report: under the headline 'Malcolm X Fails with Africans', it stated that the resolution 'proposed by Nyerere' had not been published, but believed it was in line with a previous resolution passed in Addis Ababa, 'expressing concern at racial discrimination in the US and commending action taken to combat it'. Two days later, the *Defender* printed its own assessment of Malcolm's presence in Cairo: 'It was the presence of Malcolm X in Cairo that created a sensation of unusual emotional intensity...[He] circulated a well-written memorandum [urging] the heads of African states to raise sharply before

---

37 In this article Victor Riesel also asserts that the Ghanaian delegation to the OAU was pro-Communist'. Another Californian article, 'Africa and the World', by George Goodman in the *Los Angeles Sentinel* (17 September 1964, p.6) acknowledges that when Malcolm travels 'below the Sahara he is well received'. It then quotes Ezekiel Mphahlele as saying that 'freedom would be non-existent without well meaning, enlightened whites'.

the General Assembly of the UN the question of racism in the United States as a potential threat to world peace...Eloquent and long address before a large gathering...all the members of the Summit'. (p.16)

As noted above, the American Embassy attempted to prevent Malcolm's presentation to the Heads of State. Malcolm repeated this in an interview with Milton Henry broadcast in Detroit; he recounted that, 'the information agencies of the US Government had almost successfully convinced the Africans that Afro-Americans did not identify with Africa'.[38] Did the government's determination to silence Malcolm – did the FBI director's order to institute a 'counterintelligence program' against Malcolm — including murdering him?[39]

According to Eric Norden, because the *Isis* was so crowded,

Malcolm moved to the *Nile Hilton*, sharing a room with Milton Henry, a lawyer and civil rights activist from Detroit.[40] On July 23, after dinner, 'Malcolm collapsed in his hotel room, suffering from severe abdominal pain. He was rushed to hospital...His stomach was pumped out...and that saved him...Analysis of the stomach pumping disclosed a 'toxic substance'. Its nature was undisclosed, but food poisoning was ruled out. Malcolm was hospitalised for a day and a half, but against his doctor's advice he managed to appear at the Summit Conference and give his speech. He was shaky for several days afterwards. According to Milton Henry, Malcolm believed 'someone had deliberately poisoned me...Washington had a lot to do with it'...Mrs. Ella Collins, Malcolm's sister, reported that Malcolm told her...that he felt that the CIA was definitely responsible.[41]

Malcolm recounted this incident to Jan Carew in London:

two things happened simultaneously. I felt a pain in my stomach and, in a flash, I realized that I'd seen the waiter who'd served me before. He looked South American, and I'd seen him in New York.

---

38 Ruby M & E.E. Essien-Udom, 'Malcolm X: an international man', in Clarke (1969), p.254.

39 Goldman (1979), p.211) believed that 'there was no tangible evidence for this; Washington was...slow in responding to his trip even as a policy problem, much less as grounds for assassination'.

40 Milton Henry of Pontiac, Michigan was an attorney, the president of the Afro-American Broadcasting Co., and the leader of the Black Freedom Now Party. According to an FBI report, Milton had advocated 'that Negroes are justified in using guerrilla warfare tactics in order to secure their rights...Henry was also affiliated with communist fronts in the Detroit area in the 1940s.' Malcolm, the FBI believed, had been invited to speak at a Broadcasting Co. rally on 14 February 1965. FBI papers, part 14, Memo to Detroit requesting 'public source data', 1/2/1965.

41 Norden (1967), pp.9-10.

The poison bit into me like teeth. It was strong stuff. They rushed me to the hospital just in time to pump the stuff out of my stomach. The doctor told Milton that there was a toxic substance in my food. When the Egyptians who were with me looked for the waiter who had served me, he had vanished.[42]

That Malcolm achieved admission and permission to speak at the OAU and a response to his request, bespeaks of his influence and the acceptance of at least part of his argument. Was he naïve enough to expect more? Did Malcolm not realise that the long tentacles of US international involvement and manipulation would prevent African states from challenging it in the world forum, especially over what the US would declare to be an internal matter? As the editorial in *The Guardian* had noted 'the OAU...will be too preoccupied with racial problems in their own continent...Moreover, they are looking for American support in their campaign to end apartheid in South Africa.'[43] Or, as South African author Ezekiel Mphahlele argued, 'if Malcolm listens he will learn that Nigeria's heads of state have swapped anti-American tirades for trade and foreign aid'.[44]

OAU at the United Nations

Malcolm claimed that 'several of [the African nations] promised officially that, come the next session of the UN, any effort on our part to bring our problems before the UN will get support from them. They will assist us in showing us how to bring it up legally.'[45] However, reports in the international press for the United Nations' meetings in December 1964 focus on the debates on the dues payable by members; the other major topic was the ongoing brutalities in the Congo and Western involvements in these. Thus there appeared to be no opportunity for the OAU members to raise their July resolution. However, the question of 'racism' was raised in the context of the Congo debates. As M.S. Handler reported in the *New York Times* on 2 January 1965, 'The spokesmen of some African states... in the Congo debate accused the United States of being indifferent to the fate of the blacks and cited as evidence the attitude of the United States government toward the civil-rights struggle in Mississippi. The African

---

42 Carew, (1994). p.39. Guyana-born Jan Carew has lived most of his life in Britain and the USA. He met Malcolm once, in 1965 in London. In the early 1990s after a visit to Grenada, where he found that Malcolm's mother was well-remembered, he interviewed Malcolm's brother in Detroit. Though I would agree with Louis De Caro's allegation that 'Carew has conflated memory with imagination' in his book, this account is very close to that of others elsewhere, eg Evanzz (1992), pp.255-6. My thanks to Paul Lee, email 15/4/2006.

43 Editorial, *The Guardian*, 1/7/1964.

44 From George Goodman, 'Africa and the World', *Los Angeles Sentinel*, 17/9/1964, p.A6.

45 Breitman (1966), p.84.

move profoundly disturbed the American authorities, who gave the impression that they had been caught off guard.'[46]

New Contacts

Malcolm met with many people. As noted above, the *Arab Observer* reported on 24 August 1964 that 'during the Summit he met and talked at length with many of Africa's most influential leaders. He divided his time between the Conference Hall, and the lobbies of Cairo's hotels which housed the delegates...Since the Conference he has been in almost daily contact with religious leaders and teachers...[He] has met with top Islamic leaders...[A]t the same time he has met and talked with numberless persons of all walks of life in Cairo [and] African Freedom fighters...[He] has discovered that the UAR stands firmly on the side of the twenty-two million oppressed Afro-Americans.'[47] George Goodman in the *Los Angeles Sentinel* (17 September 1964, p.A6) was determined to denigrate Malcolm and confuse his readers, by stating that 'Malcolm reportedly lives in Cairo but travels throughout cities below the Sahara and is well received. There are strong anti-American sentiments in every city of the world and it is mainly to those elements he address his tirades.'

We know that Malcolm talked with Abdulrahman Muhammad Babu, founder of the Umma Party of Zanzibar.[48] Years later Babu recalled that 'Malcolm came to my room in a very ambivalent mood, because at that very moment Harlem was burning. The youth in the uprising were calling for Malcolm. And Malcolm was in two minds. He wanted to go back, to come back and lead the struggle and be with the people in the struggle. But we wanted him to remain there in the conference so as to give us the feeling of the struggle and to convey to all the Third World leaders what America, the real America, was going through...This meeting also gave us an insight into Malcolm's own evolution. Malcolm started his political struggle at a community level. But he evolved into a national and international figure precisely because his politics were at the same time evolving. Malcolm had the vision to see the threat that a united Third-World countries would pose to imperialism.'[49]

---

46 Handler quoted in Breitman (1966), p.87.
47 This article was sent by the Cairo 'Amembassy' to the Dept. of State on 7 November 1964.
48 'Saw HE Babu' – *Notebook 7* entry for 21//7/1964. Babu's first names are spelled variously by different authors.
49 Abdul Alkalimat (ed), *Perspectives on Black Liberation and Social Revolution*, Chicago: Twenty-first Century Books, 1990, pp.123-4. S. Babu & A. Wilson, *Babu: The Future That Works: Selected Writings of A..M. Babu*, Trenton: Africa World Press 2002, pp.184-5. Speech at the International Conference of Malcolm X, 1-4 November 1990, New York.

In his Notebook Malcolm lists some of the people whom he spoke with, but seldom gives any details. He met with David Du Bois, 'Ahmed, Hussein and F.E. Boaten' who had been Ghana's Minister of Education. On July 15, he notes John Tettegah, 'most dynamic young Ghanaian', who was the Secretary-General of the Ghana Trade Union Congress.[50] A week later, he met again with Julia Wright: they discussed the OAAU. For the 24th, he lists Mrs. Padmore and Pauline Clark with whom he talked 'at length' and then had dinner. On the 25th he met with Mrs Du Bois[51] and Alioune Diop of the journal *Présence Africaine*[52]; with Julian Mayfield, and 'MBoya and he renewed his invitation for me to visit Kenya.[53] The following day he 'talked with Akbar at Isis for 2 hours...David...Rashid joined us. We discussed setting a press conference before my departure and the OAAU office for Cairo.'[54]

In his *Autobiography* Malcolm states that he met with President Nasser. (p.426) It would be interesting to know whether this was before or after President Nasser had praised the passing of the Civil Rights Act in the USA in his opening speech at the OAU. But Nasser had also to negotiate the Cold War. At a meeting in Detroit in February 1965 Malcolm stated that he had 'a chance to speak in Alexandria, with President Nasser for about an hour and a half. He's a brilliant man. And I can see why they're so afraid of him, and they are afraid of him. They know he can cut off their oil. And actually the only thing power respects is power.'[55]

Also from the *Notebook* we learn that on 15 July he was interviewed by a prominent British Sunday newspaper, *The Observer*, and there was a 'TV interview UPI'. On July 18, with 'Pitkins,' he attended the luncheon given by the London correspondents. Three days later he was 'interviewed here on the Isis for Middle East Feature Services'; on the 22nd, he was interviewed by the *London Daily Mail*. After his release from hospital, on July 25 there were 'more interviews – MENA and Vista News TV'.

50 Tettegah had chaired the second conference of International Trade Union Committee for Solidarity with the Workers and People of South Africa held in Accra, Ghana, from 9 to 11 March 1964.

51 According to the *New York Journal American* (5/8/1964) they met at the Hotel Omar Khayam, 'which was the headquarters of the violently anti-US pro-Communist Ghanaian delegation'.

52 Diop had founded this influential journal in 1946.

53 Presumably Tom Mboya, a Minister in the Kenyan government. He was assassinated in 1969, probably for accusing the Kikuyu elite, including the head of the government Jomo Kenyatta, of acquiring the most productive land from expelled Europeans.

54 David Du Bois wrote to Malcolm from Cairo on 24 November 1964 that 'there was a strong desire in Cairo to launch OAAU...Clearly indicating our allegiance to the New York OAAU, with you as it leader.' Malcolm replied on December 17, encouraging the formation of a branch and noting that he had 'enjoyed the hospitality of [your mother's] home and her office while I was in Ghana'. Schomburg Center: Malcolm X Papers, reel 3, box 3, folder 14.

55 *Malcolm X* (1992), p.81.

Returning from Alexandria on August 8, Malcolm notes that he is now residing at the Shepheard Hotel, as a 'guest of the state', and that he is busy writing his article for the *Egyptian Gazette*, and that he was interviewed by David Du Bois for the *Arab Observer*. (see above)

Malcolm's busy schedule continued: in his *Notebook* he lists many more meetings, often with un-named people, frequently with Ahmed. The only others mentioned, on 9 August are 'Uganda's representative to the UAR – talked', and on August 18, 'M. Fathi Nasr-al-Din and Khalil Mahmoud...we talked about the States and the OAAU'. The range of Malcolm's contacts is indicated by a letter he received dated 3 September, from K. Mahmud staying at the Hotel Green Valley in Cairo. This clearly followed up a conversation, as it listed 'some of the Muslim High Schools' in Nigeria looking for Muslim teachers, who would prefer having some 'suitably qualified Afro-American Muslims'.[56]

There is an undated OAAU press release among John Henrik Clarke's papers at the Schomburg Center, from the Information Bureau of the OAAU in Accra. It cites a press release by Malcolm X in Cairo, which in turn refers to a letter, which he had sent to Diallo Telli, the General Secretary of the Organisation of African Unity:

> We want the OAU to know that there are thousands of Afro-Americans who are ready to place ourselves at your service to help drive those South African murderers from the Congo. Many Afro-Americans are unemployed ex-servicemen who are experienced in every form of modern warfare and guerrilla fighting...We of this generation are fed up with colonialism, imperialism...and all other forms of racism...and we are ready to strike whatever blow is necessary to sweep the racists from this earth, at once and forever.[57]

It would appear that Malcolm had considerable trust in Diallo Telli, as, in light of the recent riots in the USA, he had sent Telli a telegram on 28 July, regarding the 'violent and brutal attacks by savage racist policemen in America against innocent and defenseless Afro-Americans'. He asked for a special meeting of the OAU to be convened in order to request the UN's Commission on Human Rights to 'launch an immediate investigation into the inhuman destruction of Afro-American life and property which the present US government seems either unable or unwilling to protect'.[58]

---

56 Schomburg Center: Malcolm X Papers, SC Micro 6270, folder 3, file 15.
57 Schomburg Center: Clarke Papers, Box 6/4.
58 The telegram was sent from the *Isis*, which seems to contradict Norden's statement that Malcolm had moved from this yacht. A copy of the telegram is in the John Henrik Clarke Papers, box 24 at the Schomburg Center.

Malcolm X also found time for involvement in Muslim groups and events, some in Cairo and some in Alexandria. From Paul Lee I learned that Malcolm had attended and made a speech at the Muslem Youth Association meeting held on the Prophet's birthday, July 21. He said that Muslems in America 'consider President Nasser as their leader' as they admire his support 'for African peoples in their struggle for independence and a decent life'. Lee then wonders if this was the same meeting, or a different one, to that recorded as a 'speech made by Minister Malcolm X on July 27' at 'a feast given in honor of Malcolm X by Shuban Al-Muslimeen (the Young Men's Muslim Association), and was attended by some of the top religious leaders of Cairo...Malcolm X was made an honorary member of the El-Shubban Al-Muslimeed, and given authority to set up branches in America.'[59]

On 22 August, according to his *Notebook*, Malcolm gave a press conference; 'Fathi, Hussein, Akbar...David...R...talked till after midnight about the importance of unity among the Afros who are abroad – Rashid, Khalid, Ibrahim and David. Port Said tomorrow.' On 25 August, on returning from a visit to Port Said, Malcolm noted 'two reporters from China...Hussein, David, Dr. Shawarbi, Akbar and I discuss "the problem"... Sheikh Ma'moun's banquet[60] – sat between Amb. for Nigeria and Sudan and Libya.'

On his return from travels to see the magnificent ruins of ancient Egyptian civilisations (see below), Malcolm notes the many people he meets. These included Dr. Asa Davis of Ibadan University, whom he had probably met during his previous visit there.[61] On 9 September, he records 'with Fathi and Al-(illegible) went to the African Association – many speeches, including mine'. He notes that he met many students.

Travels Within Egypt

On 27 July, according to his *Notebook*, Malcolm left for Alexandria. Who had arranged this trip is not known. Though he notes attending some meetings in Cairo, for example a reception at the Chinese Embassy on 1 August, the following day he was back in Alexandria. For once, he gives some details:

---

59 Email from Paul Lee, 16/8/2006. Much of one of the speeches that Malcolm gave to one of these Muslim groups can be found in the on-line FBI papers, section 4a, report by FBI New York Division, 20/1/1965. These FBI reports are quite unbelievably voluminous – and indicate the level of surveillance suffered by Malcolm X.

60 Was this the Rector of the Al-Azhar University whom Malcolm had met in July?

61 Professor Davis was a senior lecturer in History at the University of Ibadan from 1962 to 1969 and served as editor of the *Journal of the Historical Society of Nigeria*.

Camp for Muslim Youth – Abu Bakr El Sadiq Conference... long double line of Muslim youths, all were shouting "Welcome Malcolm"...It was so exciting, so unexpected...such an honor...This affair impressed me even more than my trip to Mecca: youth from everywhere, faces of every complexion, representing every race and every culture...filled with militant, revolutionary spirit and zeal.

Egypt, August 1964

The OAAU's paper *Backlash* reported in its 28 September issue that the 'students cheered Malcolm as he arrived at Abu Bekr Sediz Campus escorted by His Excellency Dr Mohammed Teufie Erveida, Secretary General of the Supreme Council on Islamic Affairs'. The paper then states that a division of the OAAU had been formed in Cairo, called the Organisation of Afro-American Students, which would set up college branches in the US.[62] Anyone interested in applying for one of the Al-Azhar University scholarships should apply to the OAAU. The photo on the cover page of the issue for 19 October is captioned 'Malcolm X receiving certificate of recognition and authority from the Rector of Al-

---

62 Nasir El-Din Mahmoud, President of the American Muslim Association, cabled President Nasser, Chair of the OAU on 28 November 1964, advising him that 'there are many U.S. military trained young Afro-Americans that if equipped and supplied, are ready to volunteer today to take up arms beside our Congolese brothers in their just struggle against US – Belgian, armed, British assisted aggression'. Schomburg Center: Malcolm X Papers, Box 14, folder 2.

Azhar, Hassan Maa'moun'. There is another cover photograph of Malcolm on the issue for 9 November: 'Malcolm X at luncheon in Alexandria – Dr. Mohammed Kazeem of Ein Champs University acting as interpreter, and Dr. Mohammed Teufie Erveida'.

We learn something more about the Alexandria meeting that Malcolm addressed from an FBI report, which quotes from innumerable US newspapers and from a Muslim Mosque Inc. press release. This stated that on 'August 4, 1964, in Alexandria, Egypt, Malcolm X had addressed over 800 Muslim students representing 73 different African and Asian countries at a banquet given by the Supreme Council of Islamic Affairs in which he, Malcolm, exhorted the students to call to the attention of their respective governments, who in turn should be persuaded to bring to the attention of the United Nations the plight of the Negro in America. At the conclusion of the banquet, according to Malcolm X's press release, one (name inked out) (Last Name Unknown) offered Malcolm X 20 free expense-paid scholarships to Al-Azer (phonetic) University in Cairo so that Malcolm X could have some of his young men trained in the (Muslim) religion.'[63]

According to Malcolm X scholar Paul Lee, the camp itself was organised by the Supreme Council, and it was the Council which 'later gave Malcolm X 20 scholarships for African American Muslims to study at Al-Azhar university'.[64]

At the end of July did Malcolm attend the celebrations of the twelfth anniversary of the Egyptian revolution?

Again Malcolm fell ill. 'I knew I had eaten something that was poisoning me', he wrote in his *Notebook* on August 6. He saw a doctor, who gave him some pills, 'and a painful injection...Told me it was the 'Spanish' I had eaten. Should be eaten only in the winter – more injections in the evening'.[65] Were the swollen ankles he noted on August 15, for which he went to see a doctor in Cairo, an after-effect of this poisoning? He makes no comment on the doctor's diagnosis in his *Notebook*.

Whatever this illness was, by 23 August Malcolm was well enough to travel again. In his *Notebook* entry for that day he recorded: 'Port Said wreath on monument to war victims...went to museum...toured city with police escort and governor's aide-de-camp...lunch at Suez Canal Authority Club (guest of pres, gov)...boat ride.' The next day: 'Said Abdullah's office...tour shipyards...return Cairo.' President Nasser was obviously taking great care of Malcolm. Indefatigable, on August 26

---

63 FBI Papers, Part 12 Report from the FBI New York office, 10/8/1964.

64 Email, 16/8/2006.

65 *Notebook 7,* entry for 8 August 1964.

Malcolm notes that had travelled to Aswan with Fathi and some others, presumably to see the dam whose Stage 1 construction had just been completed;[66] they then went to see the superb ruins at Luxor and Karnak, returning to Cairo on August 29th.[67]

Travel Outside Egypt

On September 16 and 17 Malcolm notes that he applied for visas to Saudi Arabia, Kuwait, Kenya and Ethiopia at the respective consulates.[68]

According to the 'Amembassy Jidda' Malcolm had arrived in Jedda on September 19 'for a three day stay'.[69] The 'Airgram' recounts Malcolm's previous visit in April, his introduction of 'the highly respected 'Abd al-Rahman Azzam pasha, first Secretary-General of the Arab League, and that he had become a 'an honoured guest of the government'. Malcolm made the Umra, or 'little pilgrimage' to Mecca. In the press interview published in *Al-Bilad* he apparently emphasised the benefit of his visit for his personal spiritual development. He met with Muhammad Surur Al-Sabban, the Secretary General of the Muslim World League, both in Mecca and in Jeddah. It has been suggested that Al-Sabban might have helped with financing Malcolm's travels in Africa.[70]

Malcolm called at the US Embassy to ask for additional pages to be inserted in his passport. He left for Kuwait on 23 September.[71]

Malcolm's letter from Mecca, dated 23 September, was printed in the *New York Times* (11 October 10 1964, p.13). In this Malcolm details the 15 scholarships offered by the Islamic University in Medina. Malcolm states

---

66 USA and Britain promised to finance the dam's construction. However, both nations cancelled the offer in July 1956, as they objected to an Egyptian arms agreement with Czechoslovakia, and to Egypt's recognition of the People's Republic of China. In 1958, the Soviet Union stepped in and funded the dam project.

67 From Luxor Malcolm sent a post card to some friends in New York: 'Greetings from the Ancient "Valley of the Kings" here in Luxor. After seven weeks amid the archeological sites of the Ancient Nile I feel like an expert in Egyptology, but I haven't forgotten our problem there in the States even for one minute, nor neglected it'. (My thanks to Paul Lee; email dated 4/11/2006.)

68 *Notebook 6*, entries for 16 and 17 September.

69 NARA: SOC 14-1 POL 13-10 US: Amembassy Jidda to Department of State, ref CA-2764, 10/9/1964.

70 Bruce Perry (1991, p.322) suggests that Malcolm might have approached Surur Al-Sabban for help with financing the Muslim Mosque in Harlem, and that it was in response to this request that a Sudanese scholar, Shaykh Ahmed Hassoun, was sent to New York to assist the work at the Mosque.

71 NARA: SOC 14-1 POL 13-10 US, Embassy Jidda (sic) to State Dept. 29/10/1964, 22/9/1964; telegram from Thacher, 'Jidda' to Secretary of State 22/9/1064 with copies to Kuwait and Dhahran.

that he had spent 'all summer' at the headquarters of the World Muslim League to prepare as an evangelist to the United States. The League, founded in 1962 by Surur Al-Sabban, aimed at 'co-operation and working unity in the Muslim World'.

For 24 September Malcolm notes that he is in Kuwait and receives one caller, Homeed Demerdash (sic),[72] whom he had met in Cairo. On the 27th he notes that he has 'been idle...beginning to feel wasting my time'. What had he hoped to be doing or whom had he hoped to be meeting? The following day, he writes that, 'Demerdash takes me to the Foreign Ministry – Sec. had seen me on TV in London and immediately became friendly. He took me to see – and while there two more came in'. I cannot solve the mystery of these meetings.

Notebook entry for 29 September: 'arrived Beirut–met by students–lecture on campus–overflow crowd...The students were receptive, their questions objective. There was a cross section represented. Then to Khartoum.' For the 30th the *Notebook* places him in Addis Ababa, where he gave a radio interview and talked with two representatives of Bechuanaland (the name is almost illegible) and then lists the names of many more people whom he met, without giving any more information. 'Ethiopia is a wonderful country', he said at his Homecoming Rally in New York in November. 'It has its problems...Some of the most beautiful people I've seen are in Ethiopia, and most intelligent and most dignified...I was there for about a week...'[73] On October 3 he met Babu at the airport, and the 'Minister for External Affairs...Spoke to about 50 Peace Corps at the PC Hostel and met Alice W. by accident and surprise'.[74] The next day Malcolm notes, 'BBC interview'; and on 5 October, 'to Nairobi'.

The FBI report states that on 30 September Malcolm called at the US Embassy in Kuwait in order to obtain a copy of his health certificate, which he claimed he had lost in Saudi Arabia; he was going to Khartoum, and then to Ethiopia.

On October 6 the US Ambassador in Ethiopia reported to the Department of State that Malcolm had arrived in Addis Ababa and had addressed the opening student assembly at the University College at the invitation of the Student Union four days previously. In his talk, the Ambassador reported, Malcolm drew parallels between colonialism

---

72 I have not been able to find any information on this person.

73 Breitman (1970), p.142. Malcolm states that he had been in Mecca 'for about a week'. As he explains that 'I went through Khartoum to Addis Ababa', this might just have been a flight stop-over.

74 Alice Windom, whom Malcolm had met on his first visit to Ghana.

in Africa and in the US, and repeated his call for unity and for Africans to take the United States before the UN. The Ambassador believed that the 'speech employed clever distortions of truth to lead to distorted conclusion'. 'The audience response was good', the Ambassador reports, 'with several interruptions for applause, particularly during his attacks on the US effort in Africa.' He ends his report with, 'none of the local papers or radio stations carried any account' of the speech. If there were no press reports, how did the Ambassador learn what Malcolm said? Was Malcolm under surveillance here too? We learn from another Embassy missive to Washington that unknown to Malcolm, 'there was an embassy officer in the audience during the speech'.[75]

Had Malcolm perhaps met Ghanaian Robert Gardiner, the Executive Secretary of the UN's Economic Commission for Africa, who was then stationed in Addis Ababa? It is quite possible that they had met each other while Gardiner was stationed in New York.[76]

On his departure Malcolm told the press that 'America is morally incapable of solving the Negro problem or ever seeing the problem in the proper light'.[77] But, if Malcolm had held a press conference, the media must have been interested in him. Had the Embassy inveigled it into silence?

Did Malcolm return to Cairo from Addis to attend the second Conference of Non-Aligned States taking place there on 3 October? The conference was opened by Gamal Abdul (sometimes spelled 'Abdel') Nasser and was also addressed by Emperor Haile Selassie of Ethiopia. Moise Tshombe had flown from the Congo to attend, but was not permitted to land in Cairo and was told his presence was 'inopportune' when he arrived on a commercial flight. It was forecast that 'colonialism, neo-colonialism, racial discrimination...are likely to form subject of firm resolutions'.[78]

---

75 NARA: SOC 14-1 US, Gordon Winkler, Amembassy Addis Ababa to Department of State, 6/11/1964.

76 Gardiner served as Executive Secretary 1961 - 1975. He was the UN's Special Representative in Congo 1962-3.

77 FBI report on Malcolm X #100-399321, part 14, report on visit abroad p.119.

78 *Voice of Ethiopia*, 8/10/1964, p.3; *Ethiopian Herald*, 4/10/1964; *West Africa*, 3/10/1964, p.1125; 10/10/1964, p.1131.

Lessons Learned

At a personal level, Malcolm learned that he was under threat from the US government. Malcolm noted that, 'throughout my trip, I was of course aware that I was under constant surveillance. The agent was particularly obvious and obnoxious to me...'[79] Whether his illnesses had been caused by these agents is not known, but as noted previously, Peter Goldman, Malcolm's biographer, does not believe so.

At a political level, by the end of his stay in Cairo Malcolm had realised the obstacles he faced: in his letter of 29 August, printed in *By Any Means Necessary* (pp.108-112), he says that he is not doubtful of support, but has learned 'that one cannot take things for granted'. What he was trying to do was 'very dangerous because it is a direct threat to the entire international system of racist exploitation'. He thought he might be killed soon for making this challenge. He repeated his belief in 'human rights for everyone' and emphasised that, 'our fight must never be against each other...but against the *common enemy*'. (his emphasis) 'Progress depends on this', he believed.

In his article in the 14 September issue of *Backlash* Malcolm explained the measures taken by the US government

> in order to keep the OAAU from gaining the interest [and] support of Independent African States, the racism element in the State Department...gave maximum world wide publicity to the recent passage of the Civil Right Bill...The resolution [passed at the OAU] meeting had so many frightening implications for America's future image and position in the world, especially for her foreign policy... that the American press completely smothered...the passing of the Resolution.

Malcolm had also learned that the overt 'dollarism' he had spoken about at the OAU meeting was being matched by more covert activism by the imperialists. But it was 'dollarism' that was more important. As he explained in January 1965,

> It is easy to become a satellite today without even being aware of it. This country can seduce God. Yes, it has that seductive power – the power of dollarism. You can cuss out colonialism, imperialism, and all other kinds of isms, but it's hard for you to cuss out dollarism. When they drop those dollars on you, your soul goes.[80]

---

79 *Autobiography*, pp.427-8.
80 Breitman (1966), p.199.

CHAPTER 5

Kenya, Tanganyika, Zanzibar, Addis Ababa
October 1964

Kenya, October 5 - 9

In 1887 the British East Africa Company established a level of control over the countries that became Kenya and Uganda; the British government took over in 1895, added Zanzibar, and bestowed colonial status in 1920.[1] The colony was used not only as a source of raw materials and a market for manufactured goods, but also as a place of settlement for adventurous as well as impoverished Britons. Africans living on the most productive lands in Kenya were dispossessed and these areas were taken over by the immigrants, and came to be called the White Highlands. The Africans thus forced to become labourers had to work for a pittance. From 1895 labourers were imported from India to work on the railway needed to transport agricultural and mining produce to the coast for shipment to England.

Whites were the 'unofficial' members of the Legislative Council and after WWII held all ministerial appointments. One African, Eliud Muthu,

---

1 I have retained the original spelling, punctuation and emphases in all documents quoted. There are so many books on the histories of each of the countries Malcolm visited, that I shall not give such general references.

founder of the Kenya African National Union (KANU), was appointed to the Council in 1944.²

The Kikuyu, who were about 20% of the population, and most of those dispossessed, were the majority of KANU's members. It was led, after his release from prison, by Jomo Kenyatta, a Kikuyu. The Land and Freedom Army (the 'Mau Mau') began a struggle for independence in the early 1950s; the number of Europeans killed was 68; the number of Africans killed is currently estimated to be 100,000.³ About one hundred and fifty thousand (including Kenyatta, who was NOT the leader of the Mau Mau) were imprisoned.

The Whites won the war, but the financial cost to war-impoverished Britain was high. The slow pace of movement towards power-sharing had to be quickened: the first Constitutional Conference was held in London in 1960; there the problems faced by all British colonies became obvious. When the Europeans divided Africa among themselves in Berlin in 1885, they ignored historic, language and natural boundaries. There was nothing to hold the peoples of Kenya – e.g. the Luo, Kikuyu, Masai, Meru and Kamba, together, except the British gun. How was power to be shared among the 20 disparate peoples in an independent Kenya? The problem – as we can see in 2010, has not been solved in Kenya or elsewhere on the continent.

Kenya attained independence on 12 December 1963, under the premiership of Jomo Kenyatta. Kenyatta declared Kenya a republic in 1964 with himself as president and appointed Oginga Odinga, a Luo, vice-president.

When Malcolm arrived in Nairobi, the population of Kenya, according to the 1962 census, was about eight and a half million, of whom 176,000 were 'Asians', 56,000 were Europeans and 34,000 were Arabs.

---

2 'Official' members were government officials; 'unofficial' members — seldom more than one or two — were usually appointed by the colonial government

3 This estimate is from one of the recent exposés of British atrocities, Caroline Elkins, *Britain's Gulag*, London: Pimlico 2005, pp.xiv, 366.

The year of Malcolm's visit was one of 'deteriorating relations as one cold war manoeuvre after another began to work in East Africa and we were forced to recognise that powerful agencies were in the field to subvert our national and Pan-African interests', according to Oginga Odinga.[4]

According to his *Notebook*, Malcolm left for Nairobi, the capital of Kenya, on October 5.[5] He had flown in from Beirut.

Malcolm noted that he 'saw no mixing in Nairobi and the Asians are getting worried about the future. There seems to be an "invisible force" trying to bring disunity between Africans and Asians (Israeli?).' Other aspects of the country he found far more appealing:

> Kenya, a place which really knocked me out. If ever I saw any Africans who looked like they had the potential for explosion, it's our Kikuyu brothers in Kenya...They look like they can explode, more so than any place I went on the continent. You can just see, right in their faces, energy...And as proof that they can explode, they exploded the other day. When the United States, with her criminal action in the Congo – and that's what it is, criminal action in the Congo – they marched on the embassy there in Nairobi and tore it up. And that shows you what the Africans feel.[6]

Malcolm telephoned 'Odinga's office' on October 7, obviously asking for an appointment as he noted on the following day that 'Odinga tied up with PM Kenyatta Equator Club'. (Who had initially introduced them is not known; it could well have been Pio Gama Pinto, who was Odinga's close advisor.) Malcolm and Odinga did meet: Malcolm found Odinga 'very attractive, alert, understanding and sympathetic'.[7] After the meeting Malcolm 'went to Parliament with Mr. Pinto and had dinner with several

---

4 Oginga Odinga, *Not Yet Uhuru*, London: Heinemann 1967, pp.274-5. Odinga resigned his post and membership of TANU in late 1964.

5 *Notebook 6*, entry for 7/10/1964.

6 On the Congo, see Adam Hochschild, *King Leopold's Ghost*, London: Papermac 2000; Patrice Lumumba, *Congo My Country*, New York: Frederick Praeger, 1962; Ludo De Witte, *The Assassination of Lumumba* (London: Verso, 2001) for a full exposé of the assassination. Larry Devlin, in his *Chief of Station, Congo*, New York: Public Affairs 2007, explains that the US' involvement in the Congo was in order to prevent it falling under Communist influence. The US was interested in the Congo's copper, cobalt and diamond mines. Patrice Lumumba, the elected president, was believed by the US government to be a friend of the USSR, and thus 'his removal must be an urgent and prime objective' Devlin was told. (p.63)

7 Early in 1964 while he was Minister for Home Affairs, Odinga had visited Peking. He believed that 'independent African states must be ready to wage war on South Africa' and appealed for China's help. (*West Africa*, 16 May 1964, p.557) This visit would not have endeared Kenya to either the USA or the USSR, which was on 'bad terms' with its fellow Communist state.

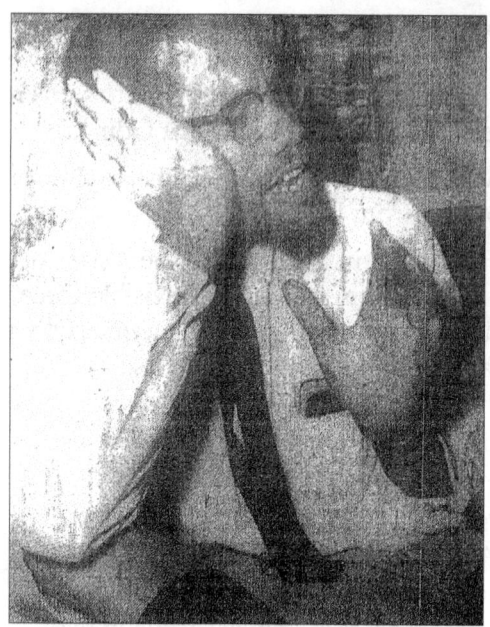

Malcolm X, pictured in his hotel room in Nairobi

MPs including Hungarian Ambassador. Invited to speak to Parliament 15th.'[8]

Oginga Odinga was a believer in democratic socialism. Though appointed by President Kenyatta as Vice-President, he and Kenyatta soon clashed, as Odinga was very critical of the President's alliance with foreign capital and the 'Western Powers'.[9]

Historian Karl Evanzz states that Malcolm had met Nairobi-born Pio Gama Pinto at the United Nations in New York.[10] Of Goanese origins, Pinto's parents sent him back to India for his education. There he became involved in the independence struggle.[11] He returned to Kenya in about 1950 and joined the independence movement. A journalist, he was imprisoned for four (some claim five) years during Kenya's freedom struggle for supporting the so-called 'Mau Mau' freedom fighters[12], reportedly supplying them with 'arms and supplies'. He also looked after the families of the 'freedom fighters, including those who had been killed'.[13] On his release he returned to journalism, publishing weekly papers in the bi-monthly English-language *Pan Africa*, for which he received financial support from Prime Minister Nehru in India. An active supporter of trade unionism, he was elected a member of the Central Legislative Assembly in 1963 and the following year helped establish the Kenya African Workers' Congress, independent of the US-dominated

---

8 *Notebook 6*, entry for 8/10/1964. Hungary was still part of the Soviet Bloc.

9 For the relationship of Odinga, Mboya and Kenyatta, and party politics, see the interesting article by 'A Special Correspondent', 'The Changing face of Kenya politics', *Transition* 25, 1966, pp.44-50. Odinga (1967, p.109), claims that Mboya was 'nurtured by the British government'.

10 Evanzz (1992), p.161. The reference cited is 'State Department file on Malcolm X'. I have been unable to find any evidence of Pinto visiting the United Nations or the USA. Dr DaCosta, who is working on a biography of Pinto does 'not believe that Pio met Malcolm X anywhere in the USA'. (Email from Shiraz Durrani, 11 February 2008)

11 India gained its independence from Britain in 1947 – part of what had been the British colony of India was then converted into the Muslim country of Pakistan.

12 The freedom fighters called themselves the Land and Freedom Army' the name 'Mau Mau' was bestowed by the colonials.

13 Cabral Pinto, 'Life and times of Pio Gama Pinto', *Daily Nation*, 20 February 2009.

International Federation of Free Trade Unions. He was assassinated almost on the same day as Malcolm, on 24 February 1965, probably for his involvement with those beginning to fight against what was described as 'Kenyatta and his clique of rightists...close to the neo-colonialists'.[14]

Pinto interviewed Malcolm for *Pan Africa*. He began by questioning why he called himself 'Malcolm X'. He then asks about the Civil Rights Act. Malcolm replied that,

> American legislation cannot solve the type of racism that has become an inseparable part of America's political, social and economic system. It takes education not legislation...[S]ince the passage of the Bill three Civil Rights workers were murdered in Mississippi...Another negro educator was murdered in Georgia... [D]uring the summer there were riots during which the police used clubs to crush scores of negroes. They used vicious dogs...The Civil Rights Bill...is only used as a propaganda trick by America to impress the African and Asian nations into thinking that she is doing something meaningful to solve the problem that she actually can't solve because it is too deep.[15]

Pinto then questions Malcolm about the importance of the Black Muslim Movement. Malcolm replies that 'most people agree in America that the stepped up militance on the part of the whole Civil Rights movement was pressed forward by the militancy of the Muslims and I must say also by the independence of the African states here on the continent'. He then went on to elaborate on this statement:

> As long as Africa was colonised, the coloniser projected the image of Africa and it was negative. And this made the people of African origin in the West not want to identify with Africa. And as the image of Africa was negative, the image of themselves was negative. But... now Africa is projecting a positive image, you find that the black people in the West are also projecting a positive image, they have more self-confidence and they are stepping up their drive in this struggle for freedom.

---

14 'Pio Gama Pinto: independent Kenya's first martyr, 1927 – 1965', *Awaaz*, #1, 2005, pp.18 – 21. The quotations is from p.20; Shiraz Durrani, 'Pio Gama Pinto: some facts about the life of a great leader and patriotic journalist', written for *Sauti ya Kamukunji*, published by the University of Nairobi Students Union in 1984. My thanks to my colleague Shiraz for this and the other article on Pinto. Odinga in his *Autobiography* (1967, p.251) says of Pinto's assassination that it 'leaves a gap in our political struggle for full freedom that few men can fill...he was an intelligent socialist'. For other aspects of Pinto's involvement in Kenya's politics, see eg, Bildad Kaggia, *Roots of Freedom*, Nairobi: East African Publishing, 1975.

15 *Pan Africa*, November 13, 1964, pp.21-2.

To the question on what he intended to do on his return to the USA, Malcolm replied

> We are involved in a programme to bring the problem of our people in the States before the United Nations and try to make the world see that the United States government is just as much responsible for violating the human rights of 22 million black people in that country, as South Africa for violating the rights of the Africans in South Africa or Portugal is guilty of violating the rights of Africans in Mozambique and Angola...Instead of continuing the struggle within the confined area of civil rights which keeps us under the jurisdiction of that government we intend to internationalise it by making it a human rights problem...and then ask the world to support us in a problem that is no longer an American problem or negro problem but is a work problem.

On October 13 the Nairobi *Daily Nation* made its readers aware of Malcolm's presence in East Africa, but said nothing of his presence in Kenya, as far as I have been able to discover.

> Malcolm X, leader of the Negro Nationalist Movement – splinter group of a Black Muslim sect – has arrived in Dar. The Government Party newspaper, *The Nationalist*, says he accused the US State Department of creating Negro leaders with the object of keeping Negroes down. He also said Africans should take a more definite line and not allow themselves to be bullied, the newspaper reported. He said he was on a world tour, and would visit Kenya and Ethiopia next. He has been in Cairo and the Middle East during the past few months. (p.1)

Zanzibar and Tanganyika, October 9 - 17

Zanzibar is an archipelago of islands about 15 miles off the coast of the country we know today as Tanzania. It was settled by Persians, Arabs, Africans, and Indian traders and was much involved in the trade in enslaved Africans. Colonised by Britain, it obtained its independence in 1963 as a constitutional monarchy. However, a popular uprising by the Afro-Shirazi party led by Abeid Karume, and the Arab, left-wing Umma Party, led by Abdulrahman Muhammad Babu, resulted in the overthrow of the Sultan on January 12, 1964. Karume and Babu led the negotiations with Tanganyika to form the United Republic of Tanganyika and Zanzibar (URTZ) on April 26 of that year. Nyerere was the President and Karume the Vice-President. (The name 'Tanzania' was adopted on 29 October

1964.) However, the islands remained semi-autonomous, with their own President, House of Representatives and flag. Despite this the union was not easy, partly due to the religious and ethnic divisions and differing political viewpoints.

The Soviet Union and China had established missions in Zanzibar, and supported its independence. This was much disliked by the USA, then vying with the Communist world for influence in Africa. Zanzibar's – and much of Africa's relationship with the USA – deteriorated considerably over the Congo. According to Odinga, the 'Zanzibar revolution was the 'start of the Cold War scare in East Africa on a large scale'.[16]

Tanganyika, also a creation of the Berlin conference as a German colony, was transferred to Britain as a 'trust territory' by the League of Nations after WWI. It was, like all these 'countries', the home of many diverse peoples. They naturally formed ethnic associations, and it was only protest against the coloniser that united them after WWII. In 1954 they formed the Tanganyika African National Union (TANU), a 'trans-ethnic' organisation under the leadership of Julius Nyerere. Nyerere and TANU negotiated and obtained independence for Tanganyika in December 1961. As he believed that a multi-party system on Western lines would inevitably lead to ethnic conflict, Nyerere created a one-party state, but fostered local involvement in decision making; however, he outlawed trade union strikes, which led to some opposition. After the creation of the United Republic, he proclaimed the Arusha Declaration in 1967, promoting a form of African socialism which also promoted self-help and a refusal of dependence on foreign aid.

A key player in the Organisation of African Unity (OAU), Nyerere was the chair of its African Liberation Committee, which had its headquarters in Dar-es-Salaam.[17] Nyerere believed in a United Africa under a single continent-wide government, which was not the desire of all the members of the OAU.

Tanzania's population in 1967 was 12 million, including 355,000 in Zanzibar, of whom about 57,000 were Arabs and 13,550 'Asians'. On the mainland there were 35,000 Arabs, 104,900 'Asians' and 22,200

---

16 Odinga (1967), p.279.

17 This Committee had been set up in 1963. Its aim was to 'unite various liberation movements and distribute funds to them and help them establish education and military training centres', according to *West Africa*. (1/8/1964, p.858). This sounds very much like the program Nkrumah had instituted in Ghana. The Committee aided 'only the liberation movements which are accorded official OAU recognition'. (G.A. Obiozor & A. Ajala (eds), *Africa and The United Nations System: The First Fifty Years*, Lagos: Nigerian Institute of International Affairs 1998, p.71)

Europeans. Africans were divided into about 130 'tribes' varying in size from 1.5 million to just under 200.[18]

In August 1964 there had been a large anti-American demonstration in Dar, led by the ruling party, TANU. Its focus was on the US involvement in events in Congo. There had also been a demonstration in Kenya.

Malcolm must have been invited to visit Zanzibar by Abdulrahman Muhammad Babu. Babu (as he was commonly called) was now the Minister of Economic Development. He had met Malcolm at what he described as a 'very interesting moment'. As Babu explained at a conference in 1990,

> I met him for the first time in Cairo, when there was a crucial meeting of the second summit of the OAU...Malcolm came to my room in a very ambivalent mood, because at that very moment Harlem was burning...Malcolm was in two minds. He wanted to go back...and lead the struggle and be with people in the struggle. We wanted him to remain there in the conference so as to give us the feeling of the struggle and to convey to all the Third World leaders what America, the real America, was going through.[19]

The two men clearly liked each other, as for undisclosed reasons Malcolm also went to meet Babu at Beirut airport on 3 October 1964. Malcolm described Babu in his *Notebook* as 'very informal and friendly. An extremely alert man and dedicated to what he believes.' (The friendship was strong, as Babu addressed the OAAU rally in New York on 13 December.)

Zanzibar-born Babu had studied in England from 1951 and worked with the Movement for Colonial Freedom, with pan-Africanist George Padmore and independence-oriented Africans resident in London, such as Mbiyu Koinange of Kenya. Babu returned home in 1957 and became involved in the independence struggle by setting up a political party. He attended the All-African People's Conference in Accra in 1958, where he recalled that meeting 'Nkrumah for the first time was a most exhilarating experience'.[20] In 1959 he accepted an invitation to visit China and the offer of becoming the East and Central African correspondent for the China News Agency. In June 1964 he had visited Peking and obtained $16.8 million aid for Zanzibar – $28 million for the union as a whole', according to *Newsweek* (6 July 1964 p.29). Babu was a staunch and committed socialist, as witnessed not only by his life but in his writings, such as

---

18 Bureau to State, *The Population of Tanzania: analysis of the 1967 population census*, Dar es Salaam, 1973, pp.160-172.

19 Alkalimat (1990), pp.123-4.

20 'Memoirs' by Babu, in 'Five Decades of Liberation & Revolution: the Life of Comrade Abdulrahman Mohamed', *Review of African Political Economy*, 23/69 September 1996, pp.321-348; the quotation is from p.326.

African Socialism or Socialist Africa?, published in London in 1981. In this he argued, for example, that the USA and Europe are 'part and parcel of the same system, whose precondition for survival is the political and economic domination of Africa and other developing countries'. (p.113)

The curious – if not anxious – American consul must have questioned Babu about Malcolm, as he reported to the State Department that Babu 'had been very impressed with Malcolm X when he met him at Cairo. Babu claimed that Malcolm X was a dynamic person who made a great impact on the African leaders.' Ambassador Attwood described Babu as 'an astute, hard-boiled, Marxist-trained correspondent for a Chinese communist publication'.[21]

In his *Notebook* Malcolm wrote '9 October Zanzibar'.[22] But when exactly he was on the island and when he was in Dar-es-Salaam is unclear. On October 12, so some three days after Malcolm had landed, the US Embassy reported to the Secretary of State in Washington that 'Malcolm X arrived DAR over weekend and gave exclusive interview to Nationalist'. 'Leonhart' then summarised the article, 'Malcolm X Raps Africa', and concluded with 'Embassy understand Malcolm X spent yesterday Zanzibar. Length of his visit DAR uncertain'.[23] As the telegram was copied to other embassies in East and North Africa, there was clearly considerable interest in Malcolm's travels and meetings.

Presumably back in Dar, Babu took 'two other Brothers' to see Malcolm at his hotel on October 12; the following day he had dinner at Babu's home with 'four other "brothers"'. 'I knew I was being "weighed"', he wrote, 'and was elated when told I'd meet the President at 6pm'. Babu reported that,

> When Malcolm X came to Tanzania, I took him to meet President Nyerere on a historic date...that very day China exploded her first nuclear bomb...Nyerere said "Malcolm, for the first time today in recorded history, a former colonial country has been able to develop weapons at par with any colonial power. This is the end of colonialism through and through." And Malcolm replied, "Mr. President, this is what I've been thinking all the way as I was coming from my hotel to this house".

And this is what Malcolm had in mind: To promote internationalism

---

21 NARA: SOC14-1 US, Consulate Zanzibar to Department of State 26 August 1964. Attwood (1967), p.156

22 The *Voice of Ethiopia* reported his presence. How this newspaper obtained news and how long it took to reach there from East Africa is not known. But it is certainly interesting that an Ethiopian newspaper should note Malcolm's arrival.

23 Lyndon B. Johnson Library: Dar-es-Salaam to [Secstate[740, copied to Nairobi 113 and Addis Ababa 44, 12/10/1964. My thanks to the librarian at the Johnson Library for sending me this.

in the Third World. He saw what American policy meant and what it could mean in the event that the Third-World population inside America could be politicised and mobilized.'[24]

Malcolm noted in his *Notebook* that he had found Nyerere to be a 'very shrewd, intelligent, disarming man who laughs and jokes much (but is deadly serious)'. At the Homecoming Rally in New York at the end of November, he recounted that their meeting had lasted three hours. Malcolm described Nyerere as a 'most intelligent man and alert and knows what going on'.[25]

Babu was not the only one to welcome Malcolm in Tanzania. Malcolm writes, 'Ed Anderson – several Africans and Afro-Americans there' in his *Notebook* for October 11. Some months later, Anderson wrote him from Dar:

> We greatly appreciated your recent visit to Dar-es-Salaam. Your influence on the minds and hearts of the people that heard your message cannot be measured. You left a host of followers and well-wishers behind. Recently my wife visited Nairobi and she had the same reaction there to your visit....

Anderson then asks Malcolm to introduce the two Tanzanian delegates to the United Nations to the OAAU.[26]

On October 14 Malcolm notes that he went to visit 'Mr Rodriguez, Afro-Cuban at Cuban Embassy' and that evening was taken to dinner by 'Otimi Kambone'.[27] 'Many other Africans were there', he noted. 'I was the guest of honour. Director of TBS was there – encouraged to postpone departure tomorrow until after all the visiting P[rime] M[inister]'s leave.'

The meeting of the Prime Ministers on October 15-16 was a 'four-power' summit of Presidents Nyerere, Kenneth Kaunda of Zambia, Milton Obote of Uganda and Jomo Kenyatta of Kenya. They discussed the situation in the Congo, the struggles for independence in Mozambique,

---

24 Alkalimat (1990), pp.123-4, 127; S. Babu & A. Wilson, *Babu: The Future That Works. Selected Writings of A.M. Babu*, Trenton: Africa World Press, 2002, pp.84-8, Speech at the International Conference of Malcolm X, 1-4 November 1990, New York.

25 *Notebook 6*, entry for October 13; Breitman (1970), pp.144-5. My thanks to Paul Lee for pointing out this reference.

26 Schomburg Center: Malcolm X Papers, reel 4, folder 5: Anderson to Malcolm, 17/12/1964.

27 Malcolm probably meant *Oscar* Kambona, the Minister for External Affairs? Kambona had been the secretary-general of the Tanganyika African National Union (TANU) during the struggle for independence and had worked closely with Nyerere. He could have met Malcolm in the USA, as he was there to give an address at the 6th Annual Meeting of the African Studies Association on 25/10/1963. Newsweek called Kambona 'the tough, bustling Foreign Affairs Minister'. (6 July 1964, p.30) He was also the chair of the African Liberation Committee. (*West Africa*, 7/3/1964, p.255)

and Southern Rhodesia, where Ian Smith, the white Prime Minister, was attempting to get Britain to agree to independence virtually under White rule. The Prime Ministers decided to call on the British government to convene a constitutional conference. This meeting was followed by a meeting of the OAU's Liberation Committee, headed by Oscar Kambona, the URTZ Foreign Minister. Southern Rhodesia and the struggles against the Portuguese overlords were on its agenda.[28]

Had Malcolm been permitted to attend either of these meetings? He did extend his stay in Dar, and wired, 'Pinto postponing arrival Nairobi', despite the previous arrangement to address the Kenyan Parliament on October 15.[29] Clearly whoever he hoped to meet during the extra days was important. There is hardly anything in his *Notebook* for October 15 and nothing at all for October 16. Given that Malcolm might well have feared that the CIA or other agents would try to procure his *Notebooks*, I assume that there are many names and meetings he did not record.

The Media in Tanzania

On October 12 Malcolm notes, 'reporter from the *Tanganyika Standard*'; 'Indian reporter interviews'. Later 'Ed Anderson; interviewed by TBC at his house'.[30] The *Standard* interview, published on October 13 as 'Malcolm X Raps USA', stated that Malcolm had said that,

> American Negroes are beginning to see that their relationship to Africa is something which cannot be denied...The right type of Negro can make a great contribution to Africa, but the type that is being sent here now by the American Government is not designed to make contributions to things African...I think American leaders are more afraid of Africanism than of Communism.[31]

The US Embassy in Dar-es-Salaam sent summaries of two newspaper reports on Malcolm: he had 'repeated his fundamental message of the need for African/Afro-American unity and warned about the Negro leadership created by the State Department'. The main points he had made, the Embassy reported, were taken from the *Tanganyika Standard* (see above):

> American State Department creates Negro leaders with object of holding Negroes down. Important to sort out genuine leaders from others. Africa should take more definite line and not allow itself

---

28 *Africa Report*, December 1964, p.30; *The Nationalist* (Tanzania) 15 & 19 October 1964, p.1.
29 *Notebook 6*, entry for October 15.
30 Tanganyika Broadcasting Corporation.
31 FBI report on Malcolm X #100-399321, part 14, report on Malcolm's visits abroad, pp.110-111, probably taken from NARA: DC 14-1 US, Leonhart, Dar-es-Salaam to Secretary of State 13/10/1964.

be bullied. America needs Africa more than Africa needs America. Regarding the forthcoming US elections, he said the choice was 'between the lesser of two evils'.

Malcolm, according to the Embassy's summary, had made the following points:

a) He does not intend return US before elections and does not wish become involved as his presence in America at election time might cause demonstrations beneficial to Goldwater. On other hand any comments he might make would not help Johnson. Choice is only between lesser of two evils.

b) Said he came to URTZ [Union of Tanganyika and Zanzibar] following visits to Saudi Arabia, Kuwait, Ethiopia. Now on world tour explain inside story Negro problem US. Hopes to meet with GURTZ (government of the Union] official and will visit Kenya and Ethiopia before departing for West Africa.

Malcolm had given an exclusive interview to '(Arab) nationalists' while in Dar-es-Salaam, the FBI claimed in its report to the State Department. What or whom did the FBI mean? Zanzibaris? Or Pinto? Or Babu? Or could there have been reporters there, perhaps from Egypt or Algeria, given the Prime Ministers' summit and Liberation Committee meeting?[32]

The headline I have been able to see, on page one of the *Tanganyika Standard* for 13 October, is, 'We're one with you, says "exile" Malcolm X'. It begins with, 'Malcolm X, a leader of the Black Muslims, lounged on his bed at a Dar es Salaam hotel yesterday and talked about many things'. He was in Africa 'for the purpose of creating a better understanding of Africans here'. The 'Negroes sent by the US government to Africa were not designed to make a contribution to things African. They are designed to create an image that will make the African feel repulsive. It is my contention that they make Africans hate American Negroes. I think American leaders are

---

32 NARA: SOC 14-1 US, Leonhart, Dar Embassy to Secretary of State and US Embassies in Nairobi and Addis Ababa, 12/10/1964, reporting on the interviews in *The Nationalist* and the *East African Standard*. (The *East African Standard* had Kenyan, Ugandan and Tanzanian editions.)

more afraid of Africanism than they are of Communism. A Communist can go to America and live where he likes, but an African can't.'

Malcolm then responds to questions about Cassius Clay, then visiting Africa, arguing that Clay must be in a 'religious turmoil' as he could no longer believe that Elijah Mohammed was 'infallible'. The article concludes by noting Malcolm's 'hopes to meet a number of Tanganyikans of all levels during his stay'. He had accepted an invitation to visit Zanzibar.[33]

On the 14th Malcolm notes, 'at Babu's for pictures', presumably again for the press.

Fortunate Meetings

On October 17 Malcolm 'caught the same plane to Nairobi with Kenyatta and Obote. Shook Nyerere's hand at airport...Upon boarding the plane the Uganda FM asked me to sit beside Obote.[34] So I ended up between Obote and Kenyatta, riding with him to Mombasa, where Kenyatta decided to spend the nite.'[35] 'Providence put us together', Malcolm told'.[36]

In his *Autobiography* (p.426) Malcolm says that he had 'private audiences' with Dr. Milton Obote, the Prime Minister of Uganda. Was Malcolm referring to their shared flight or had they met in Dar?[37] As Prime Minister Obote had deplored the 'inhuman treatment' of African-Americans in a well-publicised letter to President Kennedy in 1963, he would have had some interest in Malcolm. And Malcolm would have been equally interested in him.[38]

---

33 The article was reproduced in the *Uganda Argus* on 14 October 1964, p.2, headlined 'U.S. sends wrong type of negroes to Africa, says Malcolm X'.

34 Ugandan Milton Obote, while an unskilled worker in Kenya, became active in political circles and worked with Tom Mboya in the early 1950s. He returned to Uganda, a British colony, in 1957, and was elected to the Legislative Council and went on to establish a political party, the Uganda People's Congress. Uganda was the home of many competitive ethnic groups, it attained independence under the prime ministership of Obote in 1962.

35 *Notebook 6*.

36 Paul Lee (email 7/5/2006) referred me to Malcolm's speech at the Homecoming Rally in November, at which Malcolm had said: 'I was fortunate enough to ride on the same plane with Kenyatta...Obote, when they were going from Dar es Salaam to Zanzibar, back to Kenya'. This seems to imply that the plane from Dar to Nairobi had a stop-over in Zanzibar. Breitman (1970), p.145.

37 There are no reports on Malcolm in the papers of the British High Commissions in the newly independent British ex-colonies. I can only conclude that these are with MI5 or MI6. My request for their release elicited the usual farcical response that it cannot even be confirmed that such papers exist.

38 Evanzz (1992), p.155.

Malcolm's Report on His Visit

Reporting on his visit to the OAAU Homecoming Rally in New York on 29 November 1964, Malcolm said that he 'never went anywhere that has pleased me more than [Tanzania]. It's beautiful – all of Africa is beautiful, but in Tanganyika...it's hot, it's like Miami...' Malcolm also berated the Unites States Information Service working in Africa in this talk:

> I'm telling you, they've done a vicious job...It will make that propaganda machine that Goebbels had, under Hitler, look like child's play. Why, in every African country the USIS window has pictures in it, showing the passage of the civil rights bill to make it look like the problems of every Negro over here have been solved... They use that passage of the bill to make it appear that Negroes aren't being lynched any more, that Negroes' voting rights aren't being trampled upon any more, that police aren't busting Negroes' heads with clubs any more, nor are they using dogs and violence and water hoses to wash us down the drain...
>
> To show you how vicious they are...the USIS [has] circulated a document on me throughout the African continent – knocking me.[39]

Nairobi, October 17 - 24

Having sat 'with the Uganda FM at airport in Nairobi', Malcolm wrote in his *Notebook* on October 17, 'MBoya came and got me...couldn't reach into...went to Equator Club...met several VIPs including Dr. Munzai – Minister of Health'.[40]

Tom Mboya had led the Kenya Federation of Labour (really a political organisation), the only African group permitted to operate throughout Kenya until 1960. He and Oginga Odinga formed the Kenya Independence Movement, which became the Kenya African National Union (KANU). By 1958 Mboya was so well known that he was invited to attend first anniversary celebrations of the independence in Ghana, and later that year attended the All-African People's Conference there. The following year he toured the USA, seeing it as a 'potential source of material assistance'; he received funding for fifty scholarships to American universities for young Kenyans.[41] At independence, Mboya was made Minister for Labour; in

---

39 Breitman (1970), pp.143, 139-140.

40 This was Dr Njoroge Mungai, a cousin of Jomo Kenyatta and a member of the inner group within KANU; he had been its first secretary. He was now Minster of Health.

41 David Goldsworthy, *Tom Mboya: the man Kenya wanted to forget*, Nairobi & London: Heinemann Educational 1982, p.116-9. We do not know whether he had met Malcolm during

1963 he was moved to Justice and Constitutional Affairs, and in 1964, when Kenyatta declared Kenya a republic, he was moved again, to serve as Minister of Economic Planning and Development. By then he was much involved in the seemingly inevitable splits among activists of different ethnicities and politics once independence is achieved.[42]

> The following day Malcolm
>> received invitation to the Premier of the Uhuru film. During the intermission Tom MBoya introduced me to his wife, the Prime Minister and several others. The Prime Minister asked me how the plane ride was after he left...Don Harris and John Lewis.[43]
>
> On the 19th, 'Pinto came by' bringing an invitation to the
>> Ball tonite...Met at the door by Mr. and Mrs. MBoya. During the evening I sat with Mr de Souza (MP and Speaker). Dr. Mungai introduced me to all the VIPs again (PM, Odinga, Telli, etc)... evening was quite full...The PM is a good dancer, remarkably agile for his age![44]
>
> Mr. and Mrs. Mboya picked up Malcolm the next day,
>> and we went "out in the country" to meet the P[rime]M[inister] for the start of the Parade – the streets were crowded...VIPs joined the PM "upstairs" for tea and coffee. I sat with his daughter Jane. Later at the Equator I talked with her for 30 mins before I knew who she really was. Mr Diallo Telli also arrived.[45] We had dinner together. I sat at the table with the PM's family and Mrs MBoya. At 2pm the PM addressed a huge rally "took complete responsibility for organising the Mau Mau"...Diallo Telli was very enthusiastic in

---

this visit. See also Mboya's *Autobiography, Freedom and After*, London: Andre Deutsch 1963. A very controversial figure, whose political 'interests' changed over time, Mboya was assassinated in July 1969. According to Odinga (*Not Yet Uhuru* (1967), p.187) the USSR was offering scholarships via its Embassy in Cairo: 'by independence about one thousand had been sent to study there'.

42 Was he an agent of the CIA? Aleme Eshete in his 'The CIA in Africa', on www.tecolahacos, 24 December 2008, claims that he was; while in Ellen Ray (ed) *Dirty Work 2: The CIA and Africa* (Secaucus: Lyle & Stuart 1980,p.59) it is stated that 'Mboya was ideal for the CIA's purposes'.

43 Two visiting SNCC members. See below.

44 This was a dinner-dance in honour of Jomo Kenyatta. Ambassador Attwood reported that Malcolm had arrived with the Minister for Information and Mrs Oneko and the Pintos. Dr Mungai 'interrupted Minister of State Koinange who was dancing with Mrs Attwood to introduce Malcolm as "the leader of the whole civil rights movement in America"'. NARA: SOC 14-1 US, Attwood to State Dept. 20/10/1964.

45 Diallo Telli, from Guinea, helped found the OAU in 1963 and became its first Secretary-General in 1964. After serving two terms as Secretary-General, he returned to Guinea in 1972 to the post of Minister of Justice. In 1977 President Sékou Touré accused him of involvement in a plot to overthrow him. He imprisoned Telli and let him die of starvation.

praise of my efforts, saying I must visit Guinea and Sekou Toure[46] even if it is not at his expense.

This was 'Kenyatta Day' – the ceremonial commemoration of Jomo Kenyatta's arrest and detention by the colonial government in 1952. Malcolm's attendance at the parade was reported on page one of the *Uganda Argus* on October 21. At the end of a long article describing the celebrations, the paper noted that 'a controversial figure present at the ceremony was Malcolm "X", the leader of the Black Muslim sect in America. He has been in Nairobi for the last few days after a visit to Tanganyika.'

On 31 October Dar-es-Salaam's *The Nationalist* reported that Malcolm had returned from Nairobi and would be leaving the following day for Addis. 'Africa holds the key to the solution of the problem of African Americans', he is reported as telling newsmen. 'America won't give more than forced to.' Was he going to Addis, or perhaps to Cairo? There was a meeting there by some of the non-aligned states, to plan a major conference to discuss the need to 'fix a terminal date for colonial rule throughout the world at two to six years'. Unfortunately the overthrow of President Ben Bella of Algeria in June cancelled the meeting which had been agreed for that month.[47] Could Ben Bella have invited Malcolm to attend this gathering?

Reactions of the US Ambassador

William Attwood, the American Ambassador in Kenya, was less than happy about Malcolm's presence in this African country, which had only attained independence a few months previously. He reported that the 'warm reception' given to Malcolm was 'disturbing since his twisted account U.S. civil rights situation will no doubt be widely accepted among emotional and less sophisticated Kenyan leaders'. Clearly Attwood must have included the Kenyan ministers of state offering hospitality to Malcolm as among the 'less sophisticated'.[48]

In Nairobi, according to Attwood, Malcolm 'declared that America will never voluntarily give American Negroes freedom unless forced. Africa has the key to Negro problem solution and will determine degree of freedom they get because African leaders hold strategic power balance

---

46 Sékou Touré, president of Guinea, is usually described as initially a pan-African Marxist.
47 Peter Calvocoressi, *World Politics Since 1945*, London: Longman (1968) 1991, p.147.
48 NARA: SOC 14-1 US, Attwood to State Dept., 19/10/1964, 20/10/1964, copied to London, Dar, Kampala and Zanzibar.

in world affairs...American aid was not a favor to Africa because Africans contributed human flesh to American economy.'[49]

Ambassador Attwood added a comment to the FBI's report:

> Meeting in Parliament probably organized by one or more members and has no official character except that it does give Malcolm additional status. Malcolm commented that meeting was unofficial because otherwise 'efforts might be put forward to stop it'. He refused to identify any individuals or government that might attempt to cancel meeting, but hinted it was US.
> We doubt he will see Prime Minister Kenyatta since he has no appointment according Cabinet Secretary Ndegwa.
> Meeting with Ambassador at Malcolm's request, covered same general ground. Malcolm said he was 'no longer' a racist and 'not anti-American' but sidestepped question what he was doing here by saying he wished be out of US during election campaign in order avoid to take sides.[50]

In his *Autobiography*, Ambassador Attwood makes no comment about the OAU meeting, but he does comment on Malcolm's appearance in the Kenyan Parliament, emphasising that it was unofficial and relates that

> one afternoon at the Nairobi race track...Kenyatta and some of his cabinet were sitting in the former governor's box, and I noticed a white man in the group. Moving closer, I saw it was Malcolm X... Unfortunately we didn't know he was coming[51]...The next morning, he came to see me at the embassy...he assured me he now believed in cooperation between the races. After he left I alerted other posts of his arrival, suggesting they enlighten their African friends in advance. Malcolm X, though an embarrassment, didn't cause us too much trouble. The people he influenced were likely to be emotionally anti-American anyway...'[52]

---

49 NARA: SOC 14-1 US, Attwood to Secretary of State, copied to Embassies in London, Dar-es-Salaam, Addis Ababa, Kampala and Zanzibar. This is taken from the *Uganda Argus*, 20/10/1964.

50 NARA: SOC 14-1, Attwood to Dept. of State, 22/10/1964, with copies to all US Embassies in Africa.

51 The Ambassador had been warned by the Dar-es-Salaam Embassy staff that Malcolm was planning to visit Kenya. (NARA: SOC 14-1 US, Embassy Dar-es-Salaam to State Dept with copies to the embassies in Nairobi and Addis Ababa, 12/10/1964)

52 Attwood (1967), p.188. One cannot help but wonder whether the US government staff abroad are indoctrinated with the notion that the 'sophisticated' native is the one who is pro-American. Or that those who were anti-American were so for 'emotional' reasons only.

Attwood's superior attitude to Kenyans is unquestionable, as is his attitude towards communism: the *Times* of London (20 November 1964, p.11) reported that about a month after Malcolm's visit Attwood had issued a statement warning Africans that 'anyone who thought communist aid was motivated by altruistic motives was in for a big shock'. The implication that American aid was 'motivated by altruistic motives' is, to my mind, also more than somewhat questionable.

While the Ambassador might have succeeded in persuading the Kenyan media to turn the proverbial blind eye to Malcolm, after he had left the *Standard* carried an editorial on Malcolm (see below). Despite the pro-US views expressed by the editor, Ambassador Attwood was now worried. He telegrammed the Secretary of State and the US Embassies in Africa on 2 November: 'We disagree that Malcolm has had no real impact in Africa. He had considerable success in Kenya in publicizing his views and in getting ear of Kenyan leaders'.[53]

Reports in the Media

Curiously, the Kenya papers seem almost to have ignored Malcolm's visit. The colleague who searched the papers for me reported that he 'could not find any interest shown by the US Embassy published in the Kenyan Press regarding Malcolm's visit; in fact it wasn't much publicised. Among the daily newspapers it is only the *Daily Nation* that carried a story, on 23 October.'[54] Headlined 'Malcolm "X" praised by Kanu MPs', it reported that,

> Militant American negro Muslim leader Malcolm 'X' yesterday met Kanu Backbench MPs in Nairobi. But he failed to turn up later at a Press conference arranged by the Kanu Backbenchers Association's chairman, Mr. Z. M. Anyieni.[55]

After the meeting the Association passed a resolution expressing 'complete solidarity' with the 'Afro-American' freedom fighters. The resolution described Malcolm 'X' as an 'outstanding leader of 22 million Afro-Americans'. The resolution said that the Association expressed its 'full and unqualified' support for the Afro-Americans who had launched a

---

[53] NARA: SOC 14-1, US, Telegram from Nairobi to Dept. of State, 2/11/1964. The US government's policy in Kenya, according to the editors of *Ramparts* magazine, was 'one of selective liberation. The chief beneficiary was Tom Mboya.' This interesting article provides an analysis of the shifting US policy regarding Kenya, and the roles of the CIA and Ambassador Attwood. On his retirement in 1966 Attwood is said to have stated that 'an Ambassador who treats his CIA chief as an integral member of his Country Team will generally find him a useful and cooperative associate. I know I did'. (p.30)

[54] Email from Eric Santos, 21/2/2003. I am very grateful to Eric, the son of a Kenyan colleague, for searching the Kenyan papers for me.

[55] Anyiene was a left-winger, who fell out with Mboya and Kenyatta and resigned from KANU in 1965.

historic struggle for the removal of discrimination and segregation. 'This meeting expresses its complete solidarity with the Afro-American freedom fighters in their present struggle for basic human rights as outlined in the United Nations Charter.' (p.20)[56]

Notably it was the *Uganda Argus* that reported on Malcolm in Nairobi, in its issue of 20 October:

> 'Africa holds the key to the solution of the problems of the American Negro and can determine the degree of freedom he will get', the negro campaigner, Mr. Malcolm X, said in Nairobi. 'America will never voluntarily give us anything more than she is forced to, and since we are a minority, we don't have the force. But the African leaders hold a strategic balance of power in world affairs.' Part of his mission to Africa was to make African leaders aware of this position they hold. 'When America gives aid to African nations she is not doing anyone any favours, because Africa made more of a contribution to the American economy than Americans did – she gave human flesh'. Malcolm X said he had been surprised by the amount of support African leaders showed for the American Negro cause. 'Every person in a responsible position I have spoken to shows unlimited concern and sympathy for our problem', he said. In Dar es Salaam, he had had a three-hour talk with President Nyerere. (p.5)

On 21 October, Malcolm 'appeared on VOK-TV at prime evening time in special interview', according to Ambassador Attwood's report. In this interview on Kenyan television Malcolm claimed that the Civil Rights Act of 1964 was propaganda calculated by the US government to impress people in Africa and Asia; nothing had changed for 'Negroes' and little could be expected from the 'mealy-mouthed Negro leadership'. In fact 'Negroes' were being persecuted more vigorously than before. 'Internationalization of problem required to bring pressure on USG (US government) and on "good people" in US who would then take action to avoid embarrassment.' Malcolm stated he came to Kenya at the invitation of 'certain government members' and had previously visited Nairobi on his way to Dar-es-Salaam secretly in order to contact government leaders without publicity...refused to disclose which government leaders he had talked to. Malcolm is also reported as stating that he had 'expressed his displeasure to the Ambassador (Attwood) about an alleged effort on the part of the American Embassy to prevent Americans from meeting with him'. Malcolm said he would depart for Addis Ababa October 24 for a

---

56 Photocopy found in Schomburg Center: Malcolm X Papers, reel 16, folder 15, file 1.

four day visit, then visit Lagos, Accra, Conakry, Bamako, possibly Dakar and 'definitely' Algiers.[57]

After Malcolm's departure, a weekly paper, the *Sunday Post*, printed a longer account on November 15. Was this perhaps inspired by the US Ambassador? The article begins with very negative quotations from Ghana's *Sunday Mirror*, which calls Malcolm one of the 'parasites' who settle in Ghana because they find life elsewhere 'tedious' and goes on to argue that 'We Ghanaians have no desire to internationalise racism... Malcolm X's philosophy can be described as apartheid in reverse'. The paper then quotes from the editorial comments regarding the forthcoming *Autobiography* by the *Saturday Evening Post*. The editor believed that 'If Malcolm X were not a Negro, his *Autobiography* would be little more than a journal of abnormal psychology...[T]he militant hatred that he preaches was behind some of the violence of the summer riots in the North.' The only concession to Malcolm is the neutral caption to the excellent photograph of him: 'Malcolm X, pictured in his hotel room during his recent visit to Nairobi'. (Was the photographer – and the paper – trying to counteract pressure from the US Ambassador?)

Also after his departure, the *East African Standard* carried an editorial on Malcolm. The editor believed that Malcolm would have Negroes abstain from voting in the US elections. At Lagos he had repeated what he had said in Kenya about the Civil Rights Act – it was a 'propaganda stunt. Johnson and Goldwater – and presumably the whole white population, are to him equally bad – any Negro who votes for either is "crazy".' Malcolm, claims the editor, 'derided the policies of the Nobel Prize winner Martin Luther King and advocated a campaign of Negro violence. It was unlikely that he would gain much real support for his views in Africa, the editor believed, 'as Africans had a real appreciation of the sincere efforts the Federal government was making to solve the race problem'.[58]

The paucity of reports questions the independence of Kenya's press. As I queried above, is it possible that the US Embassy prevailed upon the local press to ignore Malcolm, despite his reception by the ruling political party and the ministers of state?

---

57 Compiled from NARA: SOC 14-1, Attwood to Dept. of State, 22/10/1964 and FBI report on Malcolm X # 100-399321, part 14, visits abroad, pp.120 – 123. This was compiled by New York FBI office as the Assistant Attorney General, Internal Security Division, 'has expressed concern over the fact that Malcolm X's activities abroad indicated a possible violation of the Logan Act'.

58 *East African Standard*, 2/11/1964, p.4.

African-Americans in Kenya

In fact, the 'American black colony' welcomed Malcolm and there were at least two parties in his honour. The first was attended by many of the Afro-Americans working at the Embassy. This upset Ambassador Attwood so much that he threatened to withdraw the funding the party-giver's institute was receiving from the US government if his staff attended the second affair. Nevertheless, some attended and 'some who didn't sent around liquor along with their regrets'.[59]

By sheer coincidence, John Lewis of the Student Nonviolent Coordinating Committee (SNCC) was languishing in Nairobi at this time. He had been on a holiday in Guinea, funded by Sékou Touré, perhaps at the instigation of his (Touré's) friend Harry Belafonte. With some additional funding from the American Committee on Africa, Lewis was visiting a number of other African countries. His plane from Ethiopia to Zanzibar developed a mechanical problem and he was grounded in Nairobi for some days. Naturally the two men had met on numerous occasions in the US; now they 'talked, then went up to his room – our rooms were on the same floor [in the New Stanley Hotel] – and we talked some more'. In his *Autobiography* Lewis reports that Malcolm talked about the lack of unity within the civil rights movement in the US. Lewis found that,

> Africa was doing for him the same thing it was doing for us – providing a frame of reference that was both broadening and refreshing. [He] was enthusiastic and excited [and] seemed very hopeful...[H]e had been struck by how the majority of the black people of Cairo were light-skinned. That had been eye-opening for him, he said.[60] He talked about the need to shift our focus, both among one another and between us and the white community, from race to class...He saw the great powers, such as the Soviet Union and the United States, using poor people, of whatever race, for their governments' own imperialistic ends. That word kept repeating: "imperialistic"...To see Malcolm X so swept up with enthusiasm was inspiring.
>
> But there was something else I noticed about him that afternoon and the next...there was a fear in the man, a nervousness was written all over him...[He was certain] that he was being watched, that he was being followed. He took a seat away from both the window and the door...[H]e had a great sense of alarm, a great

---

59 Goldman (1979), p.215.
60 Lewis (1998), pp.297-7.

sense of anxiety. In a calm measured way he was convinced that somebody wanted him killed.

Throughout his trip Lewis met Africans who wanted to 'know about Malcolm X. He became a measuring rod in every one of our encounters. The young Africans...were, for the most part, true revolutionaries, far more radical than the SNCC. This was why Malcolm struck such a chord with them...[W]e were dismissed as mainstream and it was Malcolm who was embraced.' (p.295)

In Addis Ababa

Betty Shabazz shows (left to right) a map of Africa, pointing to Ethiopia while Malcolm travels there

There is, as far as I have been able to find, no information at all on Malcolm's return to Addis Ababa. His *Notebook* entries are very brief: *October 24*: 'Jane & Mel takes me to the airport. Alice W, Osman and his wife met me at airport. Saleh Sabien? Phillipe Komtona.' *October 25*: 'with Ale??? Uncle and Ababa – Ethiopian food – Stephanie. Art Carney.' *October 26*: 'dinner with Alice, Osman and wife. Saleh, Coker (of Nigeria).'[61]

The only name I recognise (sadly) is Alice – that is, Alice Windom and Coker, whom he had met in Nigeria.

The *Notebook* entry for October 27 is 'sick. Samuel Horkins, Bill Davis and Coker. To OAU to meet D. Telli.' Diallo Telli had just

---

61 On who 'Coker' might have been, seen chapter 7.

returned to the OAU office in Addis after touring 17 countries, presumably to discuss the planning of the next Foreign Ministers conference to be held in February 1965. Did Malcolm go to Addis in order to meet with Telli?

On that day, the US Acting Country Public Affairs Officer in Addis Ababa ran into Malcolm at the Ethiopia Hotel and described Malcolm talking with some fellow guests, Mr. Samuel Hoskins of the Baltimore *Afro-American*, and Mr. Goodwin Anim, manager of the Ghana News Agency.[62] Mr. Winkler reported that,

> in substance, he [Malcolm] said that the American Embassy officials in Nairobi were opposed to his appearance on television... According to Malcolm X, there are a lot of American Negroes in Kenya...the only unorganized group in Kenya was the group of American Negroes who are living or working on this continent... Unknown to him when he made a speech at University College of Addis Ababa during a prior visit to Ethiopia...there was an embassy officer in the audience...[Malcolm X] indicated that he had expressed his dis??? [unreadable] to the Ambassador (in Kenya) about an alleged effort on the part of the American Embassy to prevent Americans from meeting with him. He added 'I know they sent word here that I was coming and they are trying to keep me from making any public speeches'...He said he was leaving for Lagos the following morning...Malcolm occasionally used 'Afro-American' when referring to Negro Americans. He acted in a cordial and polite matter, but was completely negative...about the racial situation in the United States.

Malcolm told the US Embassy official on the 27th that he was leaving for Lagos the following morning. On October 28, Malcolm records that 'DT came up on plane – introduces me to everyone – heaped all sorts of honours and praises upon me. Interviewed by Olabisi Ajala[63] (Nigerian World Tr?? [illegible]) for some Asian newspapers. Met at airport by Helen Darden.'

---

62 NARA: SOC 14-1 US, Airmail from Gordon Winkler, the Acting Public Affairs Officer in Addis to Dept of State, 6/11/1964.

63 Olabisi Ajala was born in Ghana to Nigerian parents and was brought up in Nigeria. In 1948, aged 18, he left for the USA for higher education. After attending a number of universities, he moved to Canada, then Australia. He began travelling the world in 1957 and published an account of his travels, *An African Abroad* (London: Jarrolds) in 1963. (This brief biography is taken from the book.) My colleague Professor Ayodeji Olukoju emailed me (25/7/2008) that 'Bisi (Olabisi) Ajala was a popular figure of the 1960s and 1970s, who traversed the globe on his scooter (motorcycle). A popular musician waxed the hit song, "Ajala travel (sic) all over the world," in his honour. He was also famous for his celebrated and highly publicised (soap opera) liaisons with some women (European and Nigerian). He died in relative obscurity several years back.'

CHAPTER 6

Nigeria, Ghana, Liberia, Guinea, Algiers, Geneva and Paris
October – November 1964

Compared with his previous visits, information about Malcolm's return visits to West Africa is relatively thin.

Nigeria

Malcolm arrived in Nigeria on 29 October. According to Peter Goldman, by this time Malcolm recognised that Africans would not make forthright demands of the UN and began to talk more in 'general terms about internationalising the struggle...He was bucking...the great reach of US foreign aid. Africa liked Malcolm X but couldn't afford him.' (p.218)

The Lagos Embassy reported that there was
> scanty press coverage...TV coverage limited initial arrival with no special interviews and also no public lectures or appearances... Two press conferences..."the greatest problem facing Africa is internal squabbling" focusing on racial differences in East Africa and religious differences in West Africa...Thus his impact in Nigeria considerably less than on previous visit...[1]

---
1 NARA: SOC 14-1 US, Matthews, Nairobi 4/11/1964. I could find no report in the *West African Pilot*, the *Lagos Daily Telegraph* or the *Lagos Morning Post*.

A scrutiny of Nigerian papers reveals that this information is correct. Given that previously Malcolm had received considerable attention during a very brief visit, one has to surmise that the allegation he had made in Addis Ababa (noted previously) that the US government was putting obstacles in his way was correct. At an OAAU rally in New York on 29 November 1964 Malcolm spoke of the 'vicious job' done by the United States Information Service by claiming it was representing Black Americans. This served to prevent real contacts and convinced Africans that 'we had no interest in them'. The USIS put up large posters on the Civil Rights Bill, 'claiming that our problems had ended'.[2]

Most interestingly, the *East African Standard* (2/11/1964, p.4), which had so minimised his visit to East Africa, now reported on Malcolm in West Africa. Had it not occurred to the Embassy there to suggest that the press should cease reporting on Malcolm's visits anywhere in Africa? The article stated that in Lagos Malcolm 'had expressed similar views to those he voiced in Kenya recently' regarding the Civil Rights Act and the unambitious policies of leaders such as now Nobel prize winner Martin Luther King. He advised Afro-Americans to boycott the presidential elections as there was little difference between the policies of the candidates towards Blacks.' However, the editorial ends with the following statement, which sounds very much like an Embassy press release – or an attempt to appease the USA: 'It is unlikely that Malcolm X will gain much real support for his views in Africa...where appreciation of the sincere efforts of the Federal Government to solve the race problem are recognised.'

The FBI reported that on his arrival Malcolm held a press conference, at which he analysed 'one of the greatest problems facing Africa' as 'internal squabbling'. 'In East Africa it is the Africans against the Asians, and in West Africa it is the Muslims against Christians, and all these are fed by outside forces.'[3] Clearly Malcolm realised that the USA and other western powers had become adept at the old British policy of 'divide and rule'.

In his *Notebook* for the 29th, Malcolm writes: 'TV interview. Met Simmons Oklahoma & – Hansberry. Wachuku came by.[4] On the 30th, 'Press conference. Guinea Embassy. Letter from President Asekewe (sic) wants to see me 11am tomorrow.' 'Hansberry' must have been William

---

2 *Liberator*, vol.5, no.1, January 1965, p.5, Pearl Black, 'Malcolm X Returns'.

3 FBI report on Malcolm X #100-399321, part 14, report on visits abroad, p.125.

4 Jake Simmons, a member of the Creek Nation of Oklahoma, was a prominent African-American oilman; by the 1960s he was an intermediary in multi-million dollar deals between major American oil companies and Liberia, Nigeria and Ghana. (See http://en.wikipedia.org/wiki/Jake_Simmons,_Jr.) (My thanks to Craig Sherwood for this reference.)

Leo Hansberry, who had initiated the courses on African civilizations and cultures at Howard University, Washington DC.[5] Among his students had been the young Nnamdi Azikiwe. As detailed in Chapter 3, Malcolm had met Jaja Wachuku, the Foreign Minister on his previous visit to Nigeria.

The following day's notes are:

> Essien[6] calls – suggests to cancel coming to Ibadan because of the importance of 'unfolding events' here at Lagos...President gracious and humble for a man of his power. Well informed. Had seen me on TV – took initiative to see me. Wished I had had more time to express and explain my views, especially 'committee structure' – he is student of political science – gold cuff links and silver ash tray. 'You have done so much for Africa, you deserve some African gold.'

Malcolm was indeed honoured by President Nnamdi Azikiwe. The President, having spent many years in the USA as a student, would naturally have had a special interest in Malcolm and the evolution of Black struggles in the USA.[7]

The final entry for October 31 is: 'Joseph Iffeora came by...Coker – Tangi and wife.' 'Coker' might well have been Increase Coker, descendant of migrants from Sierra Leone, who had been editor of Azikiwe's *West African Pilot* in the 1950s. Or the lawyer, H.T.O. Coker, who defended the *West African Pilot* when it was sued for libel by the Federal Minister for Information in 1965.[8] I have not been able to identify 'Tangi'.

The following day Malcolm notes:

> reporters from Pilot and Post – Essien & KM drive me to Wachuku's – 2 hours – strongly pro-West & Israel; also pro-Tshombe; very anti-Arab, anti-Nasser, Nkrumah and Casablanca Group...Interviewed

---

5 My thanks to Professor Kevin Gaines for reminding me of Professor Hansberry. Hansberry had conducted research in many African countries, including Nigeria and Ghana. On 22 September 1963, he had delivered the inaugural address at the formal opening of the Hansberry College of African Studies at Nsukka, University of Nigeria. In 1964, he became the first recipient of the African Research Award from the Haile Selassie I Prize Trust. He died on 3 November, 1965.

6 Essien-Udom, who had arranged for Malcolm to speak at Ibadan University on his first visit. See Chapter 3.

7 An Igbo (Ibo) from Eastern Nigeria, Azikiwe had studied in the USA, edited a nationalist newspaper in Ghana from 1934 until 1937, and on returning to Nigeria founded the pro-independence newspaper *West African Pilot*, which became very influential. He founded the National Council of Nigeria and the Cameroons to fight for independence and became premier of Eastern Nigeria as the ethnic divisions of Nigeria flared with approaching independence. At independence he was named Governor-General, and when Nigeria declared itself a republic, he was named President. Unfortunately 'Zik', as he was known, does not mention Malcolm in his *Autobiography, My Odyssey*, London: C. Hurst & Co., 1970.

8 Azikiwe (1970), pp. 330, 346.

by editor of *Spear*...Spoke with General Secretary All Nigerian Muslim Council.

One cannot help but wonder why the Foreign Minister had given Malcolm so much of his time. Why had he called on Malcolm on the 29th? Had he hoped to influence Malcolm, who would certainly have disagreed with the attitudes he appears to have expressed? Had the US Embassy asked him to meet Malcolm?

Malcolm concludes his notes in Nigeria with, 'I was attacked verbally by the reporters for the good statements I had made about Azikiwe. The mood among the young generation of Negroes is most impatient and explosive.'

Ghana, Malcolm's Legacy

According to Leslie Lacy at the University of Ghana in Legon, Malcolm's 'second coming caught us by surprise...but we were ready. Most of us had not gone back to our old lives. Malcolm...and all that we had seen and felt as a result of his visit, had had a converting effect upon our lives, and he had outlined specific plans for how we could aid our struggle for human rights in America...[The students] at the University had talked about Malcolm for days after he left.' A student knocked on Lacy's door on campus while Malcolm was there. 'He shook Malcolm's hand and said: "I want to say that the students do not believe what Mr. Basner said about you in the *Ghanaian Times*. None of us here like him. We wish he would go back to South Africa."' When the student left, Lacy explained to Malcolm that Basner had written an article in the *Times* calling Malcolm 'a nationalist and therefore a racist'.[9]

However, as the *Liberator* in its October 1964 (p.16) issue claimed that the OAAU Information Bureau had been set up at the Ghana Press Club on 27 August, it is difficult to understand Lacy's surprise at Malcolm's arrival. It is, of course, possible that the *Liberator's* dating is incorrect, or Lacy did not want to reveal ongoing correspondence. The Bureau had been 'formed to better acquaint the people of the African continent with the day to day struggles of the Afro-American against white supremacy and would also supply the Afro-American press with information on development in the African states', the *Liberator* stated.

That Malcolm had certainly left a legacy behind is obvious from the ongoing feud between two Ghanaian papers. According to the US Embassy,

---
9 Leslie Lacy, 'Malcolm X in Ghana', in Clarke (1969), p.218. See Chapter 3 for the controversy over Basner's article.

on 11 August the *Daily Graphic* had published an article which asked Negroes to 'Give Civil Rights Bill a Chance'. Some expatriate Negroes protested to *Ghanaian Times* concerning moderation of *Graphic* article and requested *Times* to attack its author, Eddie Agyeman. Rather than attack Agyeman personally, *Times* editor Badu reportedly decided to publish series civil rights articles by "Afro-Americans" [of] which [the] Mayfield article is the first. [This is a] pictorial article entitled 'What has Driven the Blacks into Rebellion?'... Theme of article is Negroes 'have no alternative to follow but the route to rebellion'[10]

Malcolm in front of Parliament House, Accra, May 1964. the statute of President Kwame Nkrumah was toppled during the 1966 coup.

Meetings

In his *Notebook* for 2 November, Malcolm notes:
to Accra. Met by Maya and Julian. Delphine King. Saw Cassius. Maya took me to Nana NKetsia's home for dinner with Mr Welbeck, Dr Mak and a couple of others (African culture, religion, Islam, Afro-Am's role & attitude, etc)[11]

Malcolm had spent much time with both Maya Angelou and Julian Mayfield on his previous visit, when he had also met Ras Makonnen, an old pan-Africanist. Cassius, was, of course, Cassius Clay, known as Muhammad Ali once he converted to Islam. He had won the world heavyweight championship in February 1964. Malcolm had been his tutor, his advisor, his helper, but their relationship disintegrated when Malcolm left the Nation of Islam. Thousands greeted Ali in his arrival in Accra, where he 'boxed an exhibition, visited factories and schools and met with President Kwame Nkrumah...[Ali and Malcolm] crossed

---

10 NARA, SOC 14-1, Telegram from US Embassy, Accra to Secretary of State, 13/8/1964.

11 I have been unable to trace Delphine King – this is not the name of the wife of Preston King (see Chapter 3).

paths in the Hotel Ambassador on the morning of Malcolm's departure, and Ali snubbed him. "Did you get a look at Malcolm", the champion derisively told reporters. "Dressed in that funny white robe and wearing a beard and walking with that cane that looked like a prophet's stick? Man, he's gone. He's gone far out, he's out completely. Nobody listens to Malcolm any more."'[12]

But John Lewis, as described in Chapter 3, found that Malcolm was revered, not ignored. He and his SNCC colleagues were constantly asked about Malcolm wherever they travelled in West Africa. 'Malcolm X was considered even further to the left than we – an extremist, a revolutionary. But here in Africa, among these young freedom fighters, we were dismissed as mainstream, and it was Malcolm who was embraced.'[13]

Nana (Chief) Kobina Nketsia, whom Malcolm had met on his previous visit, and N.A. Welbeck, were two senior figures in Ghanaian politics. The Nana had been imprisoned with Nkrumah during the liberation struggles against the British; he became Director of Culture and then Pro-Chancellor of the University of Ghana. N.A. Welbeck, who had been an early and active member of Nkrumah's Convention People's Party (CPP), was appointed Minister of Works on independence. In 1960 he was sent to the Congo as Ghana'a emissary to Patrice Lumumba, but was quickly expelled; Nkrumah then appointed him Minister of State for Party Propaganda.

On November 3, Malcolm records in his *Notebook* that he was interviewed by the *Evening News* and Cameron 'Dodie[14] and spent time with Julian, Leslie Lacy, Dr. Lee and Mrs. Du Bois', who took him to see Tema (the port which served Accra) the following day. He called at the UAR Embassy, and met the Ambassador, whom he noted as being a 'very nice man'.

The Chinese News Agency interviewed Malcolm on November 5, according to his *Notebook*. Then there was a press conference at the Press Club, followed by a meal at the Chinese Embassy. The entry then states

> Office of President at 12.59 he had already asked for me; he was dressed in black, very clean-looking, so relaxed but alert. Dashed to Winneba.[15] Full house. Back in time for party at (illegible) Embassy.

---

12 Thomas Hauser, *Muhammad Ali: His life and Times*, New York: Touchstone 1991, p.109.
13 Lewis (1998), p.295.
14 This was Cameron Duodu, who was then the editor of *Drum* magazine. See Chapter 3.
15 Malcolm had lectured at Winneba on his previous visit – see Chapter 3. It was the political/philosophical institute for training young freedom fighters.

So, despite undoubted pressures of his office, and from the USA, President Kwame Nkrumah made time to see Malcolm again. What had they discussed? After all, Nkrumah knew the US well, having spent many years there as a student. Did they discuss the chances of the Civil Rights Bill having any effect? Or Malcolm's lobbying of the OAU to take the case of the African Americans to the United Nations? Malcolm expressed his appreciation of the President to Shirley Du Bois, who had warned him that his life would be in danger if he returned to the USA: 'Your president, Osagyefo[16], has taught me the true meaning and strength of unity. If I can pass this on to my people, if I can show them the way – my life will be a small price to pay for such a vision.'[17] How much Malcolm appreciated Nkrumah is demonstrated by a portrait of Nkrumah in his home in New York, probably drawn by the artist Kofi Bailey then resident in Ghana.[18] Nkrumah also valued Malcolm: his 1968 pamphlet, *The Spectre of Black Power*, is dedicated to Che Guevara, Ben Barka and Malcolm.

We do not know whom else Malcolm spent time with during his four days in Ghana. Leslie Lacy noted that 'unlike his first [visit], this was quiet and uneventful'.[19] He describes Malcolm as looking 'tired, very tired... as he talked, sometimes incoherently, I felt a strange feeling of finality... Malcolm was pensive, pre-occupied, searching, he had new ideas and strategies. He was hurrying back to Harlem.'[20]

William Gardner Smith[21], a left-leaning journalist just appointed Assistant Editor-in-Chief of Ghana TV and a recent addition to the 120 or so African Americans in Ghana, recorded that he thought Malcolm was 'troubled'. He believed that Malcolm's thinly disguised fear 'emanated from the Muslims themselves'. Maya Angelou felt that Malcolm was very different from his first visit some months ago: 'There was a sense of – not desperation, but it was like the hand of fate was on him.' Smith and others begged him to stay in Accra and to bring his family. In Smith and his wife,

---

16 'Osagyefo' means 'redeemer'; Nkrumah apparently preferred to be called by this name/title.

17 Shirley Du Bois, 'The beginning, not the end', in Clarke (1970), p.127. Many feared for Malcolm's life: Natambo (2002), p.308) reports that Nkrumah offered him a 'cabinet post' and that Presidents Ben Bella and Gamal Abdel Nasser had offered him government appointments. Were these offers to save him from possible assassination and/or to use his undoubted insights and gifts in their governments? I have not been able to confirm Natambo's claims.

18 My thanks to Paul Lee for this – email 7 May 1909. (Copied from *Ebony* September 1964.)

19 Lacy (1970), pp.221-227.

20 Lacy in Clarke (1969), pp.219, 225.

21 After ten years as a journalist for Agence Presse France in Paris, Smith had arrived in Accra in September 1964 to take up a new post as Assistant Editor-in-Chief to Ghana TV; in 1965 he has also the director of the Ghana Institute of Journalism. Expelled in 1966 when Nkrumah was deposed, he returned to Paris.

Malcolm 'inspired great admiration...When we met him...Malcolm X was becoming a revolutionary. He was a great man to us.' Dr. Robert Lee, whom Malcolm again visited, recalled that Malcolm was 'very quiet; he was re-thinking and re-formulating his ideas'.[22]

Sadly, in his *Autobiography* Malcolm says little about this trip and does not name the 'American white ambassador' with whom he talked at length. The discussion with this man, he wrote 'gave me a new insight – one which I like; that the white man is *not* inherently evil, but America's racist society influences him to act evilly'. (p.427)

Malcolm also recounts that 'throughout my trip I was of course aware that I was under constant surveillance'.

Reports in the Press

The CPP's *Evening News* carried a photo of Malcolm and a brief statement of his arrival on page 1 of its 3 November issue; the following day there was a full-page (p.5) account of an interview. This quotes Malcolm as saying that,

> The most remarkable achievement made by Africa since the arrival of the whiteman is the establishment of the Organisation of African Unity...Heads of State should give maximum and uncompromising support to the OAU and the concept of a Union Government for the continent; those who don't do this are contributing to the continued presence and dominance of the West in Africa...The building of bridges of understanding and communications between Afro-Americans and Africans [will result in] co-operation in areas that are of mutual benefit to us...
>
> Osagyefo [President Nkrumah] is one of the few leaders who are genuinely working for the improvement of the lot of the Afro-American population in the United States...I respect his realistic analysis of the world situation and also his suggestions towards the solution of many of the world's problems.[23]

---

22 LeRoy Hodges, *Portrait of an Expatriate*, Westport: Greenwood Press, 1985, p.78. The quotation from Maya Angelou is from Goldman (1979), p.219. Interview with Dr Lee, Accra, Ghana 11/2/2003.

23 In February 1964 President Nkrumah, following the denial by the US Government of any involvement in the attempt on his life in January, wrote to President Johnson of the USA: there were '"two conflicting establishments" representing the USA, diplomatic mission and the CIA'. That same month Dean Rusk, the hawkish Secretary of State, asked CIA Director John McCone 'about suitable candidates to head a post-Nkrumah government'. In March 1965 Ambassador Mahoney, on a visit to Washington, discussed with McCone a coup plot hatched by Ghanaians – led by General Joseph Ankrah, whom the CIA had considered a year earlier as the possible head of a post-Nkrumah government. (John Prados, *Safe for Democracy: the secret wars of the CIA*, Chicago: Iven R. Dee 2006) On the US involvement in

> Both candidates [in the US presidential elections] do not seek the interest of the Afro-Americans...[The] Afro-Americans will continue to be suppressed and racial equality in America will not be achieved until Africa is totally free and united. Our only bonafide strength lies in the strength of Africa. If Africa is weak, we are weak. If Africans are recognised, we are recognised...Many Africans are being fooled by President Johnson. He sends peace-corps teams to Africa but pays South African mercenaries to kill Congolese citizens fighting for the liberation of their own country.
>
> China's recent atomic explosion is the greatest thing that has ever happened in the 20th century to Black mankind...Since the whiteman only understands the language of power, it is necessary for Africa, and the dark mankind at large, to have atomic power. This will make for equality...The only reason why the West is so shaken by the Chinese atomic explosion is that China belongs to the dark race.

The editors of the Party's paper were not wholly happy about all of Malcolm's statement and provided a Marxist counter-analysis on the same page:

> The Black Muslims conclude that all dark skinned men in the world are being persecuted by the whiteman everywhere and that the alignment of forces for the struggle against anti-imperialist forces will have to be black against white and vice versa. [This] cannot be a general rule for the struggle against imperialism...Imperialism exploits the colonies more than it exploits the working class of the capitalist countries themselves not because the people of the colonies have black skins but because for its purposes it is necessary for imperialism to divide the forces against which it is fighting. In other words, the difference between the degree of exploitation of the colonies and the working class of the capitalist countries is a tactical action designed to divide the proletariat of the world...To us the acquisition of the atom bomb by China is a great event because China is an anti-imperialist nation and the stronger it gets the more it would be able to reinforce the strength of the anti-imperialist front line of all oppressed people.
>
> We, however, recognise that Mr. Malcolm X's theory might be a correct anti-thesis for conditions in America where centuries of

---

the assassination of President Nkrumah, see *New York Times* 9/5/1978, p.6 and the recently released government papers on www.state.gove/www/about_state/history/vol_xxiv/s.html and xxiv/x.

discrimination has made exploitation in the raw synonymous with racial discrimination. Welcome fighting Malcolm!

On 6 November on its last page the *Daily Graphic* carried a brief report on Malcolm's visit. Headlined 'Take Negro problem to the UN', the article states that Malcolm claimed that the Civil Rights Bill in the USA was a 'camouflage to make Africans believe that the Afro-American problem was being solved...Our bone of contention is not civil rights but human rights'.

I could find no other reports in the Ghanaian newspapers of Malcolm's visit. Had the Embassy ensured that none would appear? There is some evidence of pressure on the government. In a telegram to the Dept. of State, dated 18 April 1964 the Ambassador wrote:

> I brought up press again, saying daily press had improved toward USG but that last night I read latest issue of *The Spark* which made strictly communist line attack on Alliance for Progress and condemned peace corps through attack on perman experimentation with idea. (sic) Nkrumah did not claim credit for improvement in daily press and responded only with vague comment, 'well, it is difficult'. He said he too had just read *Spark* issue, tried to side-step by saying, 'Spark is a theoretical journal; they go into these issues'. I replied that they always went into issues from one direction. Nkrumah concluded, 'maybe we should see that we can do about this'.[24]

On November 6 Malcolm wrote in his *Notebook* that 'Helen, Julian, Maya and Delphine...H & M were the last sight I saw, waving "sadly" – two very lonely women.' Who was Helen? Were the two 'lonely women' Maya and Helen?

Liberia

In his *Notebook* on 6 November for Malcolm wrote: 'Arrived Monrovia – dinner with Under-Secretary for Agriculture...dance at City Hall. Mrs. Havelock Parker'. (I found the rest of the entry illegible.)

The next day, this man who appeared so tired to everyone in Accra, began another round of meetings: 'Radio interview. Secretary of State. Mayor of Monrovia gives dinner for me at Tropical Hut...Neal's home where most of the "power structure" partied till 2am.'

---

24 Lyndon B. Johnson Library, National Security File, Country File, box 89, Ghana, vol.2.

November 8 was no less busy:
> Clarence Parker[25]...took me to another party...Had dinner at hotel with Mayor Ross and his wife. Bowie (illegible) told me that pressure had been put on him to 'Audition' my interview before playing it. This had only been done once before (Meredith) when they didn't want anything to 'embarrass' the US government.

November 9, Malcolm's last day in Liberia was also hectic: 'Sam Paine Cooper took me to Secretary of State for Agriculture (brother of Vice President Tolbert). Then to Executive Mansion where met most of the Cabinet, including Tolbert and Secretary of State Grimes again. All were friendly – also the white commercial advisor – President Tubman was too busy.' Malcolm then left for Conakry.[26]

Guinea

Guinea had been one of France's West African colonies. In 1958 the colony's vice-president Sékou Touré, became the only leader in the colonies to refuse the policy of postcolonial 'association' as part of the independence offered by France. Retaliation was swift: independence was granted immediately: France removed its staff, office and other equipment, as well as all the files, and cut off aid. Touré, a pan-Africanist with Marxist leanings, turned to the Communist bloc for help, as all the Western nations supported France's draconian action. In 1959 Guinea and Ghana formed a compact for eventual union; Mali joined in 1961; this group formed the basis of the 'Casablanca bloc' at the OAU. Touré was careful to avoid complete dependence on the Communist bloc and received some financial assistance from President Nkrumah, to whom he offered asylum when he was deposed in 1966.

The ever-busy racist Ambassador Attwood in Nairobi sent a confidential telegram to the Department of State regarding Malcolm's planned visit to Conakry, the capital of Guinea. Attwood advised that the 'most effective way inoculate Touré against Malcolm X is to stress latter's derogatory remarks about Kennedy after assassination. In view Touré's deep admiration for Kennedy, this line should help in advance Malcolm's

---

25 P. Clarence Parker III, a banker, was the Chairman of the National Investment Commission and Treasurer of the ruling True Whig Party. At the 1961 meeting of some of the African Heads of State called by Nkrumah, President Tubman of Liberia was asked to devise a charter for unity and development that would be acceptable to the whole continent. One result was the OAU, the other was the proposal, prepared with Dr Romeo Horton, for the establishment of an African Development Bank. Parker was one of the fifteen leaders murdered in the 1980 coup by Samuel Doe.

26 I have not been able to locate any information on Mrs Parker or Sam Paine Cooper.

visit.' On November 6 the Embassy in Conakry suggested to State that it 'may wish consider informing Belafonte re-proposed Malcolm X visit with direct or implied suggestion he write personal letter to Touré on subject.'[27] A few days later this request was repeated. But either the US was unable to contact Harry Belafonte, or, of course, Belafonte might well have refused to co-operate. It is curious that the FBI could only report that Malcolm was a guest of the government of Guinea. Had it not been able to recruit any informers?[28]

Sékou Touré was expecting Malcolm. In his *Notebook* for November 9 Malcolm notes that he arrived in 'Conakry at 5pm, met by - of the Foreign Ministry. Led to VIP room. Diallo Telli was just taking off. He hugged me warmly and welcomed me before his plane took off.' Malcolm was then taken to 'Sékou Touré's home where I will reside while in Conakry. I'm speechless. All praise is due Allah. They gave me three servants, a driver and army officer.'

Malcolm spent the next day sightseeing. He received 'enthusiastic welcome at Algerian Embassy (getting visa)', he wrote in his *Notebook* on November 10.

> It is difficult to believe that I could be so widely known (and respected) here on this continent. The negative image the Western press has tried to paint of me certainly hasn't succeeded...Will see the President at 6pm...The President embraced me...invited me to dine with him at 1:30 tomorrow. He congratulated me for my firmness in the struggle for dignity 'Our people need dignity more than they need money'...went to a nite club.

Sékou Touré had met Malcolm previously, when he had gone to speak at the United Nations in October 1960 on the Congo 'crisis'. Given that Diallo Telli had advised Malcolm to see Touré, it is quite possible that Telli had helped arrange this part of Malcolm's arduous – but important – journey.

---

27 NARA: Dept. of State, SOC 14-1, Attwood to Conakry, 30/110/1964; State to Conakry, 6/11/1964; Conakry to State, 9/11/1964. In September ten members of the Student Nonviolent Coordinating Committee (SNCC) were in Guinea on a visit arranged by Belafonte. According to James Forman (*The Making of Black Revolutionaries*, Washington: Open Hand Publishing 1985, p.408) Belafonte and his family and 'members of a dance troupe he had organized' were also there. *West Africa* (22/8/1964, p.949) reported that Sékou Touré had appointed Belafonte his cultural advisor; it is not clear if Belafonte was funding the African Arts Centre he was to supervise. My request to Harry Belafonte for information has elicited no response.

28 FBI report on Malcolm X #100-399321, part 14, report on visits abroad, p.125.

In the morning on November 11 Malcolm met with Dr and Mrs John George Stubenbord[29], who were apparently working on a medical project named Ship Hope. He then kept his lunch appointment with the President; two Haitians joined them. Malcolm noted that Touré

> seemed happy, cordial but always busy and aware of all around him...several times added food to my plate. After the Haitians left he spoke to me, emphasising the importance of dignity. "Attire can be purchased but not dignity – attire can be stolen from us but not our thoughts (dignity) – lawyers and legal experts don't bring freedom; freedom comes only from the efforts made by those who themselves tire of oppression and themselves take action against it – we are aware of your reputation as a Freedom Fighter so I talk frankly, a fighting language to you." The Foreign Minister and Minister of Health were present also. Sékou Touré said he would be in the States in January and would be happy to see me again there.
> Went to Algerian Embassy...Ambassador's home...We discussed many things. He was very cordial, well-informed and militant as is every Algerian I have met. They have the best "image" of Africa of any Arab nation because of their militancy.

Speaking about his experiences at the Homecoming Rally in New York in November 1964, Malcolm told his audience that Touré 'lived by keeping himself well informed. He's very much concerned with the problems and the plight of our people in this country, and has excellent advice, too, to give toward solving it.'[30]

Malcolm spent the next day 'touring – Americans – Liberian Embassy... dinner with Algerian officer'. Whether he left for Dakar that day or on the 13th we do not know as all he notes then is 'stop at Dakar airport – soon all over airport...I was again signing autographs'.

Algiers, Geneva, Paris

On November 14, in his *Notebook* Malcolm writes that he arrived at Algiers.[31] 'language barrier tremendous. Saw two Ghanaians, whom I

---

29 I have found no information on the Stubenbords.
30 Breitman (1970), p.145.
31 Did Malcolm decide to visit Algiers because he had been so impressed by the many Algerians he had met? Did he know of the meetings reported by the weekly *West Africa*? In its 31 October issue (p.1237) it noted that 'delegates from 11 Afro-Asian countries have begun preparations in Algiers for the second Afro-Asian Conference in March next year'. This was followed by a meeting of the 13 members of the committee established at the Non-Aligned Conference in Cairo (held 6-12 October) to discuss the calling of the next

knew and a man from Liberia at dinner.' The next day he was in Geneva, where he was met by Ned Willard, according to the *Notebook* entry.

> At 12:30 Fifi (the UN Secretary I had met in Cairo) came by. We talked till 5pm. She works in the UN here and is Swiss...Ned Willard's[32] – met an English couple just returned from Nigeria – we talked till 9pm.
>
> *16 November* shopping for suit and overcoat. Ned Willard's – tour city. Dr. Said Ramadan...chatted with some of the 'Brothers' – Fifi was knocking on my door as I came up the stairs – we talked till 11 and she left. I went for a walk in the rain, alone and feeling lonely.

Dr. Said Ramadan, one of the founders of the Muslim Brotherhood in Egypt, had fled to Saudi Arabia when expelled by President Nasser. There he became one of the founders of the World Islamic League, a Saudi 'charity' organisation whose goal was to spread the Islamic faith worldwide. He then decided to move to Geneva, Switzerland in 1961, where he created the Islamic Center of Geneva.[33] This meeting might well have given Malcolm much to think about, as he had also met, and had been befriended by President Nasser!

Notebook, 17 November

> Senegalese awaited me at Paris airport. Présence Africaine...checked me into Hotel du ???...met their staff, headed by M. Diop. Several of us had dinner. A asked me to come back from London at their

---

Non-Aligned conference. (21/11/1964, p.1311) There were 47 nations at this conference, 28 of them African; one of the resolutions was for full co-operation with the OAU's Liberation Committee. (*Africa Report*, November 1964, p.29) Did Malcolm know about these? Had he hoped to meet some of the committee members? Or attend the meetings? On the first of these conferences, see Richard Wright, *The Colour Curtain*, London: Denis Dobson, c.1956)

32 Ned Willard might have been the man who worked as an Information Officer for the World Health Organisation in Geneva in 1983.

33 In 1953 Ramadan 'was in the United States to attend a colloquium on Islamic culture at Princeton University, cosponsored by the Library of Congress...The colloquium was organized by the U.S. government, which funded it, tapped participants it considered useful or promising...A now-declassified CIA document labeled "Confidential—Security Information" sums up the purpose of the project: "On the surface, the conference looks like an exercise in pure learning. This in effect is the impression desired." The true goal, the memo notes, was to "bring together persons exerting great influence in formulating Muslim opinion in fields such as education, science, law and philosophy and inevitably, therefore, on politics.... Among the various results expected from the colloquium are the impetus and direction that may be given to the Renaissance movement within Islam itself."...U.S. policy at a time when virtually anyone who opposed communism was viewed as a potential ally... Over the four decades after Ramadan's visit to the Oval Office, the Muslim Brotherhood would become the organizational sponsor for generation after generation of Islamist groups from Saudi Arabia to Syria, Geneva to Lahore—and Ramadan, its chief international organizer, would turn up, as an operative in virtually every manifestation of radical political Islam.' www.motherjones.com/news/feature/2006/01/holy_warrior.html: Robert Dreyfuss, 'Cold War, Holy War', *Mother Jones*, January/February 2006.

expense on Monday for a speaking engagement...Went to see Aida Wade[34] – she showed me her albums – I walked around Paris and finally had a midnite, lonely dinner across from the hotel.

The Senegalese was Alioune Diop, Pan-Africanist founder of the journal *Présence Africaine* in Paris in 1947. Two years later he also opened a publishing house and a bookstore, which became a meeting ground for pro-independence activists. The journal became highly influential in the Pan-Africanist movement, the decolonisation struggle in the French colonies, and the birth of the Négritude philosophy. Radical African and African-diaspora authors were published by Diop, who also called the 1st International Congress of Black Writers and Artists in 1956.

US Government Reaction

Apart from trying to influence the African heads of state via its ambassadors, the governments by trade and aid missions, the peoples through the massive propaganda efforts of the United States Information Service, the US government had another idea. Why not send another African American, espousing somewhat different philosophies from those of Malcolm, to visit?[35] The choice fell on James Farmer, president of the Congress of Racial Equality, but the information sent to the American embassies in Africa claimed that

> Farmer's trip is sponsored by the American Negro leadership conference on Africa. The Department (of State) was informed by the Planning Committee of the Conference that the purpose of Mr. Farmer's trip is to attempt to present a 'true picture of the progress of civil rights in America and to state the true aspirations of most American Negroes as compared with what has been said in Africa by Malcolm X and Cassius Clay'...Addressee missions are requested to extend the usual courtesies to Mr. Farmer and to facilitate his making contact with government leaders...The Department of course wishes to be of help to Mr. Farmer in any way practical. It is recognized that in some countries too close an identification with the Embassy may

---

34 I have not been able to find any information on Wade.

35 The US would soon have something else to excite it about Ghana. President Kwame Nkrumah published his *Neo-Colonialism: the last stage of imperialism* in 1965 (London: Thomas Nelson; reprinted in the USA by International Publishers in 1966). A well documented scathing attack on the West, Nkrumah named the USA as being 'the foremost among the neo-colonialists', with the CIA at the heart of its policy implementation. (pp.239-240) William Blum in his *The CIA: a forgotten history* (London: Zed Books 1986, p.223) points out that 'Nkrumah later wrote that "the American Government sent me a note of protest, and promptly refused Ghana $35 million of 'aid". Four months later he was overthrown in a CIA-backed military coup.'

be counterproductive...All posts...also (to) offer political briefing... also encouraged to arrange for Mr Farmer to talk informally...to non-official American community...posts should cable program suggestions to succeeding posts on Mr. Farmer's itinerary.[36]

In his *Autobiography* James Farmer gives the briefest of reports: 'After a whirlwind tour of sub-Saharan Africa in January 1965[37]...I had been given letters from Emperor Haile Selassie of Ethiopia and President Julius Nyerere of Tanzania, Kenneth Kaunda of Zambia and Benjamin Azikiwe of Nigeria, expressing in glowing terms their solidarity with the struggle of their black brothers in the United States.' (p.230) Farmer then goes on to recount an un-named African American woman going to see him at his hotel and telling him that Malcolm X was about to be 'killed sometime between now (February 1) and April 1...No, no, not by the Muslims... There is another group far more dangerous than the Muslim that's going to get him...'. The woman refused to reveal her identity or give any further information. Farmer 'dropped the subject'.[38]

One has to question why Farmer says so little about his trip to Africa, following in Malcolm's footsteps. Initially an active Black trade unionist, then a founder member of the Congress of Racial Equality, in the 1960s, when he was also working for the NAACP, Farmer was the main organiser of the student sit-ins and Freedom Rides. Recognised as a militant activist, he had been sent on his travels, or so it was stated in public, by the American Negro Leadership Conference on Africa (ANLC) whose membership included just about every civil rights organisation. According to Peter Goldman, who also alleges that the ANLC had received some funding from the CIA, a rumour reached Malcolm that Farmer was being sent to 'undo what Malcolm had done in Africa...Malcolm phone[d Farmer] just before his departure. "They're saying you're going to counteract *me*. Tell me – what about me are you going to counteract?" "There's no truth in that at all", Farmer said, horrified.' The two men then met to discuss Malcolm's experiences.[39]

Was Farmer so innocent? According to Hugh Wilford, 'concerned American officials wondered how to counter Malcolm's charismatic

---

36 NARA: SOC14-1 US, Department of State to Embassies in Accra, Addis Ababa, Dar es Salaam, Kampala, Lagos, Leopoldville, Lusaka, Nairobi, Salisbury, 24/12/1964.

37 This was Farmer's second trip to Africa, claimed by Schehter et al, as 'CIA-sponsored... the first of which was in 1958, which concerned trade unions and the International Confederation of Free Trade Unions, the international trade union body set up the by USA (and others) with the aim of countering the World Federation of Trade Unions, seen by them as a communist instrument'.

38 Farmer (1985), pp.230-1.

39 Goldman (1973), p.218.

presence and the threat to US African policy it posed'. The American Society for African Culture, which shared its offices with ANLC, had been covertly funded by the CIA for some years. The Society now suggested to the ANLC that it would finance a trip to Africa for one of their members, to act as a 'living rebuttal to Malcolm X'. But Farmer, who now maintained a correspondence with Malcolm, was not a forceful supporter of America's foreign policy, so this ploy backfired a little. Farmer met US Embassy staff on his travels and defended President Johnson, whom Malcolm had called a 'Southern racist'. Farmer 'told African audiences that what Malcolm had really been promoting was a form of apartheid'. Historian Dan Schechter and his colleagues conclude that 'Farmer could be found serving as an effective, if unwitting, instrument of CIA operations.'[40]

Farmer claimed that he did not know that his travels had been funded by the CIA. On his return he said that 'President Johnson has not been well-projected in Africa. In addition, Malcolm X contributed greatly to the generally unfavourable African opinion of Johnson'.[41]

An example of the United States' concerns regarding the USSR and the fear of the spread of communism was clearly expressed by Under-Secretary of State for African Affairs, Mennen Williams. Attending the independence celebrations of Gambia, a small British colony, in early 1965 he is reported as saying that 'Gambia might become a tempting target for communist penetration'.[42]

Going Home

Malcolm was now on his way back to the USA. A tired man. Sometimes a lonely man. A man honoured by the heads of many states, by many activists and many religious leaders. How many had he met, how many discussions, formal and informal, religious and political, had he participated in? He mentions many people in his *Notebooks*, sometimes with full names, sometimes with dashes, at other times only initials, and understandable mis-spellings.[43] How many did he not even note? Malcolm told Jan Carew that on his trips to Africa, he had

---

40 Hugh Wilford, *The Mighty Wurlitzer*, Harvard University Press 2008, pp.205, 212-219; Ellen Ray et al (eds), *Dirty Work 2: The CIA in Africa*, Secaucus, NJ: Lyle & Stuart Inc., 1980, pp.64-67.

41 'The CIA as an Equal Opportunity Employer', *Ramparts*, vol. 17, #3, June 1969, pp. 24-33; the quotation is from p.32. Goldman (1979, p.218), also alleges that the ANLC had received some funding from the CIA. Angelou (1986, p.194), quotes Malcolm as stating that Farmer had been sent to Ghana by the State Dept.

42 *West Africa*, 27/3/1965, p.358.

43 Hopefully other historians, with access to research funding, will be able to locate information on the many people I have been unable to trace.

met others whose names I can't mention. They all shared some of their valuable time with me to discuss the plight of Negroes in America and to talk about colonialism, racism and the need for unity of the world's oppressed peoples. Not one of them bought the State Department propaganda about American Negroes being content with their lot as second-class citizens...[T]hrough me they were expressing their solidarity with the twenty-two million oppressed Negroes in America...Those talks broadened my outlook and made it crystal clear to me that I had to look at the struggle in America's ghettos against the background of a worldwide struggle of oppressed peoples. That's why, after every one of my trips abroad, America's rulers see me as being more and more dangerous. That's why I feel in my bones that the plots to kill me have already been hatched in high places.[44]

There was much, very much for him to think through. As Malcolm told his audience in the Methodist Church in Rochester, New York on February 16, 1965: 'during conversations with these men (he had listed all the heads of state he had met), there was much information exchanged that definitely broadened by understanding and, I feel, broadened my scope'.[45]

Five days later he was shot dead.

---

44 Carew (1994), p.84.
45 *Malcolm X* (1992), p.147.

CHAPTER 7

London and Paris
22 – 24 November 1964

London

Malcolm stopped off in Europe on his way home to New York. When had these arrangements been made? Had Ras T Makonnen, whom Malcolm had met in Ghana, alerted him to the long history of Black struggle in Britain, in which he himself had participated from the 1930s to the 1960s, before he moved to Ghana? His trip to Paris was arranged by Alioune Diop.[1] Did Malcolm hope to find politicised Black people in Britain and in France with whom he could discuss his new learning and thinking? After all, he – Malcolm – was 'having all kinds of troubles trying to develop the kind of Black Nationalist organization I wanted to build... One of the major troubles that I was having...was that my earlier public image, my old so-called "Black Muslim" image, kept blocking me.'[2] Did Malcolm hope to find that he was not so tainted by this hate-mongering image among people in Britain?

We know almost nothing about this visit to Britain: we don't know whom he met, how introductions were arranged. Our only evidence is a newspaper cutting of him among the papers kindly found for me by the Metropolitan Police. It is difficult to believe that the British secret services such as MI5 were not keeping a watch on Malcolm. Undoubtedly

---
1 Malcolm and Diop had met in Cairo – see Chapter 5.
2 *Autobiography*, p.431.

they were, but as ever the papers have not been deposited at the National Archives, and there is nothing in the files of the Home Office, to whom both the Metropolitan Police (the 'Met') and the secret services report (at least in theory).[3]

What the Met sent me is a photograph of Malcolm in front of a microphone published in the *Sunday Telegraph* of 22 November 1964. The caption states: 'Malcolm X, former leader of the Negro extremist Black Muslim movement, who now has a breakaway group of his own, addressing the Federation of Mohammedan Students' Societies at Malaysia Hall, near Marble Arch'. During this visit he was interviewed on the BBC's 'Tonight' television program.

France, Introduction to Malcolm in France, July 1964

The July/August issue of the Paris magazine *Révolution* was a special issue on 'Colonial War in the USA' and featured an 'exclusive interview with Malcolm X'. Malcolm was interviewed by by jazz writer and poet, A.B. Spellman.[4] The FBI believed that the magazine was backed by Communist China.[5] The article was also printed in New York's *Monthly Review* in May, where it was stated that the interview had taken place on 19 March. The introduction to the piece, which seemingly was omitted from the French version, described Malcolm as 'an overwhelming public speaker...his positive demagogy is unchallengeable...He is an organizer and administrator of proven ability. For these reasons, he has the potential of becoming one of the really major revolutionists in America today'. It is important to reproduce some excerpts in order to demonstrate how Malcolm's ideas changed – and changed so rapidly – after his first visit to Cairo and Mecca. (The text is taken from the FBI's version, which does not differ substantially from that in *Monthly Review*.)

---

3 Email from John M. Lloyd, Departmental Record Officer, the Home Office, 3/10/2001.

4 A.B. Spellman, author of many books and papers, poet, music critic and lecturer, emailed me (2/1/2003) that at the time – the early 1960s - he was 'one of the young African-American intellectuals, if I many call myself an intellectual, who were trying to develop a conception of revolutionary nationalism which would stress the unity of people of African heritage as a spearhead of broad and radical social change. It all seems naïve now, but it felt right at the time.'

5 FBI Papers, #100-399321, Part 12, American Embassy in France to Director, FBI, 26/8/1964. The quotations are from the FBI translation. Mr Spellman does not know of this possible connection. On a visit to Paris he met the journal's then editor, a Vietnamese communist. *The Monthly Review*, May 1964 is available on http://www.monthlyreview.org/564mx.htm

Spellman begins by asking Malcolm about his relationship with the Nation of Islam, and asks about his plans for the future. Malcolm states that he hopes to publish a periodical, 'The Flaming Crescent'. To questions about the orientation of the Muslim Mosque Inc., his policies and the future of Blacks in the USA, Malcolm replies that

> we [believe] in the complete separation of the whites from the blacks...It would be more correct to say independence than separation...[O]ne must, in a long range program, envisage their return to their African fatherland...[O]ur immediate program must allow everything which permits us to live better while we are still in the United States. We must completely control the political life of the 'black community'...We place the accent upon the youth...[W]hites cannot join us...We shall collaborate with the organizations for civil rights for the objectives which are not in contradiction with our political and economic ideas: in other words, black nationalism...The national leaders [of the civil rights movement], the leaders working full time and the people who pay their salaries, have, of course, a word to say...If this movement becomes a genuine movement for the rights of man in general, then these [African] nations could carry the case of the American blacks to the United Nations... Furthermore, outside of the United Nations, we have also the aid of eight hundred million Chinese who are ready to fight and die for the rights of humanity...We are non-violent in the face of non-violence; but, if someone employs violence against me, my non-violence does not have any more sense...The blacks have enough of non-violence. They begin to comprehend that when they demonstrate for objectives which the Government itself has declared lawful, they have the law on their side. All those who then oppose them will be in an illegal position...I know that Robert Williams had to go into exile, simply because he tried to persuade our brothers [in Monroe, North Carolina] to defend themselves against he Ku Klux Klan and other white groups[6]...The racial problem in the United States cannot be solved within the framework of the present economic and social system...The black revolution, for the moment, is not a revolution, because it condemns the system and [then] it demands it to integrate the blacks. A revolution destroys the system and replaces it by a better system.

---

6 Malcolm mentioned Williams again in a radio interview – the Joe Rainey Show, on WDAS – 'Williams was just a couple of years ahead of his time; but he laid a good groundwork, and he will be given credit in history for the stand he took prematurely'. (Sales [1994], p.77)

Malcolm in Paris, 23 - 4 November

Malcolm had been invited to speak in Paris by *Présence Africaine*, an African cultural organisation and journal. The invitation had been issued by the journal's editor, Alioune Diop, whom Malcolm had met on his brief stop in Paris in November 17. According to Chester Himes, 'there were a lot of young American blacks in Paris...who were devoutly interested in Malcolm X...the black women oldtimers on the Paris scene were all trying to seduce him...Carlos Moore had become very close to Malcolm, translating for him and selecting the people who were allowed to see him.'[7] Moore took Malcolm to see Himes, who had met Malcolm previously in New York, and knew that 'I agreed with everything about his program except his religion. I tried to tell him that the Muslims were the first people to go into black Africa and collect the blacks and [sell] them to the European slave-traders, but Malcolm saw the Moslems as the saviors of the blacks...I didn't agree with him at all. But I was in favour of his politics.'[8]

Himes writes that a hall had been hired for a series of lectures which were 'widely publicised and were attended by hundreds of people. Carlos translated for him and generally acted as his manager.' The French police did not attend the lectures, but had a van parked outside. According to Himes, a number of the Blacks present claimed to be working for the CIA. The CIA, Himes told interviewers Fabre and Skinner, 'were only interested in Richard Wright...They thought he might have had information [on] people they considered dangerous, such as Kwame Nkrumah or Frantz Fanon. The only other person they were interested in was Malcolm X'.[9] Why these 'Blacks' would make such a claim is hard to understand. However, according to Richard Gibson, it was Carlos Moore himself who worked for the CIA. But others claim that it was Gibson who was then working for the CIA.[10]

---

7 This and following quotes are from Himes (1976), pp.291-2. Himes had met Malcolm on one of his periodic visits to New York; see Edward Margolies and Michel Fabre, *The several lives of Chester Himes*, Jackson: Univ. Press of Mississippi, 1997, p.126.

8 In their book Margolies and Fabre (p.133) indicate that Malcolm's visit to Himes was a 'long private colloquy'. They note that the Harlem bookshop owner Micheaux had been 'a good friend of Malcolm X'. (p.125) Moore is described as a 'Cuban...former minor government official...who angrily denounced race discrimination in Castro's Cuba'. (p.131).
On the Muslim enslavement of Africans, see eg, Ronald Segal, *Islam's Black Slaves*, London: Atlantic Books 2001.

9 Fabre & Skinner (1995) p.78.

10 Emails from Richard Gibson 8 & 11/2/2002. Gibson states that Moore was 'an Afro-Cuban of Jamaican origin, who later wandered for several years around Africa, preaching against the Cuban Revolution without great success'. Moore had lived for a while in New York then again in Cuba, then in Algiers and Switzerland with Joseph Savimbi; then in Paris.

Lebert Bethune writing in John Henrik Clarke's *Malcolm X; the man and his times* (1969, pp.225-234) states that, 'we – a group of young black men – arrived breathless before the door of the apartment where Malcolm was waiting...Brother Malcolm wanted to hit the streets and to visit every nook and cranny of Paris where the African-American brothers hung out. There were news conferences to be held and by now the French radio was announcing the presence of "the hater of white men".' At the cafés they visited Malcolm is 'immediately surrounded by all the Africans. They all wanted to shake his hand as we walked through the streets, Malcolm was almost invariably recognised and greeted by every African.'[11]

Carlos Moore in his biography recalls that,
When Malcolm came to Paris...we were both boxed into a dangerous corner. He had freshly made a spectacular break from the Black Muslims and was embroiled in a bitter struggle with its leadership. Having lost his political base, he attempted to connect with the international revolutionary movement, which was heavily influenced by the Left. I had been in France only a month and a half when I decided to involve myself with Malcolm...I was aware that I was opening myself to extreme danger, since Malcolm was a marked man...

For further information on Moore, see www.afrocubaweb.com; Moore's refutation of such charges is in his forthcoming biography. Gibson is accused of being a CIA agent by John Henrik Clarke. (Schomburg Center: John Henrik Clarke Correspondence SCM 94-12, file 2, Clarke to Julian Mayfield 28/8/1964.) Daniel Guerin echoes this charge in a letter dated 17/3/1966. (Tamiment Library, Breitman Correspondence, box 44, file 1) In his *Portrait of an Expatriate* (Westport: Greenwood Press 1985, pp.52-4), LeRoy Hodges states that Gibson arrived in Europe in 1951 to study at the University of Rome; he was then drafted into the US military, served in Italy and Germany, was discharged in 1954, then attended the Sorbonne and by 1955 was working for Agence Presse France. He suggests that it is possible that Gibson had been instrumental in destroying the 'alleged solidarity of Afro-Americans in Paris' and might have been a CIA agent. There is more on Gibson's perhaps questionable activities in Paris in Fabre (1993), pp. 461-472. Carol Polsgrove (2001, pp.126-7) notes that Gibson was a 'prime organizer' of the Fair Play for Cuba Committee and arranged for a number of Black writers, including Julian Mayfield, to visit Cuba. Harold Cruse, in his description of the visit, does not mention Gibson.
In the emails to me Gibson states that he was a man of the left, but unaffiliated, certainly in support of the Cuban Revolution. He claims it was he who had persuaded Fidel Castro on his visit to New York in 1960 to move from a 'downtown' hotel to the Hotel Theresa in Harlem, where he had introduced Malcolm to Castro. Others claim that it was Malcolm who had arranged for Castro's move to Harlem. Gibson was then the first African American journalist to work for CBS news. He is the author of *African Liberation Movements*, London: IRR/OUP 1972.
11 Bethune was a poet and film-maker; in 1970 he was teaching at New York State University at Stony Book. According to Gibson (email 8/2/2002) Bethune, of Caribbean origin, was 'linked to the AFL-CIO's International Relations department, which we now know was CIA-funded'.

In the Congo, the national liberation drive was in full swing after the murder of Patrice Lumumba, with whom Malcolm identified viscerally, as did I. Thus Malcolm and I saw eye to eye. When he asked me to come on board, I did so gladly and began organizing a European branch of his newly founded Organization for African-American Unity. At his behest, I recruited volunteers with military and medical expertise to assist the Lumumbist insurrection in the Congo.[12]

Carlton Barrett recalls that he 'was a part of the team with Carlos Moore, Lebert Bethune, Chuck Davis and others who had formed the OAAU Paris chapter and were the welcoming party...I remember a memorable moment sitting in and listening to himself and the late great novelist Chester Himes reminiscing about their past. Later that evening there was a session with him and the executive of the African Students Union that I attended partially. I left before it really got going.'[13]

Other sources only mention Malcolm addressing one large meeting, and as he was only in Paris for two days, a 'series' of meetings is hardly possible. Lebert Bethune (see below) wrote that the audience at the Salle de la Mutualité was composed of Africans, African Americans, French students, and French workers and intellectuals. According to the *New York Militant* (7/12/1964), there 'was not an unoccupied space in the meeting room...the crowd spilled into the corridors...Malcolm explained that he was that evening speaking on behalf of the OAAU, which was formed after he and his colleagues had studied the tactics and strategies being used in Africa. After outlining the indoctrination of Afro-Americans, he stated that "the efforts of 'liberals' to solve our problems for us have been efforts to make us become more American than African. They have no desire to solve the race problem because it would mean giving up power..." Malcolm spoke on the power of the dollar, which makes "anything possible". Asked about the recent US elections, he replied that who wins is immaterial, as "it is the same system...this system which is ruling the world".'

As they are unattributed, it is impossible to know from which of Malcolm's speeches in Paris the following two excerpts were taken. They appear in *Malcolm X: The Evolution of a Revolutionary Pan-Africanist*, published by the Kwame Nkrumah Ideological Institute, as the first item in their *Great Lives in Pan-Africanism* series. The Institute was formed in

---

12 Email from Carlos Moore, 15/7/2008. As his *Autobiography PICHÓN: Race and Revolution in Castro's Cuba, a Memoir* will be published towards the end of 2008, I am very grateful for permission to quote from it. Moore, as others, questions the veracity of Gibson's writings, given his alleged CIA involvement.

13 Email from Carlton Barrett, 12/7/2008.

Washington, probably after the overthrow of President Nkrumah in 1966.

> [T]he only hope for the black man in America [is] in a strong Africa and the Afro-American becoming inseperably linked with the overall program that's existing on the African continent. The two problems must be solved together and the forces must go forward together...This is our only hope. Our hope is in a strong Africa. And when Africa is strong, our position in America will be one of respect. But if Africa is weak, we will never be in a position of respect in America.
>
> Many of the African intellectuals that have analysed the approach to socialism are beginning to see where the African has to use a form of socialism that fits into the African context.[14]

That Malcolm succeeded in setting up a branch of the OAAU in Paris is confirmed in the radio broadcast over WINS station in New York on 18 February 1965, in which in answer to a phone-in question Malcolm said that 'last November [I] was successful in organizing a good organization in the American Negro Community in Paris, and they have been working in conjunction with the African community.[15] Himes also mentions that 'Carlos found a number of young blacks who wanted to work for Malcolm'. The Kwame Nkrumah Ideological Institute quotes Malcolm, 'while establishing the OAAU Chapter in Paris' argued that it was needed as

> it's not an accident that there is no organization existing in the Western Hemisphere designed towards that end [the unity of 'all our people in the West...with our people on the African continent']. It would be a direct threat to imperialism as it really exists and to colonialism as it exits in the West. (p.11)

---

14 Kwame Nkrumah Ideological Institute, *Malcolm X: The Evolution of a Revolutionary Pan-Africanist*, Washington, (no date), p.9. This pamphlet is in the Nkrumah Collection as the Moreland-Spingarn Library at Howard University.

15 Breitman (1966), p.188.

CHAPTER 8

New York
24 - 30 November 1964

According to the *Los Angeles Times* (25 November 1964, p.10) Malcolm was greeted by about thirty supporters on his return from his eighteen week tour of Africa and Europe. He is reported as saying that the 'US government and the Congolese Premier M. Tshombe share responsibility for the shooting of the white hostages by Congolese rebels in Stanleyville. When Lyndon B. Johnson began to finance Tshombe's mercenaries... natural to expect such disastrous undertakings to produce disastrous results.' The *New York Times* (25/11/1964, p.17) carried a similar report.

On the 'Barry Gray Show' (radio station WMCA in New York) Malcolm again spoke on the Congo situation. He analysed the role of capitalism: 'the basic trouble in the Congo right now is the intervention of outsiders – the fighting that is going on over the mineral wealth of the Congo'. He also castigated the 'newspapers, commentators and some of these so-called scientists who are trying to prove that the Congolese are savage, that they are not fully developed, that they are unable to govern themselves'. By now he understood clearly the new tactics of the capitalist world: these aspersions were used to 'justify the presence of the Western powers in the Congo, and primarily the presence of the United States'.

About one thousand people attended Malcolm's 'Homecoming Rally' held by the OAAU on November 29. Malcolm spoke of his two months in Cairo. While he did not go into details of his activities, one can gauge these from his telling the audience that 'Cairo is one of the cities on this earth that has the headquarters of more revolutionary movements than any other city'. Going on to describe his travels Malcolm emphasised that there had been 'a great deal of pressure put on various segments of the African community to not open any doors' to him. The US agents, he stated, were 'running around like mad with their money...[T]hey've done a vicious job.' He went on to describe the tactics of the United States Information Service in spreading disinformation, for example, by alleging that the passage of the Civil Rights Act means that the 'problems of every Negro over here have been solved' and by 'circulating a document on me throughout the African continent – knocking me...'.

Malcolm went on to talk about the necessity of working together with Africans to solve mutual problems, and suggested that it was of utmost importance to establish 'direct communication with our brothers on the African continent...Oppressed peoples must support each other's struggles for freedom', he maintained. At the end of the rally, the secretary of the Pan-African Student Union was invited to speak on the situation in the Congo and the audience was asked to participate in the demonstration planned against Tshombe, who was due to visit the UN. The next meeting of the OAAU would be on 'The Congo Crisis', Malcolm announced.[1]

Events were moving fast. Civil war broke out in the Congo and President Johnson hastened to support Tshombe. President Ben Bella denounced the US on Algerian television 'for its role in capturing Stanleyville to prevent the overthrow of the CIA-financed regime'. President Kenyatta issued a similar statement as did the governments of Chad, Ghana and Guinea. Alex Quaison-Sackey, Ghana's representative to the UN, called the US actions 'an affront' to the OAU.[2] Malcolm and Quaison-Sackey had been close colleagues since the Ghanaian arrived in New York. Surveillance on Malcolm by the US government increased.[3]

---

1 Breitman (1970), pp.138-140, 146-48; *The Militant* 7/12/1964, pp.1, 5.

2 Quaison-Sackey had been threatened by extremists in 1960, shortly after he had arrived to take up his appointment at the UN. (Evanzz (1992), p.88) See Catherine Hoskyns, 'The African States and the United Nations 1958 – 1964', *International Affairs*, 40/3 1964, pp.466-480 for a contemporary academic assessment.

3 Evanzz (1992), pp. 262-265. Civil Rights leaders had also sent a protest to the US Secretary of State.

CHAPTER 9

England
1 - 6 December 1964

The first Africans who settled in Britain were probably discharged African regiments in the Roman armies, which conquered the island over 2000 years ago. Others came to trade, then as seamen, and during the era of the slave trade, as servants. In the 19th century some came to attend schools and universities, and stayed (as did many seamen), joining the legal and medical professions. Seamen, traders and scholars also arrived from India. How large this population was at any time has not yet been determined.

As always, after World War II Britons themselves were emigrating to the less war-affected and economically booming countries of the Commonwealth such as Australia and South Africa. Thus, needing labour, Britain recruited workers in the West Indies and in India. Other 'colonials', learning of the availability of well-paid work, raised or borrowed the money for their passage to the 'Mother Country'. As Claudia Jones explained to American readers in *Freedomways* (Third Quarter, 1964), 'over a quarter of a million West Indians...have now settled in Britain in less than a decade.' West Indians emigrated because of the 'unbearable conditions' on the islands, caused by the 'colonial-capitalist-imperialist relations [which] impoverished the agricultural economy... [They met with] extreme manifestations of racism.' Immigrants were (and are) accused of lowering moral standards, of taking away jobs and housing and were a 'social burden'.

Racial discrimination and prejudice were rife in Britain at all levels. Both were fuelled by ignorance; for example, Professor Hugh Trevor Roper maintained on the BBC television's 'History Show' that there was 'no African history to teach'.[1] Most 'coloured' immigrants were barred from any but the lowest rank jobs, often only had access to dilapidated housing, and had to contend with periodic riots against them around the country. The first post-war lynching took place in London in 1959.[2]

The government's solution in 1962, now that more labour was not needed, was to pass laws restricting immigration – these were only intended to bar 'coloured' migrants. The response of the migrants, usually supported by those who had lived here for generations, was to form organisations to support each other and to fight back, however they could.[3]

The *Amsterdam News* reported on 5 December (p.4) that Malcolm was leaving for England as he had been invited to participate in a debate at Oxford University. He is reported as saying that 'on his return he will continue organizing the OAAU as a political action group and the Muslim Mosque Inc. as a religious group. I will work with all civil rights groups', he avowed. He 'had established good relations with the seven African heads of states...sympathetic to the plight of Negroes'. He had in fact left New York on 30 November and arrived in London on 1 December.

Oxford, 2-3 December 1964

If there is any truth in the adage that 'there is no rest for the wicked', then Malcolm must have been very wicked indeed – at least in some people's eyes. Having barely had time to hug his wife and children, Malcolm set off again, this time at the invitation of the Oxford Union, that is, the Students' Union of probably Britain's most prestigious (and elitist) university.

Oxford, like other British cities, was not immune to manifestations of racial discrimination. For example, *The Guardian* newspaper reported on 27 June 1964 (p.8) that Black people following up rooms on the vacancy list were invariably told that the room had already been let. Without research, one can only guess at the level of discrimination found by students, who set up a national Student Conference on Racial Equality in 1964 (*The Guardian* 15 June, p.3) under the chairmanship of the Oxford undergraduates' Joint Action Committee Against Racial Intolerance. Most interestingly, a whole issue of the students' journal *Isis*

---

1 *West Africa*, 4 April 1964, p.405.

2 See Marika Sherwood, 'Lynching in Britain', *History Today*, March 1999.

3 The 'standard' text on the history of Black peoples in Britain is Peter Fryer, *Staying Power*, London: Pluto Press 1985. For a brief summary of the situation in these years, see Colin Holmes, 'Violence and Race Relations in Britain, 1953 – 1968', *Phylon*, 36/2 1975, pp.113-124. On Claudia Jones, see Marika Sherwood et al, *Claudia Jones: a life in exile*, London: Lawrence & Wishart, 2000.

for November 1964 was devoted to the immigration issue, and included an article on Smethwick, a racist town Malcolm was soon to visit. There is no mention of Malcolm X in the journal. When I asked one of the writers for this special issue about Malcolm's visit, she doubted that Malcolm had been in Oxford.[4]

The Debate at the Students' Union

It was the president of the Oxford Union, Jamaican Eric Anthony Abrahams, who had invited Malcolm to participate in the annual Presentation Debate. The Union promised to pay for his flight, his accommodation in London's Mount Royal Hotel for the first and fourth of December, and in the Randolph Hotel in Oxford for December 2-3. Abrahams asked him not to speak to any other organisation or on the radio or television until after the debate.[5]

The motion for the debate was a statement made by the US right-winger Barry Goldwater when he accepted the Republican nomination for the presidential election: 'Extremism in the defence of liberty is no vice; moderation in the pursuit of justice is no virtue'. Speaking for the motion were Abrahams himself, Hugh MacDiarmid, the Scottish nationalist poet and Left-wing political activist, with Malcolm as the last speaker.[6]

The conservative *Daily Telegraph* (4/12/1964) reported that Malcolm received 'a long ovation' and quoted from his speech:

> I don't believe in any form of unjustified extremism, but when a man is exercising extremism in defence of liberty for human beings, I do not consider that a vice. When a man is moderate in defence of justice for human beings I say he is a sinner. My main reason for believing in extremism in defence of liberty is because I firmly believe in my heart that the day that the black man takes uncompromising steps and realises that he is within his rights when his own freedom is being jeopardised, to use any means necessary to bring about his freedom, I don't think he will be by himself. I believe that the day they do many more whites will have more respect for them. There will be more whites than there are now on their side with this wishy-washy love thine enemy approach they have been

---

4 Correspondence with Dr Mary Kaldor, October 2002.

5 Schomburg Centre: Malcolm X Papers, reel 3, folder 15, Abrahams to Malcolm X, 27/11/1964.

6 MacDiarmid's travel and hotel expenses were also met by the Union. National Library of Scotland, Christopher M Grieve Papers: Eric Abrahams to Mr Hugh McDiarmid (sic), 23/11/1964. (Grieve adopted the name 'Hugh MacDiarmid'.) My thanks to Alan Bell of the National Library for locating these for me. It is possible that there is more relevant correspondence is some of the four other archives' holdings of MacDiarmid papers

using up to now...I do not believe in brotherhood with anyone who is not ready to practice brotherhood with our people.[7]

Despite Malcolm's eloquence and the brilliant touch of quoting Shakespeare, and the persuasiveness of his co-speakers, the motion was defeated 449 to 225.[8] In his *Autobiography*, *The Company I've Kept* (1966), MacDiarmid, who had been involved in the Peace Movement with Paul Robeson, recalls Malcolm as a 'brilliant speaker, and to my mind, an extremely able and attractive personality'. (p.27)

The speakers for the Opposition were Humphrey Berkeley, a Conservative MP, and Lord Stonham, a Labour member of the House of Lords and Parliamentary Under-Secretary of State at the Home Office.[9] Lebert Bethune, who had accompanied Malcolm to Oxford from Paris for the debate, noted that 'the flippant, drawing room comedy manner' of the members of Parliament angered Malcolm. This is a very interesting comment in terms of British racial attitudes, as Humphrey Berkeley, ex-president of the Cambridge Student Union (1948), was a very liberal man for a Conservative. In 1965 he was to vote for the abolition of the death penalty for murder, and in the following year for the legalisation of homosexual activity among adults. A sponsor of the Anti-Apartheid Movement in 1962, he became the chair of the United Nations Association and criticised various aspects of Conservative Party politics. Berkeley was also the Secretary of the Conservative Parliamentary West Africa Committee from 1959 until 1964. Could we surmise that he (like so many others) could fight for equality 'out there' but could not deal with, or be respectful towards the Black man across the aisle from him? (It is, of course, quite possible that Bethune was referring to Lord Stonham, whose politics could be considered to be to the right of the Conservative MP.)

The *Oxford Mail* (4 December 1964, p 14) also reported the standing ovation and noted Malcolm's inveighing against Tshombe, whom Malcolm described as 'not the new Prime Minister of the Congo but the murderer of the rightful prime minister'. He was a paid killer 'propped

---

[7] There is a transcript of the speech in *Malcolm X Talks to Young People*, pp.20-26 and also on www.hartford-hwp.com/archives/45a/460.html

[8] MacDiarmid, was to stand under his real name of Dr C.M. Grieve as a communist Parliamentary candidate for West Perthshire, Scotland, in the general election in 1964; he lost. (*Daily Worker*, 3/12/1964, p.1)

[9] At this time Britain was debating the imposition of further restrictions on 'coloured immigration'. In Parliament Lord Stonham said that 'it was idle to talk of a multi-racial Commonwealth of 750 million if Britain could not integrate one million of that same Commonwealth'. He agreed that controls would have to continue. (*Daily Gleaner*, 4/12/1964, p.33) Victor Collins had been ennobled as Lord Stonham in 1958; he served as the Labour government's Junior Minister at the Home Office until October 1964, when he was made its Minister.

up by US dollars', Malcolm claimed. He also attacked the press which, he said, 'gave the impression that they attach more importance to a white death than they do to the death of a human being whatever the colour of his skin'. Unfortunately as the debate was held close to the end of term, the *Isis* and the *Cherwell* (the student newspapers) did not carry reports.[10]

The Militant of New York reported the event in its issue of December 24 (p.2). It noted that there were numbers of Africans and Indians among the student audience and that Malcolm concluded his 'stirring and vitriolic speech' with a famous passage from *Hamlet*:

> To be or not to be: that is the question.
> Whether 'tis nobler in the mind to suffer
> The slings and arrows of outrageous fortune,
> Or to take arms against a sea of troubles
> And by opposing end them?

'To thunderous applause [Malcolm] declared that the latter choice was the only possible one if people are to gain their emancipation'. The paper notes that though much of the debate was broadcast, the BBC had two commentators on the programme explaining away Malcolm's accusations, especially regarding the United States.

On November 30 J. Edgar Hoover asked for the London 'Legat' (i.e. legation) to cover the debate, but this report is not included in the FBI files.[11] The British media's interest was certainly awakened: the debate was broadcast live on BBC television; Malcolm appeared on the BBC's 'Encounter' program and on Independent Television's 'Dateline' on his return to London from Oxford. It is estimated that about 10 million people would have viewed the BBC programs.

Memories of Malcolm

Recalling the event some thirty years later, Abrahams explained on Jamaican radio that there was a tradition at the Union for the retiring president to invite a person whom he most admires to participate in this celebrated debate. Though the Union was somewhat taken aback at his suggestion of both the topic and Malcolm as a speaker, it agreed, and the 'necessary tickets were sent'.[12] Malcolm was scheduled to spend four days in Oxford, and a 'whole series of events' had been organised for him. But as Abrahams had been 'gated', that is, forbidden to leave his

---

10 Correspondence with Oxford Union Society October 2001.
11 FBI Malcolm X Files Part 13, #100-399321-185, memo 30/11/1964 & Part 13a, memo 27/11/1964.
12 An example of the mistakes made by those who gather 'intelligence' is the Metropolitan Police's belief that the trip had been paid for by the BBC. (Metropolitan Police report 10/12/1964)

college after six in the evening as punishment for having participated in a demonstration protesting the arrest of Nelson Mandela, Malcolm said he would not attend these events.

> So every night he came to my apartment...Malcolm would hold forth every night during the four nights and four days he was there...He would sit there and talk to those white students. If there were forty students there at a time, thirty-six would be white. And he would talk about 'white devils' – I remember that phrase, 'white devils' – I remember sitting there and hearing him talk about white devils, and white students would clap...Here was a man talking about racial injustice, and, well, he didn't mince words. If you looked at his thoughts, they were not violent thoughts, they were reasoned thoughts...And seeing those white kids cheering this man who was talking about white oppression was really something...We had no room in my flat at night. It was like a movie house with people lined up trying to get in...The overall thing is that he would speak and they would cheer. The way in which he reached people was very reasoned. It was never abusive...This was not a man motivated by hatred of white people. This was a man who operated at a totally cerebral level...You got the feeling that you were dealing with a very careful, scholarly man who saw clear distinctions and who could illuminate those distinctions by analogy.
> I also remember walking with him in Oxford...[In conversation] Malcolm never repeated himself once in those four days. He would make a point, and then he would use an analogy to illustrate that point. His use of analogy was brilliant, and his command of the English language was something extraordinary. We spent a lot of time discussing his relationship with Martin Luther King and the whole civil rights movement in America. He told me that he and Martin corresponded and that they spoke to each other, but there were real differences between them, even though the differences were sincere and genuine ones. Malcolm never spoke disparagingly of him at all.[13]

Abrahams also recalled that one evening a very beautiful woman student offered to walk back to his hotel with Malcolm. 'She came back rather speedily, sort of surprised that there was this rare Black man who turned down a beautiful woman' – this 'reinforced his integrity' to Abrahams.[14]

---

13 Carew (1994), pp.71-76.
14 Ibid, p.74.

Another person who recalls Malcolm's visit is Judith Okely.[15] The day before the debate, she recalls, Malcolm was welcomed in the Union bar by a 'cross-party' group of Union officials, which included her, the first woman member. Judith remembers that,

> we went up to a large room with a huge table and sat around exchanging pleasantries...The men were very deferential. I remember bringing up the subject of Burke, the political philosopher...and Sartre, who argued that apparently not making a choice is still a choice. Malcolm grinned and said he liked my comment and that he would remember it for future use. We met later in some student digs in the evening for coffee, there were about 6-8 again. Retrospectively I wonder if some of the men's deference and excessive politeness was based on confusion about how to behave with a black American... The next morning an African postgrad came down to St.Hilda (a women's college) and said he had a message from Eric. Malcolm would like to meet me again at the Randolph Hotel, but I must come with another person...[Chloe Stallibrass and I] sat down...It was a very small room. Unfortunately I did not record our conversation, but my general recollection is that what he wanted to hear about was our daily lives. He did not talk about himself much...As we knew so little of him then, we could not ply him with clichés...The most unforgettable thing he said was that he was always like a hare with ears up, listening and on his guard...At one point Malcolm asked if we would like some refreshment, e.g. tea or coffee. He ordered it by room service but insisted we both hide in the bathroom when the guy delivered it. Obviously he had his reputation to protect and that is why he insisted I not come alone.
>
> I went to the debate...Everyone wore evening dress, both to the pre-debate dinner and to the actual event...Malcolm proved his brilliance at rhetoric. The great climax was when he described people including children being attacked by police dogs and water cannon in the States. The applause was thunderous. There was a standing ovation. The students recognised quality whatever their views. After the debate, Malcolm would have gone upstairs with

---

15 That women could not stand for election to the Union until 1964 demonstrates the conservative nature of the university. It was only 'full members' of the Union who could sit downstairs during the famous debates; non-members, that is most women, could only watch from the upper gallery. Judith Okely now teaches Social Anthropology at the University of Hull and is the author of eg, *Own or Other Culture*, London: Routledge 1996 and with Helen Calloway, *Anthropology and Autobiography*, London: Routledge 1992.

the others officers and speakers...I believe he had not expected such publicity and adulation.

Tariq Ali, then an Oxford student and Treasurer of the Union, a radical leader of the sixties, now a political commentator, writer and film-maker, accompanied Malcolm X to the debate, which he chaired, as we can see from the film of the occasion. He recounts the debate in his autobiographical *Street Fighting Years*:

> We sat together in the debating chamber. He looked around the audience and said he'd never addressed so many well-dressed whites. (Evening wear was obligatory – but not, of course, for Malcolm.) His speech was, by common agreement, the most brilliant to have been heard in that hall for many decades. The entire audience was spellbound by his use of words, his imagery, and surprisingly, his total lack of demagogy...When it was his turn to close the debate he had allowed his voice to rise a bit and the repressed anger had been felt throughout the hall. He explained why he refused to continue bearing the name of a slave-owner and demonstrated how slavery had degraded the whites and oppressed the blacks. He reminded the Oxford Union that Britain had played a leading part in the slave trade and many of the so-called nobility had grown rich by trading in black human beings. The hands of the British ruling class were stained with the blood of blacks who died of disease in the crammed quarters of the slave ships or were worked to an early grave in the New World...At the end of his speech, which had evoked the struggles of black America and the three continents, Malcolm X received an emotional standing ovation. Few who heard that speech could have forgotten its impact.

After the debate, 'we retired to his hotel', Tariq Ali recalls. He questioned Malcolm about the Black Muslims. Malcolm responded that he

> did not trust them either and had established his own group...He did not believe in non-violence. On this he was firm, unrepentant, and refused to compromise. Martin Luther King plays into their hands... he tells people to turn the other cheek. You can't deal with bullies like that...Blacks are a powder keg. King wants to spray the keg with water. I think we have to light the fuse. It's the only way to teach them to respect us.

Tariq remembers that Malcolm X was 'a great admirer of Cuba and Vietnam...His real anger was reserved for what America was doing to

Vietnam'. When Tariq had to return to his college, on shaking hands with Malcolm he said he hoped they would meet again before long. Malcolm replied: 'I don't think so. By this time next year I'll be dead.' The stunned student asked questions. Malcolm explained that,

> since his break with the Nation of Islam, he had been moving in other directions. He had realized that race alone could never be a sufficient criterion for achieving social change...He had allied openly with the enemies of Washington in Havana, Hanoi and Algiers. These facts meant that, 'they have already ordered my execution. They don't like uppity niggers. Never have. They'll kill me. I'm sure.' 'Who?' He shrugged his shoulders, as if to say that the question was too foolish to merit a reply.[16]

In an undated letter to me, written late in the year 2000, Jan Carew wrote that

> Malcolm's frequent visits to Britain provided him with an intellectual cross-fertilization which he could not get in the US. In a curious way his stay at Oxford and the night-and-day sessions he had there was one of the high points of his life. It gave him an opportunity to become a purely cerebral being. He was able to sift through and synthesize his world experiences and bring into focus an ideology that broke out of the chains [of] a manichean black/white US experience [which] had somehow atrophied his vision. But he also knew very clearly that, in his own words, 'Vision without action is a hallucination'. That is why his Oxford Union debate, his sojourn at Oxford when he met a variety of students, and his speech at the LSE are so important.

Manchester, 3 December 1964

From Oxford Malcolm went to Manchester, England's second largest city. It had been a cotton manufacturing town, dependent in the 19th century on US slave-grown cotton.[17] A shipping canal linked the city with the port of Liverpool; colonial seamen looking for shore work and other 'colonials', attracted by the ready availability of work, had settled there since at least the mid-19th century.[18] Post World War II, both the colonial

---

16 Tariq Ali, *Street Fighting Years*, London: William Collins 1987, pp.41-3.
17 On this relationship, see Marika Sherwood, 'Manchester, Liverpool and Slavery', *North West Labour History Journal* #32, September 2007.
18 When the anti-slavery campaigner Thomas Clarkson visited the city's cathedral in 1787 to give a lecture, he found 'some fifty' Blacks clustered 'around the pulpit'. Thus the city's Black

population and the university had grown considerably. It was estimated in 1965 that there were about 10,000 West Indians, 2-3000 Indians and some 7,000 Pakistanis living in the city.

Manchester was by no means free of racial discrimination. For example, in 1960 there had been a protest against the colour bar by the Anti-Apartheid Movement outside the Old Trafford cricket ground; in 1962 some of the 'coloured population', claiming they were not wanted in White clubs, formed the Manchester Colonial, Sporting and Social Club; in 1964 the local Licensing Justices did not uphold objections to the renewal of a license to public house which had refused to serve Blacks; in 1965 the Pakistan Welfare and Information Centre was established to deal with various problems, which presumably included housing as 'some owners in select parts of Manchester [were] letting houses stand empty rather than let them to coloured families'.[19] According to those I interviewed, the city was very segregated, with the West Indians and Africans living in Moss Side and Pakistanis in another district called Chorlton-on-Medlock.

What was the situation like at the University? Though in 2001 the Chancellor claimed that in her student days there in the 1960s the 'students [were] passionate about racial equality', it is not possible to verify her claim. It is certainly not demonstrated in the Student Union newspaper, the *Manchester Independent*, which mentions neither Malcolm's visit or his death. From January 1964 to March 1965 the paper mentioned racial issues four times: it noted that the 900 'overseas' students at the University found their fellow students disinterested and ignorant of their countries and were not 'integrated' into the main student body (10 March 1964). Dan Brennan (mentioned below), the Union's President, supported the Union's decision not to affiliate with the Anti-Apartheid Movement (26 May 1964) though its local branch and its student members had been trying to persuade shopkeepers not to stock South African goods (4 September 1964). A student from Thailand was assaulted in the city by someone who said 'Bloody Chinese, why don't you go home?' (5 November 1964). The Union also decided not to repeat previous invitations to Sir Oswald Mosley, the leader of the fascist party in Britain, to address the students; President Brennan stated that this was 'no especial insult to the British Fascists for their beliefs...' The paper also printed, without comment, an

---

population is of long-standing. Ellen Gibson Wilson, *Thomas Clarkson: A Biography*, London: Macmillan 1989, p.37.

19 There has been no research on racism in its many manifestations in Manchester; the above are taken from a folder of newspaper cuttings on 'Racialism, colour prejudice' in the Local History Library. For a glimpse of the history of Black peoples in the area, see Marika Sherwood, *Manchester and the 1945 Pan-African Congress*, London: Savannah Press, 1995. See also Eyo Basey Ndem, 'Negro Immigrants in Manchester', MA thesis, University of London 1953.

interview with some visiting Americans, one of whom said he would never 'date a Black woman' and believed that Martin Luther King was a 'radical'. A letter in response to this called for 'fellow citizens [to] blend and dissolve into their society' (24 November 1964).[20]

The Invitation to Lecture

The Federation of Students' Islamic Societies (FOSIS), an independent organisation, had been founded in Britain in 1961; its first officials were Iraqi, Malay and Mauritian students. Having learned of Malcolm's forthcoming visit to Oxford, Hoossain Rajah of Mauritius, who was then a second-year student at Manchester University, thought it would be good to have Malcolm speak there.[21] Hoossain wrote me that

> It was done on the spur of the moment...At that time I was reading American Politics, so I was personally interested...I approached Dr. Said Ramadan through Ebrahimsa Mohamed (a fellow student) when I heard he was coming for the Oxford Union debate. Dr. Said, the head of the Islamic Centre of Geneva and the brain behind the formation of the Federation of Students' Islamic Societies of UK and Eire (FOSIS) decided to sponsor his visit.[22] We contacted Malcolm and asked him to give lectures at the universities of Manchester and Sheffield.

Hoossain, now back in his native Mauritius, explained to me that it was decided, with Malcolm's agreement, to enlarge his tour for FOSIS:

> Mr. Ebrahimsa Mohamed, the secretary of FOSIS was asked by Dr. Ramadan to accompany Malcolm X during the tour Ebrahimsa and myself organised.[23] We organised lectures in Manchester, Sheffield

---

20 It is interesting to note that the paper in its 1961 issues (the only others I looked through) is far more concerned with the world 'out there' than the 1964 issues. For example, it advocated independence for Algeria and held a debate on the issue as well as a march, then bemoaned that so few students had participated; it reported lengthily on the death of Patrice Lumumba and debated the forthcoming (anti-) Immigration Bill.

21 Hoossain Rajah, who has very kindly answered my many queries about Malcolm's visits, has worked in international marketing including stints with the UK Dept. of Trade and Industry as leader of trade missions to the Gulf states, and elsewhere. A lecturer and writer, and deeply involved in Islamic activities, he is currently in the process of establishing a small private university and research centre in the Mauritius. Unfortunately, FOSIS, though it still exists, is staffed by volunteers and has not kept its old files. Thus it has no way of locating members who might have met Malcolm.

22 Malcolm had met Dr Said in Geneva a few months previously. See Chapter 7.

23 Malcolm had preserved a telegram from Ebrahimsa Mohamed, as the General Secretary of FOSIS, which reached him in New York prior to his departure. This listed Malcolm's engagements as: reception London Tuesday; then meetings Manchester and Sheffield on Friday; London Saturday.

and London.[24] Dr. Said Ramadan [wanted] to give the opportunity to Malcolm to explain his stand on the question of racism in the US and also to clear the misconception the media had of the man.[25] At a question asked by Michael Parkinson about the image of him portrayed in the press, Malcolm replied by another question: 'Do I look like the devil and do I have horns on my head?'[26]

Malcolm's Experiences in Manchester

Mr Hoossain recalls that Malcolm

stayed for one day at my home in 3 Parrswood Road in Withington, South Manchester. The man was very humble – he did not ask to be housed in a hotel. He ate what my wife and myself gave him (we were both students). He prayed the Friday Prayer at the Islamic Cultural Centre in Victoria Park - then an old Victorian House

now the Manchester Central Mosque. His shoes got lost among others and he said: 'who would pick my shoes?' When we found his shoes – huge ones – we found that they had huge holes in them. What a sense of humour and humbleness. He did not even have a decent pair of shoes.

At breakfast, my wife asked him, 'Coffee black or white?' The man replied, 'integrated coffee'. This speaks about the man. The whole thing was to be a small public lecture at the university,

---

24 Mr Mohamed granted me an interview despite being heavily involved, as the Secretary of Muslim Aid in London, with funnelling aid to starving and bomb-spattered Afghanis. He had studied Law at Manchester.

25 As related by Mr Mohamed, Dr Said Ramadan had been one of the founder members of the Muslim World League, an organisation of scholars and public leaders. He was the son-in-law of Egyptian Hasan al-Banna, the founder of the Muslim Brotherhood, which aimed to rid the Moslem world of colonial powers. It had been founded during the British occupation of Egypt post WWII. Dr Ramadan had been forced to flee Egypt, and sought asylum in Geneva, where Malcolm X visited him once. (Interview with Mr Mohamed, London 6 February 2002)

26 Michael Parkinson, then and now a famous television interviewer, has no recollection of this interview. Phone call from Mr Parkinson's office on 31/8/2001 in response to my letter of 1/8/2001.

but a friend of mine – a Jewish friend, as a matter of fact – contacted the press. That's how the whole thing blew to a big meeting. I was a bit scared at the time that this meeting would not prejudice my studies. The people of the UK at that time were not as broadminded as they are now. I had a lot of convincing to do to get the Student Union to allow us to organise the lecture. Initially the Union was not prepared to give us permission to organise the lecture. It was the policy of the Union to bar all 'extremists'. I was able to convince the then President of the Union that Malcolm will not be controversial and that he was going to address the Oxford Union. He held an emergency meeting and we were given the permission just two days before Malcolm's arrival.27 The photo [which shows a crowded hall with people standing at the back] I have sent you of the audience shows how well attended was the meeting which was held after lunch at the Main Debating Hall of Manchester University Union. The posters we had put around the union only said: 'Malcolm X Speaks'. The door of the Union had to be closed one hour before the meeting as the hall was already packed. That day the university came to a standstill.

Professor Worsley, Prof. of Sociology, requested a meeting with Malcolm and he had lunch with us at a small restaurant just behind the University, the Bombay Restaurant. The owner, Mr. Nazir Uddin, treated us to the lunch.

What I can recall of the man was his sense of humour. He spoke about racism in US, about his conversion to Sunni Islam. He spoke about the 'Bullet and the ballot' and the 'Chicken comes home to roost' to do with the assassination of President Kennedy. These are quotes which are now often quoted. He did realise that a few months later he would also be assassinated. I have a small excerpt which somehow is still in my possession. It is what he said about extremism:

'My reason for believing in extremism, intelligently directed extremism, extremism in defence of liberty, extremism in quest of liberty, is because I believe in my heart that the day the black man takes an uncompromising step and realises that he is within his rights, when his own freedom is being jeopardised, to use any means necessary to bring about his freedom or put a halt to injustice, I don't

---

27 The Islamic Society, only in its second year of existence, only had about 15 members. Hoossain Rajah noted that 'It has been recorded by the Student Union that the meeting organised was the biggest in the history of the University. Credit was also paid to us for the orderly conduct of the lecture by the University and by the media.'

think he'll be by himself...One of the reasons why I'm in no way reluctant or hesitant to do whatever is necessary to see that blacks do something to protect themselves is I honestly believe that the day they do...there will be more whites on their side...'[28]

Professor Peter Worsley, now retired, who with his wife graciously invited me to lunch, recalled that he had first met Malcolm X when they were waiting to be interviewed on the BBC's '24 Hours' program. Claudia Cardinale, the beautiful Italian actress, was talking with Kenneth Allsop while they awaited their turn. Professor Worsley at first did not realise who the man with the gingerish hair was. Then they chatted and this resulted in Professor Worsley being asked to chair the forthcoming lecture at Manchester.[29]

It seemed to me that in recalling those far-off events, Peter Worsley had been a little shocked over an exchange during his lunch with Malcolm and Hoossain. Discussing the 'Third World' with Malcolm against the background of the growing friction between the Soviets and the 'First World', Peter had suggested that 'it could all blow up into a third world war'. Malcolm replied that 'that might be better than what we've got'. However, the relationship was not soured by this contretemps: Professor Worsley, then known as the Red Professor, received a postcard from Malcolm dated 25 January 1965. The card is of the Statue of Liberty in New York. Malcolm had written on the back: 'The statue is here because the real liberty is missing. They give us the symbol. Malcolm X.'[30]

How was Malcolm received by the students? The then Student Union (SU) president is now Lord Daniel Brennan, QC. He recalls that there had been a 'great to do...but eventually free speech prevailed'. He remembers the hall being 'jam-packed', and Malcolm X as 'probably the most influential Black leader at that time'. His talk was a 'historical survey of slavery and the Black situation. Malcolm promised to lead Blacks to the promised land, by any means necessary. He was a most charismatic speaker, slow, clear and powerful – there was an edge to it. There was tremendous tension about the man; I found him quite a frightening person, because of the undertone of violence. But he did not preach violence...He certainly made an impression, whether positive or negative.'[31]

---

28 Emails from Hoossain Rajah, 30/7/3002 and 17/8/2001.

29 Peter Worsley is the author of the seminal *The Third World*, Chicago: University Press, 1964; and eg. *Knowledges*, London: Profile Books 1997. I think this was, in fact, the interview on the BBC's 'Tonight' program.

30 Interview with Professor Peter Worsley, London 12/9/2001. He had, in fact, left the Communist Party at the time of the Hungarian uprising in 1956.

31 Telephone conversation with Lord Brennan, London 22/5/2002. My request to Lord Brennan to approve the transcript of our conversation elicited no response.

That the hall was crowded is also confirmed by Anna Ford, then a student and now Chancellor of the University, who emailed that she remembered 'Malcolm X giving a rousing speech to a packed hall. He was highly intelligent and charismatic and made a lot of sense to students passionate about racial equality.'[32]

'The hall was so crowded we had to part the crowd to get to the platform', Peter Worsley recalls. 'The atmosphere was expectant, but almost hostile. Generally the students would have been anti-Malcolm. There was not much knowledge or sympathy for Blacks. Malcolm was seen as a rabble-rouser. There were a number of Jewish students and Malcolm was a Muslim![33] Sensing this, Malcolm's first words were: "Before I begin, I want to read you a few surat from the Koran". He went on to wow the students, but  slipped once into what was taken to be an anti-semitic remark, which drew a gasp from the audience, which was, in fact, by then pro-Malcolm. But he recovered quickly...'

Though at a conference in Manchester where I recently spoke on Malcolm's visit two members of the audience denied that there could have been an anti-Malcolm feeling, the local Jewish newspapers indicate that there certainly was an anti-Muslim atmosphere.[34] The Jewish papers

---

32 Email dated 31/8/2001.

33 I want to thank Gerry Greenberg, the editor of the Manchester *Jewish Telegraph*, for attempting to find the Jewish students who had attended the meeting. Unfortunately our pleas brought no response.

34 I contacted both the men, whom I had not known previously. Steve Cohen replied that he had not been a student at Manchester at that time; he wonders whether there hadn't been any Jewish Malcolm-supporters, given 'the number of Jews on the left at that time'. Malcolm, as far as it has been possible to ascertain, received no support from the Left in the UK. When I questioned Professor Worsley about this, he wondered whether the Manchester Jews could have been influenced against Malcolm by an article in *Life* magazine, which

reveal very strong Zionist politics. This was based on the 'situation' in Palestine. Israel had invaded Egypt in 1956; in September – December 1964 the *Times* reported almost continuous Israeli 'skirmishes' with Jordan and Syria. Israel was planning on using the River Jordan for irrigation, without consultation. When the Arab countries considered diverting the tributaries feeding the river; Israel said this would constitute a 'hostile act' (10 September 1964, p.13). In September the formation of the Palestine Liberation Organisation had been approved at a meeting of the Arab Heads of State (11 September 1964, p.11). At the time of Malcolm's visit, an Arab boycott of Israeli goods, and Arab attempts to persuade other countries to join in this had been going on for some months.

Hoossain Rajah recalls that there 'were always conflicts between the Arab Society and the Jewish Society in the Student Union'.[35] An Israeli Embassy official was permitted to give a talk entitled 'Israel Looks to the Future' at the Student Union in February 1965. When the Arab students challenged the speaker the official refused to enter into a discussion and stated that Arabs had started the war of 1948 and that 'Arab belligerency is more apparent than real and a device of a crumbling autocracy to stem the tide of liberalism'. This lecture was the preamble to an Israel Week, a week of photo exhibitions, film shows and music. The Arab students responded by publishing a 'propaganda pamphlet', which they distributed during the first part of the Week, until they were stopped by the President, Dan Brennan. *The Jewish Gazette* (5/2/65, pp.5, 11) described the pamphlet as a 'counterblow to Israel week, condemning Jews as the sole source of any disturbances in any part of the world'. Presumably the Arab students had to destroy their already prepared second pamphlet. Unfortunately Lord Brennan does not recall this incident. I have not been able to locate a copy of the pamphlet.

The local *Manchester Evening News* gave a somewhat different picture of Malcolm X to its readers. Its 4 December article (p.19) is headed 'Black Muslim chief lashes out on Congo', thus immediately misinforming readers. The unidentified reporter wrote that,

> At a Press conference before speaking to Manchester University students, he said, 'You don't get action until you get mad. All we American Negroes want is to be treated and recognised as human

---

linked him with the US Nazi Party. The Nazi Party had certainly attended the 1961 Nation of Islam (NOI) convention and some other NOI meetings. In January 1965 Malcolm sent a telegram to the Nazis repudiating them. See R. L. Jenkins & M.D. Tryman, *The Malcolm X Encylopaedia*, Westport: Greenwood Press, 2002, pp.73-74. (My thanks to Diana Lachatanere, the Schomburg Center Archivist, for sending photocopies of these pages.) The international edition of Life magazine, which is what would have been available in Manchester, only carried an article on Black Muslims on 9/9/1963. This does not mention the US Nazi Party.

35 Email from Hoossain Rajah, 1/5/2002.

beings and we won't get that until whites see us thinking like human beings. In other words, no sheep, however loving and non-violent, is left alone by a pack of wolves.

Policies of men like Martin Luther King just persuade American Negroes to be a meal. The American Negro must show the white man he has human reactions, which means defending his freedom. Bloodshed would be justified. To let a dog bite you and not protect yourself is sub-human.'

Asked whether the wave of killings of Whites by Negro youths in New York was inspired by him, he said America always looked for a scapegoat – 'usually it's me'. Malcolm then continues his analysis:

America is too bankrupt morally to take the steps its intelligence says it should take to get to the root of the problem. President Johnson sent paratroopers to the Congo to murder innocent Congolese. He supports the leader, Tshombe, who is responsible for the killing of the rightful Congo Premier. The Congolese see hired killers – mercenaries – killing their people indiscriminately and realise there is a state of war. So they take hostages to stop the advance and if they had been half the savages they are made out to be, not one hostage would be alive. The Congolese are only fighting for what they believe in – and the fact that mercenaries had to be brought in by Tshombe is proof of what the Congolese people believe. It was the threat of spreading Mau Mau activity that made most of Africa free', he added.[36] 'I only believe all men should be free, and I accept any man who will accept me.

The *Manchester Guardian* (5/12/1964, p.4) reported that, 'the coloured American Muslim leader gave a warning yesterday that American Negroes would achieve their long-denied rights either by the ballot or the bullet'. He explained the formation of the OAAU and repeated that it intended to take the issue of African Americans' human – not civil – rights to the United Nations. The United States, he argues was

Just a tricky, deceitful, hypocritical, racialist society. It is a hypocritical country...It is where I was born – I am not un-American or anti-American – but I am against what they are doing to us and I am against the hypocrisy they use to try to make the world believe that they are making honest steps forward.

He was 'warmly applauded by the students', the article concludes.

---

36 On the 'Mau Mau' see Chapter 6 and eg, Donald L. Barnett & Karari Njama, *Mau Mau from Within*, New York: Modern Reader paperbacks, 1966.

We have another account by 'An eye witness', published in *The Islamic Banner* of March 1993, which also mentions the crowded hall, the massing media, and describes Malcolm as being 'simple and humble with the believers but tough with the disbelievers...He was just an ordinary Muslim and he believed in the equality of men...When he stood in front of the crowd it was as if an electric shock had touched them. All were stunningly silent. He made people laugh, he made them cry and he made them think rationally...Malcolm's ability to handle the press was unparalleled.'

The anonymous author of this article also states that, 'the stereotype image of Malcolm...in our minds was that of a savage man and a violent and provocative black Socialist leader'. Clearly the media had achieved its aim of alienating people, even Muslims in Britain from Malcolm. However, I was curious about this author's negative attitude towards socialism and during our long conversation I questioned Ebrahimsa Mohamed about this: he believed that the students of that time were confused about the difference between Marxism and socialism. 'Muslims', Mr. Mohamed told me, 'have no problems with socialism'.

After the lecture there was another TV interview. Then a rush back to Hoossain Rajah's home for refreshments before leaving for Sheffield in a Volkswagen Beetle. 'Poor Malcolm', says the anonymous author in the *Banner*, 'he was so tall he had to fold his legs all the way to Sheffield'.

Sheffield, 4 December 1964

Sheffield, a smaller industrial city than Manchester, also had a 'colonial' population by the time of Malcolm's arrival, and a newer, post-war university. The day before Malcolm was to address the students there had been a student meeting regarding an article in a new publication by the University's Debates Committee. This argued that, 'we stand by Smethwick' and advocated that the 'coloured immigrants', who were inferior, should go back home. (For the significance of Smethwick, see Chapter 12.) At the meeting the Student Union officials, while espousing free speech, condemned 'racial prejudice and extremist ideas'. Ebele Maduekwe, president of the 320-strong Afro-Asian Society, said that the article was 'disgusting and totally unnecessary'.[37] Sticking to its free-speech stance, the student paper *Darts* published four letters in the same issue: one condemned the publication of racist views in student magazine; Maduekwe's letter welcomed the article: 'We feel much better fighting an

---

37 *Darts* (the paper of the Sheffield Union of Students), 26/11/1964, p.1. I must thank Lawrence Aspden, the University Library's Curator of Special Collections, for sending me copies of this paper. Copies of *The Debater* are not available.

open political campaign than an insidious polite racial snobbery'. Two letters supported the racist: one did not like the idea of living next to a non-European; the other thought that 'the case for a total ban on immigration' would be the only solution to the 'ordinary working-class voters who have seen their home-town ruined by the activities of these aliens'.

The media was uneasy. The national *Daily Mail* reported on 2 December that, 'Sheffield University students plan to heckle Malcolm'. *The Sun*, probably the most right-wing national paper (it is difficult to call it a *news*paper) advised its readers that 'Negro Malcolm...will visit a British university with a racial problem on Friday...' The *Sheffield Telegraph* on the same day reported that 'the secretary of the Islamic Circle last night denied his society were likely to cause racial trouble by inviting Malcolm X...Mr. G.U. Siddiqui...said, "Malcolm is in this country at the invitation of the Federation of Islamic Students Societies...He was invited to come in August, but was unable to do so..."'.[38]

Malcolm's FOSIS host in Sheffield was Ghayasuddin Siddiqui, the secretary of the University's Islamic Circle. Dr Siddiqui, then a Pakistani doctoral student in chemical engineering, told me that there were many Muslim students at the university; the Islamic society had been formed prior to his own arrival. Malcolm was escorted to Sheffield by two engineering students, Salah Shahey, an Egyptian doctoral student and the other from Pakistan.

---

38 Clippings in Schomburg Center: SC Micro 6270, reel 3, folder 15.

The Student Union was not very happy about the invitation to Malcolm, but had acquiesced, and the secretary of the Union chaired the meeting. The meeting for Malcolm was the largest that had ever been organised by the students – about 700 attended. Dr. Siddiqui remembers that Malcolm was asked many questions by American students whose accents Malcolm recognised. He dealt with the questioners partly by reminding them of some snippet of their local history. Another memory is of Malcolm saying that 'Martin [Luther King] was nobody until we came on the scene'; and asking to be stopped should he 'go off the rails' during his speech, which, he said, sometimes happened when he was tired.

According to a student columnist, 'The elegance of his argument, [and] the contemptuous rhetoric which no Sheffield student dared to challenge, made him persuasive and interesting...' He was accorded 'a respectful hearing' and, according to the student union, was 'the only person in the history of the Union who has received a standing ovation from 700 students'.[39]

After the speech the 'eye witness' recalls that 'we went to have some dinner at the home of a PhD student from Egypt, who served us macaroni and mince meat, a meal which Malcolm ate for the first time and much enjoyed'.

And tired he must have been. According to the *Banner's* 'eye witness', who had accompanied Malcolm from Manchester,

> When we saw Malcolm departing on the midnight train to London, we realised that Malik Al-Shabazz (a name he preferred) had not slept for at least two days. He hardly had a moment to prepare for any of the speeches he delivered nor for the press and TV interviews. We realised that no one could have had such stamina, such a clarity of mind, such wonderful simple character, be such a friendly brother with so much knowledge about so many topics and attract so much attention from the enemies of Islam, without the blessing of almighty Allah.

The Sheffield Media

The local papers printed what *they* undoubtedly considered the most important statements made by Malcolm: he was now the chair of the OAAU; had left the Nation of Islam because 'they did not practise the true religion of Islam'. When asked whether he included JFK among 'those in the top seat at the White House who hate coloured people', over 'murmurs

---

39 This was kindly sent by Paul Lee, email 4 January 2007, referencing [Neil Rackham], 'Rackham Rites', *Darts*, 10 Dec.1964, p. 2; 'Today's Diary'.

of anger' Malcolm replied that it was 'better not to speak about the dead'. He stated that,

> I believe in the brotherhood of the human race and don't care to know anybody who is not prepared to be my brother...Education rather than legislation will solve the problem...I am in favour of using any means necessary to obtain fundamental rights.[40]

The caption on the front page photograph in the *Sheffield Telegraph* (4 December) was 'Malcolm X hissed by seven hundred'. Immediately activists on campus collected two hundred and twenty five signatures for a petition sent to the paper, stating that the report 'grossly misrepresented' what had taken place. The Student Union Secretary also sent a protest, 'expressing his dismay at the violent distortion in the report, which he felt was especially ironic in view of Malcolm X's opening remarks. in which he had stressed the danger of an irresponsible press'.[41] *Darts* also carried an article attacking the press for not reporting 'the applause, the obvious pleasure and interest expressed by Union officers and students, and very little about the arguments put forward by Malcolm X...The elegance of his argument, the contemptuous rhetoric which no Sheffield student dared to challenge, made him persuasive and interesting. He deserved a fair press – and he didn't get it.' (p.2) The Editorial also attacked the local press for misreporting by pointing out that only about 50 hissed – and that was when Malcolm 'declined to answer the question about Kennedy'.[42] What Malcolm had said was, 'They say you shouldn't speak of the dead', not what the paper had reported.

The last page of the paper carried a cartoon of two Santa Clauses. The Black one says to the White: 'You may object, pops, but I intend to deliver this load by any means necessary'. There is also a long report on Malcolm:

> Over 700 people crammed into Graves Hall for a meeting of the Islamic Circle, expecting to hear a defence of black racialism in America...Malcolm X now Chairman of the Organisation for Afro-American Unity surprised a crowd of potential hecklers into an attentive and appreciative audience by his stylish speaking... [After outlining the history of the 'Muslim movement' in the USA, he said] 'The Afro-American Negroes have a problem which goes far beyond religion. When you take away a man's freedom, you take away his life. They have castrated us morally, economically and spiritually. We were made to hate ourselves – be ashamed of

---

40 *The Star* (Sheffield), 4/12/1964, p.13.
41 *Darts*, 10/12/1964, p.1.
42 This refers to the recent murder of US President Kennedy.

ourselves, the pigment of our skin, the shape of our nose and lips and the texture of our hair.' With the emergence of the African Negro as a new political force in the world, the Afro-American was stimulated...to demand that his fellow Americans accord him equal respect...The lot of the Afro-American has improved in the past twenty years, but only when the need for manpower was such that his white fellow citizens were forced to make better jobs open to him, but 'there was no change of heart...We are not fighting for civil rights, we are fighting for human rights. To get it I would use any means necessary, any time'...His handling of questions was nothing short of masterful, and only once did he misjudge his audience reaction when he evaded a question on President Kennedy...No other questions challenged his coruscating and laconic wit...when pressed he elaborated on the term 'by any means necessary' saying, 'I didn't spell out terrorism – but I didn't rule it out...If a man is not willing to die for his freedom, he does not deserve to be free.'[43]

London 5-6 December

Malcolm left on the midnight train for London, accompanied by Ebrahimsa Mohamed. The pace of activities did not diminish. Despite having had very little sleep, Malcolm was taken to lunch at London's Islamic Cultural Centre with members of the Islamic Circle and in the evening he gave a talk to about three hundred students crowded into the Hall of the Malaysian Islamic Study Group at Bryanston Square, as arranged by Mr. Mohamed. Undoubtedly exhausted, but perhaps also elated, Malcolm left on the 11:15am flight for New York on 6 December.

Dr. Martin Luther King was also in London on those days, and addressed a crowded congregation at St. Paul's Cathedral. Malcolm had addressed some 300 Muslim students. *The Guardian* (7 December, 1964) reported him as noting Dr. King's presence: 'I'll say nothing against him. At one time the whites in the United States called him a racialist, an extremist, and a Communist. Then the Black Muslims came along and the whites thanked the Lord for Martin Luther King'. The paper then describes 'Mr. X' as 'relaxed, mellifluous and reasonable. He has the assurance of Dr. Billy Graham and the details are swamped by the powerful generalities of his message. And no one should doubt the power. Since breaking with his old leader Elijah Muhammad a year ago, Mr. X

---

43 In its issue of 21/1/1965, *Darts* carried an article on 'the plight of the American Negro', contrasting their situation with that of 'Britain's coloured immigrants [who] pose no real threat to the social stability of the country.... Their alleged sins are committed unwittingly...'

has talked for and more like an African Nationalist and has moved more formally towards Islam.'

Malcolm Under Surveillance

The level of surveillance over Malcolm while he was in Britain is quite astonishing and gives a glimpse of the fears of the FBI and the State Department. For example, just for this one brief trip, the FBI sent Malcolm's flight details to 'Legat, London' on 27 November. There is then an inked out paragraph, followed by, 'it is desired that you attempt to determine the nature and purpose of subject's trip to London'. Three days later, in another Cablegram, the FBI tells the Embassy to expect Malcolm for the Oxford University debate and says, 'it is desired you arrange for coverage of this debate'. On the 30th of November Hoover, the FBI Director, sent flight details by 'coded teletype' and the request to 'follow subject's travel and activities closely and keep Bureau advised', to ten agencies.[44]

Curiously, I could find no reports on Malcolm's visit in the FBI files. But there are a number of withheld memoranda as well as ones completely inked out. Some years ago, while researching material for another book at the US National Archives, I had a long conversation with an Archivist about surveillance materials which might emanate from British agents/agencies. If I understood him correctly, there is a mutual understanding between the agencies across the Atlantic that if one withholds reports so will the other. And in Britain much is withheld – including all surveillance reports on Malcolm X.

On his arrival at JFK airport in New York, he was met by two people whose licence plates had been issued to the 'governments of Tanganyika and Kenya', according to the FBI report.[45]

---

44 FBI Malcolm X Little, BUFILE 1000-399321, Malcolm X Little, Part 13a, FBI to 'Legat' London, 27/11/1964; FBI to 'Legat' London, 30/11/1964, copied to the Foreign Liaison Unit; J Edgar Hoover to Director, Bureau of Intelligence & Research, Dept. of State; CIA; Assistant Attorney General; London; Foreign Liaison Unit; Chief US Secret Service; Assistant Chief of Staff, Intelligence Dept., Army; Director Naval Intelligence; Office of Special Investigations, Air Force; Chief, Counterintelligence Division, 30/11/1964.

45 FBI file #100-399312, part 13a, memo 8/12/1964.

CHAPTER 10

USA
December 1964 – February 1965

Just over a week after his return, despite his inevitable tiredness, the needs of his family, and of the fledgling OAAU, Malcolm addressed the Harvard Law School Forum.[1] There he noted that the

> attitude of African statesmen towards the USA had acquired a 'new tone and a new tempo' in the ongoing debate at the UN and elsewhere on the Congo...When the colonial powers saw they couldn't remain in Africa, they behaved as somebody playing basketball...The colonial powers were boxed in on the African continent. They didn't intend to give up the ball. They just passed it to one that was in the clear, and the one that was in the clear was the US. The ball was passed to her, and she picked it up and has been running like mad ever since. Her presence on the African continent has replaced the imperialism and colonialism of the European. But it is still imperialism and colonialism.[2]

At yet another university meeting, this time Barnard College in New York and reported in the *Columbia Daily Spectator* (19/2/1965, p.3) Malcolm again spoke of what today we call 'globalisation':

> We are seeing today a global rebellion of the oppressed against the oppressor, the exploited against the exploiter...The Negro revolution

---

1 There are separate FBI Papers on the OAAU, available on microfilm These reveal that the FBI was routing information on the OAAU to the New York Police Department, the Department of Justice, the Secret Service, the State Department and the Army, Navy and Air Force.

2 Archie Epps (ed), *The Speeches of Malcolm X at Harvard*, New York: William Morrow 1968, pp.161-182. He spoke at the Law School on 16 December 1964.

is not a racial revolt...[Western industrial nations] deliberately subjugate the Negro for economic reasons. These international criminals raped the African continent to feed their factories and are themselves responsible for the low standards of living prevalent throughout Africa.

In complete contrast, but including this analysis of America's interest in Africa, on 12 December at HARYOU, a self-help organisation for the youth of Harlem, Malcolm addressed 300 at a seminar for the young 'men and women training for the Harlem Domestic Peace Corps'.[3] Malcolm repeated his charges against the press, 'which can make the victim seem like the criminal and the criminal seem like the victim'. The example he used of these distortions was the reporting of the situation in the Congo, which, *inter alia*, pictured those killed by the Africans, but not the Africans slaughtered by the White hired mercenaries. That the US was protecting its business interests in Africa, was never revealed by the media, he emphasised.[4] He was prepared to work 'with other civil rights groups to obtain better housing and quality education for Negroes'. But, he asked, 'how are you going to fight a violent man non-violently? Africans', he assured his young audience, were 'deeply interested in the rights movement' in the USA, and 'Negroes should try to strengthen the bonds between themselves and African nations.'[5] Asked about going back to Africa, Malcolm said Africa would welcome those who could make a contribution. But what was important was reaching out and 'developing mutual understanding, mutual effort towards a mutual objective'. When asked about 'Red China' (then seen as 'evil' by the USA), Malcolm replied that, 'it is good to have centres of power on this earth that aren't controlled from either Paris, London or Washington DC'.[6]

The following day at an OAAU meeting at the Audobon Ballroom, attended by about 500 people, Malcolm spoke, reportedly mainly about the situation in the Congo. Abdulrahman Babu, whom Malcolm had first met in Cairo, spoke after Malcolm, emphasising that all 'black people were united in opposition to Tshombe in the Congo'. The next speaker

---

3 On Haryou, see Harlem Youth Opportunities Unlimited, *Youth in the Ghetto*, New York: Haryou 1964.

4 OAAU's *Blacklash*, 22/12/1964, p.4. The US had at least one known CIA agent in the Congo from 1961: James T. Harris who was working for the CIA-funded American Society for African Culture. 'The CIA as an Equal Opportunity Employer', *Ramparts* 7/13, 1969, pp.24-33. See also Larry Devlin, *Chief of Station, Congo*, New York: Public Affairs, 2007.

5 *NY Herald*, 13/12/1964, in the Allan Morrison research file, Schomburg Center: Sc Micro R3537.

6 Breitman (1966), pp.21, 215.

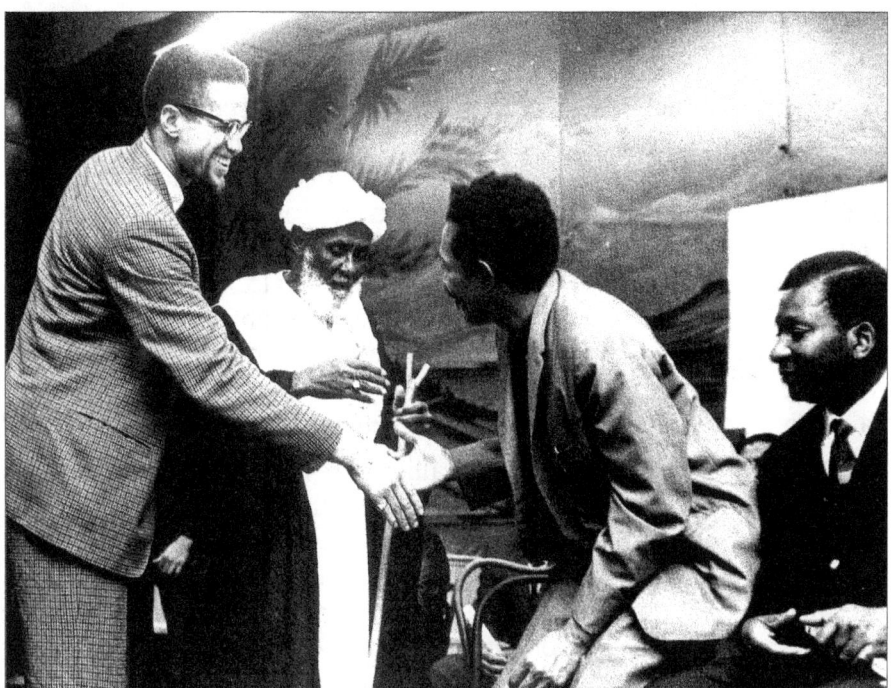

Harlem, Audubon Ballroom, December 13, 1964. Malcolm greets guest speakers at an OAAU meeting, Sudanese Sheik Ahmed Hassoun from Mecca (in Tuban) and Abu Mohammed Babu, radical government minister from tanzania, whom Malcolm met in Tanzania

was 'Shaykh Ahmed Hassoun of Sudan who spoke briefly about the Islamic religion'.[7]

That Malcolm was putting his words about working with other groups into practice is demonstrated by an announcement the N.Y. Amsterdam News (19 December 1964, p.63) that 'a group of the city's more militant civil rights officials, including Jesse Gray, Malcolm X, Milton Galamison and William Strickland of the Northern Students' Co-ordinating Committee, will lead discussion at an all-day conference, "Black Revolution – a struggle for political power", on 19 December at Mt. Morris Presbyterian Church'.[8] The National Guardian reported this meeting in its 26 December issue (p.4). The delegates had discussed that 'political power can be built by the people for liberation from white-dominated political control and economic exploitation'; unity was stressed. Malcolm urged that leaders should 'take into consideration the basic needs and desires of the people. Lumumba articulated the needs of the people, above the consideration of the tribe'. The resolution he proposed on the Congo was 'unanimously adopted' and

---

7 FBI Papers, reel 9, FBI New York memorandum, 15/12/1964.

8 Milton Galamison, who had studied at Lincoln University at the same time as Kwame Nkrumah, was active against segregation in education and housing in Brooklyn; Jesse Gray had led rent strikes in Harlem. I could find no other report of this meeting.

a protest demonstration was planned. Malcolm was among the six elected to the Interim Committee.

The *Amsterdam News* (19 December 1964, p.53) stated that Malcolm would be at the rally to support the Mississippi Freedom Democratic Party to be held on 20 December. Among the committee were Milton Galamison and Malcolm X. Also in December, Malcolm was a co-sponsor with the Harlem Progressive Labor Club of a rally whose aim I have not been able to discover. Babu (see below) was a speaker. Malcolm introduced him as 'Africa's leading revolutionary', who would be able to tell 'us what a revolution really is: a revolution, not a wading-in, sitting-in, or singing-in. We have to know what it costs. Many of us, if we knew, would have to say we're not ready to pay the price. But here is a brother who can tell us.'[9]

After Malcolm's return, OAAU rallies were held weekly, but there was no set format, except that Malcolm spoke at them all. There were guest speakers at some, as indicated below. At the rally on the theme of 'Political power in the Ghetto', Malcolm noted that 'most African and Asian nations are turning away from capitalism toward some form of socialism...He explained that European economies depended on the exploitation of their African colonies, and that the United States and Europe had kept Latin America, Asia and Africa from industrialising to keep them as a source of cheap raw materials and a market for finished products.'[10]

Che Guevara, due to speak at the December 14 OAAU meeting, for reasons unknown cancelled his appearance. Guevara was in New York to speak at the General Assembly of the United Nations in the debate on the Congo. Carlos Moore claims that Che had a long discussion with Malcolm, and that it was decided to hold a meeting regarding the events in Congo, which Guevara would discuss.[11] Had Guevara kept the appointment, would he have repeated at least some of what he had said at the United Nations on 11 December? Is it possible that, given how at least some of their interests were mutual, Che had discussed his forthcoming speech with Malcolm?

> Imperialism, particularly US imperialism, has tried to make the world believe that peaceful co-existence is the exclusive right of the great powers...The time will come when this Assembly will acquire greater maturity and demand guarantees from the United States government for the lives of the Negro and Latin American

---

9 *National Guardian*, 9/1/1965, p.12.

10 *The Militant*, 20/12/1964.

11 Moore hypothesises that Castro might have feared an assassination attempt on Guevara and ordered him not to expose himself on an open platform. (Carlos Moore, *Castro, the Blacks and Africa*, Los Angeles: UCLA 1988, p.189)

population residing in this country. How can they presume to be the 'guardians of liberty' when they kill their own children and discriminate daily against people because of the colour of their skin, when they not only free the murderers of colored people, but even protect them, while punishing the Negro populations because they demand their legitimate rights as free men? We understand that today the Assembly is not in a position to ask for explanations of these acts, but it must be clearly established that the United States is not the gendarme of freedom but rather the perpetrator of exploitation and oppression of the peoples of the world and of a large part of its own population.[12]

African representatives were determined not to let the UN drop the Congo issues. Tewfik Boutorra, whom Malcolm knew, was reported in the *New York Times* on 23 December as being the 'Algerian...leader of the effort to get the Security Council to take up charges that the United States – Belgian action in Stanleyville constituted aggression..."When the twenty assassins of the black Americans in the Mississippi have been freed", the Algerian declared, "we are within our rights to ask where racism is and who shows it?"' Thus Malcolm had succeeded in his attempts to have the position of African-Americans linked to world events at the UN.

When other African countries also condemned the US, both regarding the Congo and the treatment of African Americans, according to M.S. Handler in the *New York Times*, '[t]he African move profoundly disturbed the American authorities, who gave the impression that they had been caught off guard'.[13]

At the OAAU meeting Malcolm introduced a message of solidarity from Che with the words 'a good friend of mine'. The message ended with the words 'united we will win'. This received 'a big cheer from the audience'.[14] Guevara's place was taken Abdulrahman Babu, already known to OAAU audiences. Babu, then Tanzania's delegate to the United Nations, had probably just arrived from Havana, where he been invited to join the celebrations of the 11th anniversary of the Revolution.[15] Babu

---

12 Jay Mallin (ed), *Che Guevara on Revolution*, Coral Gables: University of Miami Press 1969, pp.112-126.
13 Quoted in Norden (1967), p11.
14 OAAU *Blacklash*, 22/11/1964; *The Militant*, 21/12/1964, p.1; FBI Papers, Reel 9, Report from New York 15/12/1965.
15 *Sunday Citizen & Reynolds News*, 29/11/1964, p.16. The paper also notes that Babu had worked as a Post Office clerk in London's Notting Hill district, which by the 1960s housed a large population of West Indian origins, as well as the fascist National Party. *National Guardian*, 9/1/1965, p.12.

stressed the need for unity and discipline, the message that Malcolm had spread throughout Africa. Equally important was leadership that wasn't 'for sale'. The USA and other imperialist countries 'just don't seem to understand that African countries are determined to plan their own destinies'. Malcolm, in his introduction, again castigated the press: 'whenever they can't control someone they call him irresponsible or subversive'. Both men spoke of the Congo and the atrocities committed there, perhaps especially by Cuban anti-Castro mercenaries.[16]

The films Malcolm had taken during his trips to Africa were shown at OAAU rallies on January 3 and 10. Malcolm gave a running commentary. The first screening was introduced by Okello Odongo, the Assistant Minister of Finance in Kenya. According to the report in *The Militant* (11/1/1965, p.8) in Kenya Malcolm had been 'given time on the government radio station and had many top level meetings with government officials. The US embassy protested against such honors being given to Malcolm X, a person not held in high esteem by US spokesmen. The protest was rejected by the Kenya government.'

If his new analysis of US interests and machinations, and of the international systems of exploitation, and his contacts with African leaders and with Che Guevara were not enough to lead to the hatching of plots on his life, Malcolm gave the government another reason. This was his association with the Socialist Workers Party (SWP) and his movement towards a more explicit socialist philosophy. According to Nelson Blackstock, 'when Malcolm announced his break with the Nation of Islam, the SWP looked forward to working with him...Malcolm soon accepted an invitation to speak at a Militant Forum, sponsored by *The Militant* newspaper...DeBerry spoke at a couple of classes at the Muslim Mosque Inc., and Malcolm continued at OAAU rallies to urge the audience to buy *The Militant*.'[17]

---

16 Carlos Moore claims that Malcolm and Guevara discussed this use by the USA of White Cuban mercenaries in the Congo. He goes on to state that by February 1965 the OAAU had 'recruited about one hundred militant black Americans for direct participation in the African revolution', and that Che had intended to incorporate these in the Cuban-recruited 'internationalist brigade'. Malcolm's assassination prevented this taking place, but Cuba did send a brigade to Zaire. (Moore (1988), p.205)

17 Nelson Blackstock, *Cointelpro*, New York: Vintage Books 1976, pp. 111-112, 75; Breitman (1968), p.37. The latter is a good source on the OAAU and Malcolm's relations with the SWP/Militant. Clifton DeBerry, a Black man, was the SWP's nominee in the presidential elections in 1964. *The Militant* was the SWP's newspaper and carried reports and interviews with Malcolm. The 'Negro' policies of the SWP evolved from discussions in Mexico between Leon Trotsky and a number of SWP activists headed by C.L.R. James in 1939. These revolutionary decisions and discussions can be found in George Breitman (ed), *Leon Trotsky, on Black Nationalism & Self-Determination* (1967), New York: Pathfinder Press 1978. See also Quincy Lehr, 'Black Liberation and Revolutionary Socialism: American Trotskyism and the Black Question 1928-1963', essay prepared for Professor Winston James, Columbia

Malcolm told Jan Carew that,

> The only Marxist group in America (sic) that offered me a platform was the Socialist Workers party. I respect them and they respect me...that is, with the exception of the Cuban Communists. If a mixture of nationalism and Marxism makes the Cubans fight the way they do and makes the Vietnamese stand up so resolutely to the might of America and its European and other lapdogs, then there must be something to it.[18]

In January Malcolm admitted in an interview he granted to the Young Socialist Alliance that he, 'would be hard pressed to give a specific definition of the overall philosophy which I think is necessary for the liberation of the black people in this country'. How had this come about? He explained that, during a discussion in Ghana the Algerian Ambassador, 'who was extremely militant and a revolutionary', had questioned his (Malcolm's) definition of his philosophy of black nationalism by asking 'where would this leave me?' The Ambassador, Malcolm explained, was a white man. 'He showed me where I was alienating people who were true revolutionaries dedicated to overturning the system of exploitation that exists on this earth by any means necessary...So, I had to do a lot of thinking and reappraising of my definition of black nationalism. Can we sum up the solution to the problems confronting our people as black nationalism?' Later in the interview Malcolm said he had had the opportunity to 'sample the thinking' of the African presidents and prime ministers he had met. 'I was impressed by their analysis of the problem, and many of the suggestions they gave went a long way toward broadening my own outlook', he added. Not surprisingly, given that most of these African leaders were men of the Left, Malcolm believed that, 'as the nations of the world free themselves, capitalism has less victims, and it becomes weaker and weaker. It's only a matter of time in my opinion before it collapses completely...It is impossible for capitalism to survive: it has become cowardly, like the vulture and it can only suck the blood of the helpless.'[19]

On January 7 Malcolm addressed the 600 people gathered at the Militant Labor Forum in New York; it was the third time he had spoken at the Forum. In his speech, entitled 'Power in Defense of Freedom is Greater than Power in Behalf of Tyranny', he explained that he had set up the OAAU

University, May 2001.

18 Carew (1994), p.36.

19 The interview, printed in the *Young Socialist* March-April 1965 is reprinted in Breitman (1970), pp.157-166. On the reaction, see Harold Cruse, *The Crisis of the Negro Intellectual*, New York: William Morrow & Co., 1967, p.409.

taking the Organization of African Unity as a model...[Our] African brothers were winning freedom faster...getting recognition and respect and their independence faster than we are so we looked to them for a model of how to conduct the struggle in America...In 1964 oppressed people all over the world made some progress...All these people realised that power is the magic word: power recognizes only power...By the time I returned last month, the Muslim Mosque Inc. had received official recognition and support by all of the official religious bodies in the Muslem world[20] and the Organization of Afro-American Unity had also received official recognition and support from all of the African countries I visited and from most of those I didn't visit...But, in the USA, for Afro-Americans, 1964 was a year of delusions and illusions. The Civil Rights Act was only a safety valve – designed to lessen the explosion, but not to solve the problems of black people.'[21]

Malcolm's dilemmas as a revolutionary and now left-leaning Black leader and thinker is revealed in a conversation he had with Harry Ring on 25 January before taping an interview for station WBAI. In a letter to George Breitman, Harry Ring, recalled that,

Malcolm expressed his views on some of the problems facing a leader of a mass movement – how to raise the consciousness and understanding of the followers without presenting ideas that seemed so far in advance that they would not be acceptable to many in the movement and how to avoid being labelled in such a way as to become isolated from the ranks.

Malcolm felt it necessary for his people to consider socialist solutions to their problems. But as the leader of a movement it was necessary to present such a concept in a way that would be understandable to his people and would not isolate him from them. It is easy, he commented, for people who are isolated and who have more of the responsibilities of leadership to stand on the sidelines and make militant-sounding declarations. Most often such people simply repeated dogma and were not seriously trying to advance the struggle.[22]

In the actual interview with Ring, broadcast on WBAI on 28 January, when Ring asked whether Malcolm was responsible for Africans seeing a

---

20 Sheikh Hassan was sent by Saudi Arabia to help the Mosque follow the true path of Islam.
21 *The Militant*, 18/1/1965, p.2, a fuller version of the text is in the issue for 25 January.
22 NYU, Tamiment Library: Breitman Papers, Box 44, file 2: Harry to Dear George 14/4/1965.

similarity between the US's behaviour in the Congo and the treatment of Blacks in Mississippi, Malcolm's response contained these words:

> New African nations are linking the problem of racism in Mississippi with the problem of racism in the Congo and also the problem of racism in Vietnam. It is all part of a vicious racist system that the Western powers have used to degrade and exploit and oppress the people of Africa and Asia and Latin America...[T]he oppressed people make up a majority [in the world and] as a majority [we] can demand not beg.
> Ring: How is Vietnam related?
> Malcolm: Vietnam is a problem of oppressed and oppressor...Our action will be one of unity of the oppressed.

This referred to the momentous linkage which had been made at the United Nations; 'on December 10...African ambassadors repeatedly compared racism in South Africa to racism in North America, just as Malcolm X had requested...The first to make the link was...Guinea's Foreign Minister' who questioned whether thousands of Congolese citizens had been murdered 'because [they] had dark skins just like the colored United States citizens murdered in Mississippi?' He was followed by Mali's Foreign Minister. Twelve days later the *New York Times* reported that 'Charges of colonialism, neo-colonialism and imperialism are being levelled at the United States in the 24-member United Nations Special Committee on Imperialism'.[23] Malcolm's lobbying was reaping dividends as further evidenced by M.S. Handler's article in the *New York Times* (2/1/1965, p.6), which stated that Malcolm X had 'prepared the political groundwork in the capitals of Africa for the recent concentrated attack on American racism in the debate on the Congo at the United Nations'.

But forces of destruction were at work. John Henrik Clarke, in a letter dated 6 January 1965, warned Julian Mayfield in Ghana that,

> Earl Grant...one of the people closest to Malcolm X had some information that you need to know. Quite a lot has been done to break up the OAAU. The organization is now in shambles. There is much more to this than I have time to tell you. Some pressures from the highest level in Washington and elsewhere were brought to bear in the destruction of what could have been the greatest force to emerge among the black people in this century.[24]

Did Earl Grant discuss this 'information' with Malcolm? Was Malcolm aware of these forces? Did Malcolm perhaps accept new invitations to visit

23 Evanzz, (1992), pp.267, 271.
24 Schomburg Center: SCM 94-21 John Henrik Clarke Papers, Clarke to Mayfield, 6/1/1965.

Europe partly to get away from these immediate pressures? Did he need more time to think and to garner support? Whatever the reality, he once again set off for England and France.

CHAPTER 11

Britain and Paris
February 1965

London, 6 – 8 February: The Committee of African Organisations

Malcolm arrived in London at the beginning of February and checked into the Mount Royal Hotel.[1] He had come at the invitation of the Committee of African Organisations (CAO), who had invited him to address their first Congress. The Committee had been set up in about 1960 to bring together British-based African organisations involved in common struggles. Its headquarters was at Africa Unity House, partly funded by Ghana.[2] The theme of the Congress was 'Charting the path of African Revolution means attacking imperialism, neo-colonialism in all its forms. Oppressed mankind, organise to achieve unity'. The other speakers were Ambassador Khalifa from Algeria, Raymond Kunene, the representative of the ANC from South Africa, and Basil Davidson, the superb historian of Africa. Malcolm was, yet again, in the company of political activists from Africa.

---

1 Schomburg Center: Malcolm X Papers, Reel 1, folder 5: Mt Royal Hotel, Marble Arch 6-9 Feb.
2 See Marika Sherwood, *Claudia Jones: a life in exile*, London: Lawrence & Wishart 1999, p.117, n.29. The UK was an important centre, Mr Amoo-Gottfried told me, because of the many African and West Indian students there, as well as many exiles, such as the ANC of South Africa.

The invitation had been issued by Kojo Amoo-Gottfried, a Ghanaian who had met Malcolm twice during visits to the United States. From his letter to Malcolm, dated 22 December 1964, we learn that Malcolm had called at the CAO office on his previous visit to London, and Amoo-Gottfried, the president, had invited him to dinner.[3] In between visits, Mr. Amoo-Gottfried told me, he had kept in touch by telephone, mainly with Betty Shabazz. In his letter the president expressed their 'glad[ness] about our discussion – though short due to lack of time. Invitation to address conference will be sent soon'. The invitation asked Malcolm to speak 'at our closing rally in solidarity with our Southern African and Afro-American struggle for freedom...'[4] Mr. Amoo-Gottfried told me he found Malcolm, *inter alia*, to be a 'very honest man. There aren't many to whom you'd trust your life'.

Malcolm wrote to Kojo on 30 December 1964 assuring him that he would, 'do anything in my power to cooperate in whatever you can arrange there that is for the good of our people. Please give my very best regards to all of our brothers and sisters.'[5] In his letter of acceptance, dated 21 January 1965, Malcolm had to ask the CAO for a 'roundtrip ticket and hotel expenses', as 'the tremendous amount of travelling I did...during 1964, mostly at my own personal expense', had exhausted his funds. The CAO duly booked him into London's Mount Royal Hotel.

Malcolm attended the Congress from 6 February, and addressed it on February 8; he thus had ample opportunity to mix with the Africans and West Indians attending.[6] He was 'a good listener and very receptive...At the conference he was very positive', Mr. Amoo-Gottfried told me. 'He attended all the sessions and spent a lot of time with us. His re-thinking was very intense...He was now dealing with imperialism and was very concerned about Algeria...He was always getting people to interact, getting them linked up...You had to collaborate so you could see who were the bad guys and who the good, Malcolm said...Had he lived, his movement would have been terrific.'

---

3 Interviews with Mr Kojo Amoo-Gottfried, a retired Ambassador, East Legon, Ghana 7 and 12 February 2003. I must thank my colleague Dr Hakim Adi, for giving me Mr Amoo-Gottfried's address. During our interviews Mr Amoo-Gottfried repeated a number of times that he had been 'very concerned about Malcolm's safety.'

4 Schomburg Centre: Malcolm X Papers, Reel 3, folder 15, letters from Kojo Amoo-Gottfried, 22/12/1964 and 17/1/1965. In his letter Amoo-Gottfried I noted that 'David Du Bois came to see me on his way back to Cairo'; clearly international linkages were strong.

5 I have here to express my grateful thanks to Mr Kojo Amoo-Gottfried for copies of his correspondence with Malcolm. Unfortunately some letters have been destroyed by flooding.

6 See Malcolm X (1992). p.38.

The weekly *West Africa* (20/2/1965, p.218) reported, 'the francophone FEANF, based in Paris sent delegates from Guinea, Mali and Congo, Brazzaville. There was also an observer from the World Assembly of Youth and from the Students' Union of Poland'.[7] Other delegates represented Liberia and Ghana.

According to *West Africa* the conference began with a seminar on 'Educational publishing in Africa and its role in the African Revolution'. This was followed by Mr. Khalifa speaking on Revolutionary Africa. He argued that 'imperialism, colonialism and neo-colonialism in Africa must now be halted either by peaceful means, or violence, according to the circumstances'. Mr. Kunene, speaking on behalf of the Liberation movements stationed in Britain, said the 'revolution in Africa would depend on how speedily "we remove the occupation forces of white minority governments in Southern Africa".' Basil Davidson, the historian, urged a union of African states, as 'only union will deal with the neo-colonialists effectively'.[8]

Malcolm had certainly found himself in well-informed and highly political company. He rose to this challenge in a far-ranging speech. He recorded that he had been asked to 'describe to them the rate of progress being made by Black Americans in our struggle for human rights, and the stage or type of race relations that exists between the Black and White Americans, and whether or not progress has been made in race relations'.

West Africa reported that Malcolm 'urged African journalists to project objectively the African image to counteract the imperialist press distortion of facts about Africa..."The imperialist press...through skilful manoeuvring are able to keep the Africans on the continent apart from their brothers in America and elsewhere"...It was about time the African press stopped following blindly what the western press write...'

The *Ghanaian Times* (10/2/1965, pp.1, 5, back page) reported Malcolm saying that 'failure to establish a Continental Union Government would be disastrous. History will record them as having failed both the Africans on the continent and the people of African descent abroad in the most crucial moments of their history...Leaders who do not co-operate will be doing a greater service to the imperialists than Moise Tshombe...'

There is a long report of Malcolm's speech in the February issue of *West Indian Gazette & Afro-Asian/Caribbean News*, published and edited

---

7 Unless stated otherwise, the report of the conference is taken from *West Africa* 21/1/1965, p.106 and 20/2/1965, p.218.

8 Sadly, Basil Davidson, this most remarkable historian of Africa and man of the Left at age 90 was, I was advised, too frail to respond to eager historians, as he had so readily done in the past. The quotation is from *Ghanaian Times* 10/2/1965, p.2.

by Trinidad-born activist Claudia Jones, who was probably one of the instigators of the formation of the CAO. Claudia, a communist, had died of a massive heart-attack about five weeks before Malcolm's arrival. Had she lived, undoubtedly Malcolm would have been taken to the *Gazette* office, which had become an almost compulsory stop for all visiting Black activists and dignitaries. The paper described Malcolm as the 'militant leader of the Negro Liberation movement of the United States' and noted that he had given the closing address. Malcolm argued that European imperialism was dependent on American imperialism. He was happy that Africans were realising that 'the monster' operating in the Congo was the same as that oppressing US Negroes. He spoke of US activities in the Congo and against Cuba. He outlined the progress being made by the civil rights movement, the obstacles it faced and situations it was attempting to correct. Malcolm attacked the media, which 'spreads distortions' and was used by 'the oppressors to create a negative image of people of the African race...[for example] it presented an image of the people of Kenya as being barbarians'. This 'science of imagery' was the 'strongest weapon of imperialism...[It] makes the African freedom fighter appear like a criminal.' He explained the reasons for his break with the Black Muslim Movement in 1964 as being due to 'quite a few people amongst them [having become] conservative. Some had economic stakes. They didn't want to rock the boat.' He had formed the Organization of Afro-American Unity, in order to 'put the struggle on a wider basis, on an international basis...We can point at the unity and the common interest of the people against the common enemy'. No, he was not a racialist. 'Muslims don't believe in judging any man by the colour of his skin...We don't condemn him because he's white but for *what he does*.'[9]

Resolutions, formulated by the 'three commissions on the political, economic and social and cultural revolution in Africa', were adopted in the closing session. These supported the Congolese people and denounced those supporting the Tshombe government, and warned the UK's Labour government to go 'further towards "one man, one vote" in its policies' towards Rhodesia/Zimbabwe.

Was it at this Congress that Malcolm might have met Basil Robinson and William Lutterodt, of the Pan-African World Pioneers? He received a circular from them, dated 7 February, in which the Pioneers wished to 'extend our friendship in this great struggle to free Africans from the evils of Colonialism and Imperialism'.[10]

---

9 *West Indian Gazette*, February 1965, p.4; Breitman (1966), p.188; *Peace News*, 12/2/1965 (copy amongst Metropolitan Police papers).

10 Schomburg Center: Malcolm X Papers, reel 3, Folder 15. I could find no information on

Paris, 9 February 1965

The following day, 9 February, Malcolm flew to Paris where he was scheduled to address a meeting sponsored by the Federation of African Students in France, and the Afro-American community. There is a telegram among his papers dated 23 December 1964 from the 'Afroam Center': 'Happy you'll be here next month'.[11] However, on landing in Paris he was detained by the French authorities and put on the next plane back to London. Chester Himes reported that, 'along with Carlos Moore, a number of disciples met him at the gate and he instructed Carlos to carry on the lecture as he would have done had he been there.'[12]

The American Embassy in Paris reported that Malcolm was due to speak on the 'Afro-American Struggle for Freedom'. 'He was en route from London to Geneva to visit the Islamic Center there.[13] The French Minister of Interior barred his entry because it felt his presence here may cause demonstrations and other trouble...No American believed involved. French police making further enquiry. London and Bern advised.' The Embassy duly reported Malcolm's immediate return to London to the London Embassy. But why would the Paris police have decided to investigate? Is it possible that this was the influence of the US Ambassador? A much deleted memorandum to the FBI Director ends with 'attached is classified 'Confidential' in order to protect (crossed out) thus having an adverse effect on the national defense interest.'[14]

The US Embassy in Paris was less well informed than the *New York Herald Tribune*, (European Edition,10/2/1965, p.3), which reported on Malcolm's non-admission and noted that the invitation had come from both the African students and the

> Committee of Members of the Afro-American Community... recently organised, [which] represents about 20 Afro-Americans... among the estimated 2,000 Negroes from North and South America

---

    this organisation or its officials. Lutterodt must have been from the old Ghanaian family, associated with the colonial governments if not the trade in enslaved Africans, which had sent its children to be educated in England for centuries.

11 Schomburg Center: Malcolm X Papers, reel 3, Folder 16.

12 Himes (1976), p.292, for all quotations.

13 As noted previously, Malcolm had visited the Center in 1964. I can find no indication that Malcolm intended to go to Geneva; he would not have had time to do so.

14 FBI: Malcolm X Little Papers, Part 15: Memoranda dated 9/2/1975 with 'decoded copy of 'Airgram' from 'Legat' Paris #68; 'Legat' Paris to Director FBI 10/2/1965; SAC New York to FBI Director 11/2/1965. (Paul Lee believes that 'legat' stands for 'Legal attorney'; but it could just as easily stand for 'legation', ie consulate or other sections of an embassy.)

in Paris. Most of the community are American Negroes...Despite the proscription of Malcolm X, the Prefecture of Police maintained its authorisation for the meeting, so the sponsors decided to go ahead later tonight with a quickly organized 'protest' session. About 200 persons attended...The speakers denounced the ban on Malcolm X, white mercenary intervention in the Congo and American raids on North Vietnam, all interpreted as attacks on non-white peoples.

The paper also noted that Malcolm had spoken in Paris the previous November, and there had been no riots.

Interviewed on his return to London, the *Lagos Morning Post* (13/2/1965, p.11) in an article headed 'Malcolm X Raps France', reported that Malcolm said that the 'decision to exclude him [was] part of an international conspiracy to prevent the black men in the West from identifying with his brother in Africa...All coloured people in the world had to identify with Africa...They had to stop thinking of themselves as British, French or American, they had to think black and be independent.' At the Paris airport he had not been allowed to telephone the US Embassy, and had gotten the 'impression that it was the embassy that had asked them not to let me in'.[15] *The Times* (10/2/1965, p.11) reported that he had been barred from France as the authorities thought his presence may 'disturb public order...[I]t seems that it is because of what is held here to be the violence of his comments that his presence has been considered undesirable..."The authorities would not even let me contact the American Embassy", Malcolm said. "I was shocked. I thought I was in South Africa."'

On the same day the *New York Times* (p.3) reported that Malcolm had been refused entry by the order of the government, as it was felt that his presence would be 'undesirable'. He now planned to spend the rest of the week in London.

A very different explanation for the French authorities' behaviour is offered by Eric Norden in *The Realist,* where he claims that a 'highly-placed North African diplomat' told him that his country's intelligence department had been quietly informed by the French that the CIA planned Malcolm's murder and 'France feared he might be liquidated on its soil'.[16] This explanation is echoed by Chester Himes: 'French intelligence got a rumour that the CIA was supposed to kill him and stopped him at the airport and would not let him enter France'.

---

15 Malcolm's telephone interview regarding this is in Malcolm X (1992), p.34-41; the quote is from p. 35.

16 Breitman (1970), pp.167-168; Norden (1967), p.12.

Back in London, Malcolm spoke by telephone with a Paris supporter. In this wide-ranging interview, reprinted in *By Any Means Necessary* (pp.167-175), he reiterated that 'the Afro-American community in France and in other parts of Europe *must unite with the African community*...This unity will give our struggle a type of strength of spirit that will enable us to make some real concrete progress, whether we be in Europe, America or on the African continent.' He would have addressed this issue had he been allowed to land, and would have advocated 'a regionalist approach'. Most interestingly, he analysed the newly formed European Common Market as a regionalist approach: it 'looks out for the common interests of Europeans and the European economy' and could almost be taken as a model for Africans and those in the African diaspora.

The Black-owned British paper, *Magnet*, reported the Paris débacle in its 'Letter from Paris' column. The meeting Malcolm had been due to address was held without him, partly to protest against the French government's action, and also to hear the message Malcolm succeeded in sending by telephone. This, according to the paper, emphasised that 'he was not a racist and had never preached the ascendancy of one race over another by force or by any other means'. The main speaker, Carlos Moore, denounced the action of the authorities. The 'Letter' concluded that 'in spite of the banning, Malcolm X did leave his mark in Paris. He may have served to tighten the bonds between Afro-Americans and Africans just as tightly as if he had been allowed to enter.' Chester Himes wrote that 'Carlos opened the hall of La Salle Mutualité and when the audience was seated read Malcolm's lecture as he would have done'. Lebert Bethune, in the essay on Malcolm previously mentioned, concluded that 'the influence of Malcolm X in Europe was a profound one, primarily on the radical youth of Europe'.

The *Magnet* report concludes with a note that, 'apparently by co-incidence', the French Security Police had been interrogating a number of 'Afro-Americans who were involved in trying to get Malcolm X to speak in Paris'.[17] Chester Himes noted that the Salle de la Mutualité 'was surrounded with a dozen or more police vans with instructions to arrest everyone in attendance'.

Richard Gibson recalls that Malcolm called him from the Mount Royal Hotel on his return from the aborted trip to Paris. 'I do not know how he had obtained my phone number and address', Richard wrote to me on 11 and 12 February 2002. 'After polite questions about my first wife Sarah, whom he had met at the Hotel Theresa, he told of his surprise at the French refusal to let him enter their country...He knew of my French connections.

---

17 *Magnet*, week beginning 27 February 1965.

I told him frankly of my serious doubts about Carlos's political orientation in view of his right-wing Cuban and other connections...I have also heard that the French feared the Americans wanted to assassinate Malcolm in Paris, but I don't believe the tale has ever been corroborated. Frankly, I think the US Embassy strongly warned the French Government not to permit Malcolm to speak in France.'[18]

Reporter Alan Scholefield of *The Scotsman* (15 February 1965, p.1) talked with Malcolm on his return from France and quotes him as saying,

> I believe the only solution to the South African problem is the same solution that was used in Algeria or the one that is being used right now in Viet-Nam...Luthuli[19] is used to keep oppressed people in check and keep them from using bona fide methods to produce bona fide results...The real leaders in South Africa are Subukwe and Mandela.
> *Will your organisation help African revolutionaries?*
> Yes, we believe it is one struggle in South Africa, Angola, Mozambique and Alabama. They are all the same struggle.
> *What are your comments on the spread of racialism in Britain?*
> ...America is dictating today to almost the entire world...American racialism is like a cancer spreading all over the world and it is having its effect in Britain...I think today that many Africans are beginning to see that America and South Africa are not so very different.

On the New York radio station WINS on 18 February, Malcolm explained to a caller that he had 'dispatched a wire to Dean Rusk, the Secretary of State here today, demanding an investigation into the reason why the French government could ban an American citizen and no reaction come from the American Embassy whatsoever'.[20] The Secretary of State was spared the problem of deciding how to respond as Malcolm was murdered a few days later.

---

18 Richard Gibson and his wife had been on the editorial team of *Révolution Africaine*, the weekly organ of the Algerian FLN. One can speculate that Malcolm got the Gibsons' address from the Algerian ambassador in Ghana. At this time Gibson was living in London and working as a freelance journalist mainly for African American newspapers. On the somewhat enigmatic Gibson, see also Fabre (1993).

19 Albert Luthuli, a Zulu, elected President of the African National Congress in 1944; then spent many years in jail. There was a serious dispute among ANC leaders from the late 1950s re different approaches to be taken to achieve freedom from apartheid rule.

20 George Breitman (1966), p.188.

London, 9 - 11 February

It was on the evening of his expulsion from the Paris airport that Malcolm attended the 'grand, very British reception' at London's Commonwealth Institute to celebrate the first issue of the black-owned weekly, *Magnet*. The editor, British Guiana-born actor, journalist and writer Jan Carew, introduced Malcolm to 'friends, acquaintances, diplomats and journalists'. There is a photograph of Malcolm reading the *Magnet* at the reception. This was a fortuitous meeting as the two men, almost the same age, but with very different backgrounds and experiences, 'began to have real conversations the night of the reception and continued over the next two days until his speech at the London School of Economics...'.[21] Anyone who was anyone in the Black world in Britain attended the launch, so Malcolm must have made many new contacts. Paul Lee believes that Malcolm had met Manchanda, Claudia Jones' colleague at the *West Indian Gazette*; could it have been at this launch?[22]

David Roussel-Milner, whose mother was closely involved with Claudia Jones, recalls seeing Malcolm X that evening. He remembers that just 'seeing him was quite a memorable experience...He seemed surrounded by an aura not just of his bodyguards but of a charisma which you could almost touch and he did not even have to speak.'[23] Another person who remembers Malcolm from this visit is Dylan Dalton. Dylan had heard Malcolm speak in Brooklyn some time previously, while she was visiting relatives there. 'He started me thinking on who I was', Dylan told me. She had bought some tapes of Malcolm's speeches, 'and even sent some to St. Lucia', her birthplace. 'He was the turning point for many of us. There was no turning back after I heard him.'[24]

---

21 These conversations (and others with Malcolm's family and colleagues) resulted in the very moving memoir of Malcolm, *Ghosts in our Blood* (1994), from which this account is taken. (p.viii) But one must recognise that Carew wrote his book some thirty years after his conversations with Malcolm. See 'The Gentle Revolutionary: Essays in Honour of Jan Carew', special issue of *Race & Class* 43/3 Jan-March 2002.

22 Email from Paul Lee 28/4/2006. Claudia Jones had died a few months previously.

23 Letter from David Roussel-Milner, 10 April 2000. On Roussel-Milner, see Marika Sherwood, *Claudia Jones: a life in exile*, London: Lawrence & Wishart 1998. Malcolm had no 'bodyguards', only colleagues who tried to protect him (or be seen with him?)

24 Telephone conversation 14/2/2002.

Trinidad-born Michael de Freitas, later known as Michael X, ran into Malcolm the following day at the restaurant in Africa Unity House, where Malcolm was eating with the CAO President and some others. He invited Malcolm to visit him at his home that evening. He was 'tired and tense', de Freitas recalled, and was at first a little 'apprehensive' of de Freitas' White partner. '[Malcolm] was a man with a fantastic wealth of information and never went anywhere without his little black case which was a mobile library of statistics.'[25] Malcolm 'told us a bit about the Organisation of Afro-American Unity'; then they listened to some music, especially records of Aretha Franklin of whom Malcolm was 'particularly fond'.[26]

The London School of Economics & Political Science, 11 February

On 11 February Malcolm was due to talk to the students at the London School of Economics and Political Science, reputedly the most politicised and left-wing of London's universities. He had been invited by the School's Africa Society, whose president was Tanzanian Lloyd A. Binagi; the Secretary, according to the invitation letter from the students, was George Uwechwe.[27] This invitation was for November 24, to speak on 'The Afro-Americans in the 1960s'.[28] But Malcolm had arranged to return to the USA on that day, so the talk had had to be postponed.

Beaver, the student newspaper, in its 18 February issue described the 'packed audience' that listened to Malcolm talk on the 'relationship between

---

25 Ebrahimsa Mohamed also remembers this 'little black book'.

26 Malik (1968), p.141. This is a commissioned *Autobiography*. De Freitas became a Muslim and a charismatic leader of the Black Power movement in Britain in the mid-1960s. Also a crook, a drug dealer and a gambler, on losing his leadership position he fled to Trinidad, his birthplace, to escape arrest. There he was eventually charged with two murders, and despite international efforts to exonerate him, was hung on 16 May 1975. See Derek Humphry & David Tindall, *False Messiah: the story of Michael X*, London: Grenada Publishing 1977. Dylan Dalton, mentioned above, helped the authors of this book. According to Mr Kojo Amoo-Gottfried, what had first attracted de Freitas to Malcolm had been Malcolm's past criminal record. Another biography (James Sharp, *The Life and Death of Michael X*, Waterford: Uni Books 1981), also details de Freitas' criminal life prior to his involvement with civil rights in the UK. Sharp says that 'Malcolm X's death affected Malik a great deal and his short contact with the American seems to have given him some purpose in life'. (p.21) Sharp, as the other authors, gives no information on when or where de Freitas converted to Islam.

27 Another Union official was a Ghanaian named Karikari, an Asante name. Sadly the Dr Karikari currently at the University of Ghana is not his namesake from the LSE. That Lloyd A. Binazi was the president I learned from my colleague Hakim Adi. (email 19/9/2002) George Uwechwe might have been the founder of the legal firm of G.W. Uwechwe in Nigeria. I have not been able to find information on these Union officials.

28 Schomburg Center: Malcolm X Papers, Reel 3, folder 15.

the African states today and the Black Muslim movement'. The paper reported that Malcolm believed 'the relationship was one of mutual dependence...The growth of the brotherhood of Africans and Afro-Americans has been retarded by colonialism.' Malcolm repeated his accusations against the media which distorts images of Africans, 'but now that the Africans can project their own image on our continent, our attitude to ourselves has begun to change...We are not for violence in any shape or form but we owe it to our manhood and our humanity to defend ourselves when the people who are supposed to defend us do not. You have had a generation of Africans who believed they could negotiate, but the new generation believes that if something is yours by right you don't negotiate – you fight for it.'

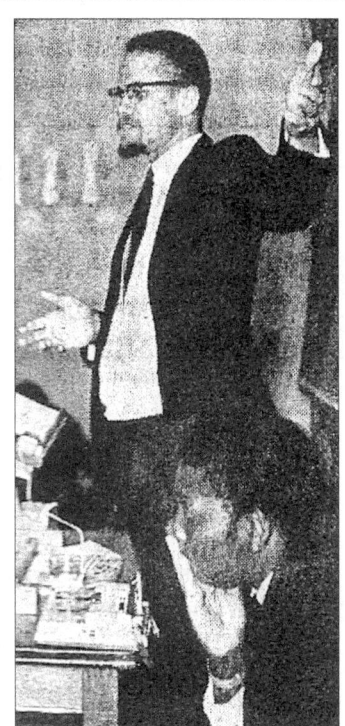

The *Times* (12/2/1965, p.7) reported that, 'there was standing room only. Frequently he was applauded. Once or twice he was interrupted.' Malcolm

> made it clear that he did not believe in indiscriminate violence against whites. He was not a racialist and did not believe in any form of segregation. But the race problem in the United States was extremely wrong and in that case extreme action was necessary. He felt that if violence was used on coloured people, they had the right to use violence in self-defence.
>
> Malcolm X sees the attitude of the white west as a relic of outdated colonialism. Speaking of America, he said: 'They send the Peace Corps to Nigeria and hired killers to the Congo. What is the Peace Corps? Exactly what is says', he added amid applause. 'Get a piece of your country.'
>
> He said that some coloured people had come to this country which in the past was so proud of its lack of a colour problem. 'This problem makes the French, British and Unites States realize that, whereas in the past the African revolution took place on the outside of the house, it is now on the inside of the house and it is causing concern.'

In the version of the speech published in *Malcolm X Talks to Young People* (1992), the 'central theme of [his] talk was the US intervention against liberation forces in the Congo'. From the *Final Speeches* (pp.46-64) version of this masterly and far-ranging speech, much of which is as relevant today as it was forty years ago, we learn that Malcolm decried, as he had done so often, the USA's involvement in the murder of Patrice Lumumba. He went on to analyse the importance of the Congo to the West in terms of its mineral wealth and strategic location. The US bombed the Congo disregarding African civilian casualties. If the Congo was not brought to heel quickly, the Western powers would become as 'bogged down' there as they were in Vietnam. How will Ian Smith be dealt with, Malcolm asked. Africans can't afford to believe that their freedom can be a matter of negotiation: 'if something is yours by right, then fight for it', Malcolm advocated.[29]

Malcolm also spoke of the negative image the western powers had crafted and imposed on Africans and those of African descent, including the West Indians in Britain. But, since Africans had been gaining their freedom, this self-image was shifting.

Next Malcolm addressed the issues raised by the Bandung Conference of 1955,[30] which, he maintained, had been 'one of the first and best steps towards real independence for non-white people...Africans lost all fear of their overlords.' Therefore the old colonial powers 'could not stay there by force and America, the new colonial power could not stay there by force. So they came up with a friendly approach, philanthropic imperialism... Africans found it hard to fight against dollarism.'

Malcolm then analysed the situation in the United States and concluded by calling on all oppressed people everywhere 'to take action against the common oppressor'.[31]

According to de Freitas, Malcolm 'completely captivated his audience... when it came to question time nobody challenged anything he'd said. They

---

29 See also speech as reported on www.hartford-hwp.com/archives/45a/460.html. Ian Smith was the Prime Minister of Rhodesia: a White man elected by a White electorate in a British colony. He was then in the process of negotiating Rhodesia's independence with the British overlords on terms that would have continued to deprive Africans of just about everything. After guerrilla warfare and generally ineffective sanctions by the Western powers, in 1978 Smith was eventually forced to accept universal suffrage and the country was reborn as Zimbabwe.

30 The Afro-Asian Conference, held in Bandung, Indonesia, drew together countries and movements opposed to imperialism. Despite divisions between the pro-Communist and other interest groups, a resolution opposing colonialism was passed and the UN Declaration on Human Rights upheld. For one man's perspective, see Richard Wright, *The Color Curtain*, London: Dobson Books, 1956.

31 Some of the speech was also reproduced in *The Spark* (Ghana) 2/4/1965, p.8.

simply asked him about his future plans...At the end of his talk, Malcolm was surrounded by people...' An editorial in *Beaver*, the student paper, the on 4 March stated that

> There is no doubt that Malcolm X was an orator and political leader of genius...His political analysis and corresponding moral values did, however, seem to affect his listeners in two distinct manners. [The editor suggested that Malcolm had failed to convince the] liberals...who felt that they could never sacrifice negotiation even while violence was being officially administered.

However, the editor believed that to many

> coloured students and some whites, Malcolm X meant much more... He had obviously acquired a far more mature grasp of practical political organisation...It is, I feel, precisely because of his rapidly developing political ability that he became a menace to the Black Muslims and the white power structure. For this reason he was assassinated.

Finally the editor hoped that the 'public press' would cease misreporting Malcolm's views.

Tom McGrath, then Features Editor for *Peace News* attended this meeting and recalls that,

> I was absolutely stunned by him. A lithe, tall man wearing spectacles...and looking, for all the world, ready for action...The majority of the audience were black-skinned and I remember feeling highly conspicuous...His words had a sharp edge to them and he had a razor wit. Everything about him was quick and alert...A third white man...suddenly his voice rang out: 'That man shouldn't be allowed to say things like that.'...There was a scuffle. Malcolm was still at the microphone...He stepped forward and grinned. Speaking with an exaggerated American drawl [Malcolm said] 'That was the voice of White Liberalism speaking'. We all laughed. It was a relief. Malcolm certainly had the gift of comedic timing...
> Soon they invited questions...Many were really statements of support by representatives of revolutionary parties from throughout Africa...[Malcolm] listened to each person very closely and responded to them in detail. He was never cursory.

McGrath had been distressed by some things that Malcolm had said about Martin Luther King, and questioned him. He did not note down what Malcolm had said in response, but recalls that it was,

That one day I might come to realise why it was sometimes necessary for someone in his position to sometimes be a bit free with regard to the truth. But what Malcolm said was much more elegant and concise. From an older to a younger man. Whatever he said it was with great courtesy and it shot through me like a flare of revelations. I was in no position to question Malcolm in such a way, I felt touched for a moment by revolutionary realism. And I was humbled.[32]

Dr. Cornel DaCosta, then a newly arrived students from Mombasa, recalls that he

was pleased to see that he [Malcolm] was incredibly articulate and a man with a cause that he seemed to want to draw others into. He gave a clear picture of racism and black disadvantage to the audience of mostly young white people, but I can't recall what he might have said about his involvement in the Black Muslim Movement However, although very keen, I did not get a chance to raise a question nor talk to him personally as he was rather mobbed by others and then escorted out quickly by his minders.[33]

That evening De Freitas and his wife drove Malcolm around the 'areas of London where black people lived...I took him to Notting Hill and the other ghettoes[34]...[Malcolm] suddenly asked me: "What are you guys doing in England? And what do you aim to do in the future?" Malcolm continued to look me in the eye and he said: "Brother, I will give you your first lesson in leadership: the head can never tell the feet they are going the wrong way."'

The report by the *Times* Special Correspondent, mentioned earlier, indicates that the reporter had interviewed Malcolm. The interview had begun 'while he [Malcolm] was eating chicken in the Islamic Cultural Centre' in London. He quotes Malcolm as saying:

Most students are potential revolutionaries. Your western countries don't have trouble because you have brain-washed them. But in Asia and Africa students are more politically mature. These politically mature students in Britain will play a part in making changes when things are unjust. If the change takes place in time, maybe it can be

---

[32] Taken mainly from an email from Tom McGrath to Paul Lee, very kindly forwarded to me by Paul. I subsequently found Mr McGrath and we emailed (1/5/2008; 11/7/2008) and spoke on the telephone.

[33] Email from Dr Cornel DaCosta, 25/6/2007.

[34] There were no US-style ghettoes in the UK, but in some areas there was a sizable minority of Black peoples.

peaceful. If they don't take place in time, they would take whatever measures are necessary.

If a person who is Asian, African or West Indian cannot live in a neighbourhood, that is unjust.

He recognised that the situation in Britain was different from that in the United States, but added, 'when you have an illegal, immoral and unjust situation it should be changed'. In reply to being asked whether he would become further involved in Britain, Malcolm replied: 'I can't say. Necessity is the mother of invention.'

Smethwick, 12 February 1965

The following day Malcolm was due in Birmingham, a large industrial city, which at one time manufactured the guns and shackles used in the trade in enslaved Africans.[35] He had been asked by the Indian Workers' Association (IWA) to go to Smethwick, a nearby, somewhat dilapidated town.[36] At the recent parliamentary elections, for the first time ever, a Conservative had won the seat for the town. Peter Griffiths' campaign poster read: 'if you want a nigger for a neighbour, vote Labour'.[37] 'Badges with similar wording' were distributed by the local Nazi party, according to Joe Street's recent article on these elections and Malcolm's visit.[38]

The IWA, an anti-racist and anti-imperialist organisation founded in 1958, had many Marxists in its ranks. Its Birmingham committee had been campaigning against racism in the town, which had increased after the election of Griffiths, an ex-head teacher, who had demanded segregated schools. (In 1963 Griffiths had warned pupils not to enter immigrants' homes as they would be in 'grave moral danger'.[39]) Jagmohan Joshi, the

---

35 De Freitas, travelling by train with Malcolm, noted that Malcolm always related whatever he happened to be doing to his purpose in life. On the train, Malcolm got onto 'the subject of communications and expatiated on the absolute necessity of building an effective communications network amongst our people'. (p.144)

36 The IWA was a campaigning organisation which had also been associated with Claudia Jones. It was Shirley Joshi, the wife of the IWA General Secretary, who met Malcolm in London to pass on the invitation. Letter from Shirley Joshi 1/11/2001.

37 A comment published in *West Africa* (31/10/1964, p.1214) regarding the loss of this traditional Labour seat to the Conservatives is very interesting: it 'must force the new government (Labour) to treat such areas as an urgent national concern...immigrants are proving essential for many sectors of Britain's economy'. The new government did not listen.

38 Joe Street, 'Malcolm X, Smethwick, and the Influence of the African American Freedom Struggle on British Race Relations in the 1960s', *Journal of Black Studies*, May 2007.

39 Quoted in N. Deakin (ed), *Colour and the British Electorate 1964*, London: Pall Mall Press 1965, p.81.

general secretary of the IWA, tried to press the Labour Party to 'publicly combat this example of racial prejudice'.[40]

Smethwick was a town with a declining population and thus there was no shortage of housing. (Such shortages were – and are – often blamed on immigrants.) About 6% of population was 'coloured'. The local council was planning to buy up all the houses in Marshall Street, in order to rent them exclusively to Whites.[41] Smethwick's Immigration Support Committee had campaigned for the 1961 Immigration Bill to curb 'coloured immigration'; in 1964, two years after the Bill had been approved by Parliament, some 6,000 signed a petition in support of further restrictions.[42]

The local Labour Club was not affiliated to the national Labour Party, but hosted Party meetings. The Club decided to exclude all people of colour because it feared that 'all the coloured members of the Midland Red Social Club' would want entrance.[43] The Club also refused permission for the Labour Party to hold an 'outgoing' party for the defeated Labour candidate. Harold Wilson, the Labour Prime Minister, publicly denounced the Club and all forms of racial prejudice. When Wilson visited Smethwick he did not use the Labour Club.[44] The local Trades Union Council, which very unusually for that time had a Black man, L.H. South of Jamaican origins, representing the Electrical Trades Union, also stopped meeting at the Club premises.[45]

---

40 Daily Worker, 17/11/1964, p.3 & 8/12/1964, p.3.

41 Daily Mirror, 5/12/1964, p.3, 8/12/1964, back page. The Guardian (24/2/1965 p.7) and the Daily Worker (24/2/1965, p.1) reported that the Council was going ahead with its plans to buy up houses in Marshall Street in order to 'prevent it from becoming a coloured ghetto'. Most of the houses were old and dilapidated – all that the newly arrived immigrants could afford.

42 Smethwick Telephone, 26/6/1964. A researcher counted that 55% of the 'election story inches [in the Telegraph] were devoted to stories mainly about immigration'. (Deakin [n..39], p.90)

43 The Times, 17/11/1964, p.6. The 'Midland Red' was the local bus company which employed numbers of Black people.

44 My thanks to Avtar Jouhl for this information and for reading the draft of the text on Smethwick.

45 Daily Mirror, 17/11/1964, back page, 21/11/9164, p.9. Daily Worker, 4/12/1964, p.3. Wilson's statement had little effect.

Black peoples in Smethwick and Birmingham had been subjected to considerable racial abuse and discrimination for some time. For example, the day before Malcolm's visit, in the magistrate's court, one of four youths charged with smashing 'a blackie's window' said, 'I'm not sorry for what I have done, I did it because I don't like them.' On 10 February *The Times* (p.6) reported that a publican who had lost his licence for overcharging an Indian lecturer, had just had his licence renewed on appeal. About ten days after Malcolm's visit a bomb went off outside an Indian food shop in the High Street. There was a Racial Preservation Society in the area, and four months after Malcolm's visit a local paper reported that the Grand Wizard of the Ku Klux Klan of America had been invited to visit the town. Fiery crosses were nailed to activists' homes in the area at that time.[46]

According to Shirley Joshi, at Smethwick Malcolm

> met some of the Indian Workers' Association members and discussed the issues around the alleged demand of Marshall Street residents to have no more black people located in the street. As I recall Malcolm X drew parallels between this and the segregation which African Americans experienced in the U.S.A. The visit of Malcolm X followed his trip to Africa and he had some discussions around the issue of imperialism with IWA members.[47]

Presumably, the IWA had 'engineered' Malcolm's visit to coincide with that of the BBC, hoping to get more publicity for the racist policies of the local council. The BBC had planned a visit to Smethwick, as it was making a film of the new Black paper, the *Magnet*, which was investigating the goings-on in the town. According to some reports, the BBC hoped to confront Malcolm with Griffiths, but the MP claimed he was too busy. Malcolm said that he had heard that blacks in Smethwick are being treated in the same way as Negroes were treated in Alabama – like Hitler treated the Jews'.[48] He was photographed by many next to the sign for Marshall Street. According to the biographers of Michael de Freitas, Malcolm spoke with a few Marshall Street residents. One man he found particularly interesting, as he asserted that, 'If this man was representative of the rest them, boy,

---

46 *Daily Mirror*, 24/11/1964, p.5; *The Sun*, 13/2/1965, p.1; *Smethwick Telephone*, 12/2/1965, p.24; *Midland News*, December 1965; *The Birmingham Planet*, 10/6/1965, p.36; *Birmingham Post*, 10/6/1965; *Hindustan Times*, 10/6/1965. There is much on Smethwick in the files of the IWA at Birmingham City Archives, MS2141, Box 3.

47 Letter from Shirley Joshi, (who is a lecturer at the University of Central England), 1/11/2001; telephone conversation with Avtar Joshi, a long-standing senior official of the IWA, 13/2/2002. He tried, but could not obtain more information. My grateful thanks to Avtar for his help.

48 *The Times*, 12/2/1965, p.6; *Birmingham Post*, 13/2/1965, p.1.

you are in for trouble in this country. Coloured people must organize themselves against any resistance.'[49]

The response to Malcolm was furious. A shopkeeper is reported to have said that, 'it's disgusting that the BBC should bring that man here. They are trying to stir up trouble in this street all over again.' The Mayor of Smethwick said the visit was 'deplorable' as he believed the sole intention was to 'create more tension in the town'. *The Daily Mirror* (13/2/1965, p.8) reported the Mayor as saying that 'it makes my blood boil that Malcolm X should be allowed into this country'. The *Birmingham Post* (13/2/1965, p.1) carried the BBC's denial, though Malcolm had arrived in Smethwick in a BBC car – and was followed by a retinue of press cars.[50] The paper also reported the Smethwick Conservative Group leader's criticism of the visit, which, as Malcolm was 'an extremist', could only 'stir up the immigrant situation'. The leader of the Labour Club held similar views, as did the chairman of the Birmingham Conference of West Indian Organisations.[51] Peter Griffiths, the MP, issued a 'get out of Smethwick and stay out directive to extremist elements, both black and white' on the following Saturday, reported the *Smethwick Telephone*. (19/2/1965, p.3). The chairperson of the Birmingham branch of the West Indian Standing Conference denied the relevance of Malcolm by saying that 'Conditions here are entirely different from those in Alabama. The West Indians are not the sort of people who would want to follow Malcolm X'.[52] The *Daily Mirror* columnist Cassandra (15/2/1965, p.6) asked 'what is the BBC doing messing about with Malcolm X in Smethwick? He has uttered as much hate-laden racial trash as Colin Jordan – the BBC ought to know better.' Jordan had served in the military during WWII, then gained a history degree at Cambridge; by the 1960s he was the virulent leader of the largest fascist organisation, the British National Party.[53]

---

49 Humphry & Tindall (1977), p.46.

50 That he was not involved in getting Malcolm to Smethwick was reiterated in a letter to me by the BBC's Julian Pettifer, 20/6/2000.

51 *Daily Telegraph*, 4/12/1964, p.17; *The Times*, 17/11/1964, p.6.

52 *The Times*, 13/2/1965, p.6. Perhaps Malcolm's comment on self-hatred made at the LSE is pertinent in trying to understand this statement: 'West Indians were running around here in search of an identity and instead of trying to be what they are, they want to be Englishmen'. (*Final Speeches*, p.54) On the experiences of the first generation of post WWII Caribbean immigrants, see the following accounts and novels: Sam Selvon, *The Lonely Londoners*, London: Wingate 1956; Colin MacInnes, *City of Spades*, London: MacGibbon & Kee 1957; Donald Hinds, *Journey to an Illusion*, London: Heinemann, 1966; George Lamming, *Water with Berries*, London: Longman 1973; Trevor Carter, *Shattering Illusions*, London: Lawrence & Wishart 1986; Joan Riley, *The Unbelonging*, London: Women's Press 1985 and *Waiting in the Twilight*, London: Women's Press 1987.

53 Curiously, the present leader of the National Front, the successor to the BNP, is also a Cambridge history graduate!.

Even *The Times* reported the visit on 13 February (p.6). It had alerted its readers the previous day of the intended visit and claimed that Malcolm's expenses had been paid by the BBC. 'The English are becoming increasingly racialist and the Smethwick situation could develop into a brutally violent affair', *The Times* reported Malcolm saying. It criticised Malcolm's knowledge of the situation in the UK on the basis that 'he had not realized that the Government's immigration restrictions also applied to white immigrants'. (What the paper did not tell its readers was that these restrictions were never in fact applied to Whites, as I, a Hungarian/Australian 1960s immigrant, can testify.) On the 15th the paper reported Malcolm's response to the contention that he should not have been allowed to set foot in Smethwick: 'Nobody is doing me any favours...by permitting me to appear on any platform. I have my views...if they want to listen to them, good. If they don't want to hear them, good. Where I have spoken I have been invited.' Peter Griffiths, the Conservative MP, was not to be dismissed so easily: on 18 February he asked in Parliament if Malcolm X could be declared an 'undesirable alien to prevent future entry'. The government spokesman replied that it was 'not justified in refusing admission in the future, but will keep it under review'.[54]

Malcolm's 'tour' of Smethwick was even noted in the USA. In a report carefully noted as 'London, 13 February, Special to the *New York Times*' the paper reported on 14 February (p.24) that Smethwick was a symbol of 'racial problems' in Britain. Malcolm had spent three hours there, and is quoted as saying 'if coloured people continue to be oppressed, it will start a bloody battle'. The *Los Angeles Times* reported the visit to 'Smethwick, 'the midlands hotbed of racial problems in the UK', and the Mayor's anger. 'Why had Malcolm tried to equate Smethwick with Birmingham, Alabama', the horrified Mayor asked.[55]

Less than ten days after Malcolm's visit, *The Guardian* reported (24/2/1964, p.7) that Smethwick Council was going ahead with its plan to buy up all the houses in Marshall Street in order to 'prevent it becoming a coloured ghetto'. The Labour Club did not renege on its decision to bar Black peoples from its premises.[56]

---

54 *The Times*, 19/2/1965, p.17; See also *Final Speeches*, pp.65-67. According to the papers on Malcolm X sent to me by the Metropolitan Police on 9/11/2001, the Home Office Immigration Division asked the Met whether it was compiling a report on Malcolm X. Unfortunately the reply has not been forwarded to me.

55 *Los Angeles Times*, 14/2/1965, p.E20). The article also noted that Malcolm had been refused entry to Paris. Most interestingly, the article ended with a comment that the Labour Party, which had initially opposed limiting immigration, now 'under political pressure, has veered towards the Tory position lately' - ie, of imposing further limits on immigration.

56 *The Times*, 21/11/1964, p.8

It should be noted here that Martin Luther King, en route to Oslo to collect his Nobel Peace Prize, had stopped off in Britain a few days before Malcolm's visit to Smethwick. He was not castigated in the papers for warning 'against coloured ghettoes...There is a growing problem of race relations in the UK'. He is reported as 'lashing out against the colour biased immigration laws', which had recently been enacted and were being re-debated in Parliament.[57] According to the New York edition of the *Pittsburgh Courier* (19/12/1964, p.21), Dr. King was highly praised by the BBC for his anti-violence stance. When Malcolm was asked on radio what he thought of this, he replied that it was 'bankrupt'. Nelson Mandela also practised non-violence, Malcolm is reported as saying, 'and discovered to his dismay that it just doesn't work'. The Civil Rights Bill has not been 'effective in improving the lot of the American Negroes', he concluded.

Birmingham

From Smethwick Malcolm returned to Birmingham where, according to the *Birmingham Post* (13/2/1965, p.1), he held a press conference in Julian Pettifer's hotel room. He is reported as speaking about the OAAU and emphasising that 'he had done nothing to fan the flame of hatred in Britain. "I have avoided incidents; I have avoided anything that could create an incident. I have been as inconspicuous as possible in seeking to nourish my interests."' Michael de Freitas, who had travelled to Birmingham with Malcolm, also reported the press conference, at which Malcolm dealt 'with the questions from the press with vigour and aplomb. It seems that Malcolm had a number of his own old comments thrown at him by the newshounds, and had to explain again and again what the context and time of each comment had been. There were lots of questions and answers like that, but unfortunately, nobody printed what he's said in the papers next day', de Freitas notes. (Not held sufficiently newsworthy, I presume.) After the press conference, Malcolm left to address a meeting of the Islamic students at Birmingham University.

The meeting at the University was not a private or an exclusively Muslim meeting, but one on race and racism, according to Dr. Robert Moore, who was a researcher at the University at that time.[58] The meeting was chaired by Dr. Ahmed Qidwai, a lecturer in Chemical Engineering and associated with the Federation of Islamic Students. Priestly Hall at the University was packed. The student newspaper, *Redbrick* (17/2/1965, p.9), does not make clear the nature of the meeting, as it states that '[p]

---

57 See eg. *Daily Mirror*, 7/12/1964, p.6; *Daily Worker*, 7/12/1965, p.1.
58 Telephone conversation with Professor Moore, 19/6/2000.

ress-men flocked to the Union, but a strict check on Guild cards kept non-members out of the private meeting of the Islamic Society'. Malcolm explained the foundation of the OAAU, which, he is reported as stating, believed in 'maximum retaliation'. To 'strike back', he explained, 'is only intelligent self-defence...A racist speaks in brute force; we must reply in the same language'. 'Mr. X did not disappoint us', the reporter wrote. 'In polished style, with the skill of a true demagogue, he described the Muslim faith: I am a Muslim and I believe in Islam, which means peace, but I do not believe that I may not protect myself.' The brief article concludes with an expression of relief that there had been no disturbances during the meeting, in contrast to the 'furore caused earlier in the day when Mr X was filmed in Smethwick'.

Professor Robert Moore recalls that Malcolm told the audience that 'You had an empire on which it was said the sun would never set. Why, now, every morning when that sun rises he don't know where to look'. Malcolm spoke on the Black struggle in the USA, and linked it with struggles in Africa. Both required new models of struggle. Would the civil rights model, as practised by Martin Luther King Jr., achieve anything, Malcolm asked. 'Malcolm was rather aggressive in his comments on Christianity', Professor Moore remembers, 'so when I got a chance to ask a question I pointed out that the founder of Christianity was a working class man of colour from the middle east. Malcolm wagged his finger at me and said, "Yes, that's right, but you are going to get into a lot of trouble saying things like that".'[59]

De Freitas wrote that Malcolm had a 'constant theme, of human rights for the black man and how any organisation to fight for these rights in the parts of the world where people were deprived of them must be set up on an international basis. Unity, he pointed out, was strength, and he warned of the white man's strategy of setting up black men as puppet leaders so that the black people were divided amongst themselves and never really achieved anything.'(p.145)

After the University meeting, the students took their guest to dinner at a Muslim restaurant. Lewis Chester, a *Sunday Times* journalist, told biographer Derek Humphry that he had met Malcolm 'at an Indian restaurant [where] Malcolm had been talking to about a dozen blacks over the dinner table. He was almost luminous and everybody was basking in his aura'.[60]

---

59 Email from Robert Moore, 15/11/2001. Jesus Christ continues to be depicted as an unmistakeable White man – with blue eyes and blond hair - everywhere in the world.

60 Humphry & Tindall (1977), p.48. The story told by Lewis Chester to Humphry contradicts de Freitas' own version of how he changed 'de Freitas' to 'X'. Chester recalled that he had asked 'a man next to me "What are you?" and he answered "I am his brother." I thought he was

London, 12 and 13 February, 1965

Did Malcolm return to London late that night or the following day? According to de Freitas, he and Malcolm, 'spent several hours visiting the various black centres in London and putting our plan (the formation of a London branch of the OAAU) across to the West Indians we met. We found a whole lot of enthusiasm...We were so successful that we began to work out organisational details and [planned] for Malcolm's return to London in the summer to attend the public launching of the organisation in Trafalgar Square.'

Malcolm, de Freitas records, attended Friday prayers at the Regent's Park mosque and in the evening there was a get-together of activists. De Freitas recalls Malcolm criticising the Black middle class in America who did too little to 'lift the black man up, and the writers for endless intellectualising'.[61]

The Metropolitan Police report states that Malcolm left for the US on February 13, on the 12:30pm TWA flight for New York. So he could only have attended Friday prayers in London very late that night, as he was in Birmingham that afternoon and evening.[62]

Check-in time at Heathrow airport was usually two hours before departure time, so Malcolm would have had to be at the airport, about an hour from London by public transport, at 10:30am. This leaves little time for visiting either a mosque (early on Saturday morning?) or Black centres. So what are we to make of de Freitas' account? As he wrote his commissioned *Autobiography* soon after Malcolm's murder, one should probably not doubt his memory, but might question his veracity. Given the position he had acquired by 1965/6 as the Black Power movement leader, de Freitas/Abdul Malik may have enhanced or embellished the plans he said he and Malcolm were forming. He claims that London-based Africans had not been approached regarding the formation of a branch of the OAAU. But this seems hardly credible, given that not many days previously Malcolm had spoken at the CAO Congress and had spent some time with Kojo Amoo-Gottfried. Would they not have discussed the

---

being evasive so I asked him again, and he replied, "Call me Michael X."'

61 Malik/De Freitas, 1968, pp.146-7. De Freitas did set up an organisation:: he had been discussing this with Ray Sawh, an Indo-Guyanese residing in London, as well as with Jan Carew and Abdullah Patel from Bombay. Called the Racial Adjustment Society, or RAAS, it was set up later in 1965. I can find no mention of the OAAU in the biography of de Freitas or in Sawh's *Autobiography, From Where I Stand*, London: Hansib 1987.

62 Heathrow Airport to Metropolitan Police, 13/2/1965. The report notes that MI5 were informed of Malcolm's departure.

OAAU branch in Ghana? Wouldn't Malcolm have also raised this at the meeting at the London School of Economics?

Abdul Malik's credibility was also questioned by Richard Gibson in 1967, when he described the Trinidadian to Julian Mayfield as 'a well known fraud, [who] jumped on the stage to collect what coins and publicity he could. [He] is a grim farce and one built up cynically by the bourgeois press in the country (Britain) as a black bogeyman. To justify the far more real white fascists.' One reviewer of de Freitas' (now Abdul Malik) *Autobiography* found it to be the work of a 'self-asserting opportunistic young man anxious for personal recognition and material well-being'.[63]

The *New York Times* (14/2/1965, p.24) reported Malcolm's return and quoted him as saying at the airport that, 'General de Gaulle had too much gall in keeping me out of France'.

Malcolm's humour and gift with words is wonderful!

---

63 Schomburg Center: Julian Mayfield Correspondence MG339, file 5/6, Gibson to Mayfield 17/8/1967; review by R.Manderson-Jones in *Race & Class*, 10/3, 1969.

CHAPTER 12

The Return

Malcolm arrived back from London on flight TW703 on the afternoon of the thirteenth of February. His round of speeches continued; he explained the new analyses he was developing. For example, at Columbia University on February 18th he told the students that, 'It is incorrect to classify the revolt of the Negro as simply a racial conflict of black against white, or as a purely American problem. Rather, we are today seeing a global rebellion of the oppressed against the oppressor, of the exploited against the exploiter.'[1]

When interviewed by the Illinois judiciary to see if he could testify in a case, Malcolm responded that he could not, as he had been invited to attend the Bandung Conference to be held in March in Jakarta. But this was not to be.

Three months away from his fortieth birthday, just before he left London, Malcolm had told Jan Carew that, 'the chances are that they will get me the way they got Lumumba'. He was correct.

On 21 February 1965 an assassin's bullets ended the life of one of the most remarkable men of our times.

The only African leader, as far as we know, who sent a message to Malcolm's family was President Kwame Nkrumah:

> I have received with profound shock the news of the death of your husband at the hand of assassins. Your husband lived a life of dedication for human equality and dignity so that the Afro-

---

1 Breitman (1968), p.91.

New York, Kennedy Airport, November 24, 2964. Malcolm returns home to Betty and the children and also to a family reunion with his mother and siblings in Lansing.

Americans and people or color everywhere may live as men. His work in the cause of freedom will not be in vain.[2]

That the bullets were actually fired by NOI members now seems unquestionable. But were they by any chance paid/instigated/encouraged by a US government agency/department?

And, given the thorough surveillance of Malcolm, how come the CIA/FBI could not prevent the assassination?

---

2 Shirley Graham DuBois, 'The Beginning, Not the End', in Clarke (1969), p.127

CHAPTER 13

The Post-mortems

The murder of Malcolm had repercussions and responses around the world. Below is a glimpse of some of the immediate responses.

London – Reaction in the Black Media

Kojo Amoo-Gottfried of the Committee of African Organizations (CAO) recalled in his interview with Hakim Adi that he had met Malcolm after his talk to the CAO congress and that Malcolm had been 'very concerned about his safety and security'.[1] On 23 February the CAO issued a statement on Malcolm's death:

> [at our conference] we were able to get an unprejudiced and clear understanding of both the man and his policy. He won over many in his audience amongst whom were his most incisive critics. He dispelled much of their lack of sympathy created by a biased press and based on unfamiliarity with his real aims. He was certainly no rabble-rousing demagogue, but possessed a composure and clear-headedness which was highly incompatible with the image of a fanatic that had been and is being projected by his detractors. He was neither leader nor prophet of the lunatic fringe...He was staggeringly honest and sincere...This great nationalist leader never preached one thing and practised another...

---

1 Email from Dr Hakim Adi 19/9/2002.

Malcolm X regarded the use of force in self-defence where violence is unleashed against the Negro people's demands for freedom and for human rights as justifiable only because the hand that prevented them had been unamenable to negotiation and peaceful demands. He had little faith in those who, while breaking his head with a cudgel, exhorted him to be passive and love them...Malcolm X aimed essentially at the forging of stronger links between Negroes in America, Africans and all oppressed peoples in Asia and Latin America, and that is precisely why he was murdered...We condemn this ignominious act which is another futile phase in the policy of the imperialists to keep the majority of mankind in a subordinate status and thereby maintain their precarious and moribund domination... The most fitting tribute to Malcolm is to overcome differences among us and to unite all oppressed peoples, build unbreakable unity and carry forward the cause for which Malcolm X gave his life...We express solidarity with his aims and work, which no act of brutality can undermine or obliterate.[2]

The CAO also sent telegrams of condolence to Betty Shabazz and to Brother James at the OAAU, in both of which they reiterated their promise of support. Malcolm's 'uncompromising militancy against US imperialism and racism crucial to fight for freedom and dignity. Malcolm's blood launched Afro-American revolution. You shall not falter nor surrender', the CAO told the OAAU. A subsequent letter addressed to both concluded with a promise: 'Malcolm has laid down his life in order that we shall be free. He has not died in vain. We solemnly pledge to you that in us you have the assurance and support of a family confidently resolved that you shall witness and live in the certain realisation of the vision of our Brother Malcolm.'[3]

About two weeks after the murder, the CAO also organised a demonstration in London, which was attended by more than one hundred people. The march to the US Embassy, behind banners of Lumumba and Malcolm, was led by the president of the CAO, who was allowed to hand in a Protest Note to the ambassador. This, according to *West Africa* (6/3/1965, p.273) 'condemned United States imperialists' brutal and criminal murder of Malcolm X. The Note demanded that the real culprits, who CAO believed, were hired by United States imperialist agents, be brought to justice.' The banners held aloft by the marchers carried protests

---

2 New York University, Tamiment Library: Breitman Papers Box 44, Excerpts of the CAO statement appeared in *West Africa*, 27/2/1965, p.246.

3 Tamiment Library: Breitman Papers.

such as 'We know why Malcolm died'; 'Yankee monsters commit another murder'; 'We condemn Yankee hypocrisy' and 'How many more must die?'

The statement mentioned above was distributed at the march, according to New York's *Militant* (29/3/1965, p.6)

The Union of African Students in Europe also sent condolences and stated 'Glory for his uncompromising courageous struggle against US racialist imperialism and for freedom, justice equality to all mankind. Assassination cannot stop final victory.'

The front page of the February 27 issue of the Black weekly, the *Magnet* bears a portrait of Malcolm with the headline 'Malcolm X: Tragedy of the American Society'. The introduction to the brief report states that 'Not everyone will agree with his views...He was the leader of the Black Mosque, a breakaway group from the Black Muslims'. Having gotten the name of Malcolm's mosque wrong, the writer then describes the Black Muslims and goes on to quote James Baldwin's remarks on the assassination: '[it is] an act which has sprung from the moral climate of America...' The writer goes on to recall that two weeks ago he had chatted with Malcolm about the 'leaders of the Negro revolt in America', whom Malcolm went on to call Uncle Toms. The editor disagrees, and calls Malcolm a 'militant racialist'. While suggesting that discovering who killed Malcolm might be unimportant, he castigates the US for deeming its 'negro citizens third class'. He goes on: 'Though one could not have agreed with the violent views of Malcolm X...one must feel sympathy for a man who was thrown up out of the heartlessness of this land. The death of Malcolm X does not augur well for America...The lesson, we believe, is that few countries in the modern world can afford to create a racialist. England cannot afford this!'

The *Magnet's* 'Letter from Paris' in the issue of April 10-23 carried a report of the memorial service held for Malcolm in Paris at the Muslim Mosque. Prayers in the Mosque's conference hall followed prayers in the 'inner sanctum', which only Muslims could attend. Carlos Moore spoke again, 'reminding those present that, although we may not have understood the prayer or shared Brother Malcolm's religious affiliations, we were beholden to his political creed and that at times the two were even inseparable'.

The other paper catering to Britain's (or at least London's) Black population, *Flamingo*, had interviewed Malcolm on 10 February, but did not print this until April. It is banal, questioning Malcolm on the Black Muslim movement, mixed marriages and 'moderate' civil rights leaders.[4]

---

4 The interview is reproduced in Steve Clark (ed), *February 1965: The Final Speeches*, New

These two papers seem to bear out Malcolm's comments on the media as well as on some West Indians in Britain.

UK National Papers

The British national papers were also at a loss. *The Guardian* (22/2/1965), a left-wing paper, reported his death on page 12 and in its brief piece noted that Malcolm had 'often advocated violence as a means of settling social problems'. His break with the Black Muslims was supposed to have been due to a power struggle. The reporters at the paper clearly had not agreed on a 'line' on Malcolm as this report is very far from the thoughtful editorial of 11 July the previous year, detailed above. The following day, in its 'London Letter' column (the paper was then published in Manchester), James Baldwin, then visiting Britain, is quoted as saying that 'the Western world has to become aware that the colour problem does not exist as an "isolated act of God", but is embodied in our Western civilisation'. Perhaps to atone for its negligence, misrepresentation and lack of understanding, on 27 February the paper published an article 'Black and White' on its editorial page. Taken from his speech at the LSE, this is a more accurate account of Malcolm's views, but it lacks any kind of introduction. Could the paper still not come to terms with Malcolm?

The Observer, a left-wing Sunday paper, in an article headed 'A Myth is Born', published on 28 February (p.2), also lacked understanding: 'Malcolm, who was no more than a controversial extremist leader in life, is becoming an international symbol in death', it reported. This was based on the many telegrams of condolence pouring into the OAAU from all over Africa, many of which 'compared Malcolm with the late Patrice Lumumba'. However, while even this paper did not know how to interpret Malcolm's life and death, it perhaps made up for its ignorance by printing long excerpts from Malcolm's *Autobiography* in this and the next issue.

The New Statesman (26/2/1965, p.310), a weekly left-wing paper, demonstrated more insight: 'the murder will have an impact outside America...In Africa and Asia it will come to have a personal effect... [Malcolm] was a superb orator...his fanaticism changed the tone of public debate...At the LSE the coloured intelligentsia listened to him with mounting enthusiasm. This is what we believe, they were saying afterwards...Malcolm X did not believe in separatism, an American Bantustan policy. He was not advocating violence: "We owe it to our

---

York: Pathfinder 1992, pp.42-45.One of the founder journalists of *Flamingo* was Dominican Edward Scobie, who became a lecturer at Rutgers University and at City College New York, and authored *Black Britannia: a history of Blacks in Britain*, Chicago: Johnson Publishing 1972.

humanity to defend ourselves", he had said.' The writer thought that Malcolm and Martin Luther King were moving closer – 'together they would have made a formidable force', he believed.

The Economist (27/2/1965, p.888) printed a report emanating from New York, but unsigned. This argued that, though Elijah Muhammad had more followers than Malcolm, Malcolm 'commanded a national, indeed an international audience. His call to violence and his political extremism were exactly what was likely to appeal to young militants among Negro intellectuals...His advantage over the other Negro leaders lay in the very fact that he was unencumbered with the principles which the educated man, black or white, never questions. Malcolm X was in this sense potentially dangerous...Soon a day may come when orthodox Negro leaders will miss Malcolm X sorely. For he might have been able to harness the political energy of the Negroes in the North. He was a revolutionary; the civil rights leaders are still reformers.'

The left-wing weeklies also noted Malcolm's assassination. *The Socialist Leader* (27/2/1965, p.2) believed that, 'if there was no racial discrimination there would be no need for organisations like the Black Muslims or the one Malcolm X was in. Violence is not a solution. But in certain situations the use of force might be necessary – but try the non-violent first.' *Peace News*, which had reported Malcolm's speech at the CAO conference and demonstrated its interest in Black issues by printing excerpts from Donald Hinds' forthcoming autobiographical *Journey to an Illusion*[5], reported the murder on page one of the issue of 26 February. While noting that 'the voice of Malcolm X was important' it believed that his following had been exaggerated and that his importance was a 'symptom of a social disease which for example CORE and the SNCC... are acting boldly and effectively to cure'. To its credit, on 12 March 1965 (p.11) the *News* printed a long letter from Baron Jakob von Vexhüll of Christ Church College in Oxford, which set out Malcolm's importance and corrected the misquotations in the article.

> Further to the left, the Communist Party's *Daily Worker* carried the news of the assassination on its front page, and mentioned Malcolm's trips to the universities of Manchester and Oxford. The report demonstrates the paper's lack of knowledge of Black issues.[6] Interestingly the *Worker* gave space to the distinguished philosopher Bertrand Russell on 24 February: murder is a terrifying indication

---

5 *Journey to an Illusion* (London: Heinemann 1966) was republished by Bogle L'Ouverture in 2009.

6 I discussed this in 'The CPGB and Black Britons 1920-1938', *Science & Society* 60/2 Summer 1996, pp.137-16. The CPGB had not changed by the 1960s: see my *Claudia Jones: a life in exile*, London: Lawrence & Wishart 1999.

of the disintegration affecting American society. A society in which people are shot down at will is a society which will plunge the world into disaster. Malcolm X was reviled in the United States and Britain by the established press...because he showed that the same standards which promoted cruel and unrelenting wars of atrocity in Vietnam, in the Congo...were responsible for the suffering of the Negro in the Unites States.

The right-wing weekly *Spectator* (26/2/1965) carried a piece written in New York by Murray Kempton: 'Now that he is dead, it is odd how sad we are and how pitiful he seems...feeling we all had that Malcolm had been a creation of journalism. Yet he was more than that. By taking his stand and enduring, Malcolm X created a nation and a little part of every Negro had a small allegiance to him.'

The Times (22/2/1965, p.10), the leading 'establishment' daily, called Malcolm a 'vigorous, articulate and contentious man, a tremendously effective orator', whose 'declared policy was the establishment of a non-sectarian black nationalist party'. The next day, it also quoted James Baldwin and noted that Malcolm has 'repeatedly claimed that there was a plot to kill him'. The editorial on the following day (p.13) predicted the weakening of the 'entire black nationalist movement'. Malcolm, this editor stated, had 'wanted the limelight and got it' by splitting with the Black Muslims...'He talked...of the eventual destruction of whites', but achieved nothing. In the US, he believed that 'a minority can gain its rights only by proving its moral claim in equality'. (Is it because he saw outrageous supremacist attitudes during his visit to Britain, that James Baldwin told the *Times* that 'Britain is no longer white, and what happens to you now depends on whether you accept that fact'?)

The *Daily Mirror*, a tabloid generally thought to be in support of the Labour Party, described the assassination on its front page, noting Malcolm's visits to Smethwick, and stated that he had 'formed his own extremist group, the OAAU'. On 23 February the columnist Cassandra wrote that the 'murder of Malcolm Little – who bore the alternative melodramatic title of Malcolm X – was a wild, bloody and brutal affair. But it was entirely in keeping with his philosophy of advocating violence and bloodshed in all racial matters. Little's business was hatred and he pursued it with murderous intent and unending zeal...Little's criminal background was harnessed to considerable intellectual ability of a deadly kind. He used his articulate powers to advocate bloodshed as a political solution which makes it not very difficult to regret his demise'.

That much of the British media, Black or White, could not really 'see' or 'hear' Malcolm was not a phenomenon of the 1960s. Such incomprehension is, I think, 'alive and well' forty and more years later.

Tom McGrath, who had met Malcolm at the conference held at the London School of Economics, published this poem in the left-wing paper, *Tribune* (3/4/1965, p.10). It seems to me to reflect the breadth Malcolm's meaning to a White political activist.

Consolations

There may have been other considerations
    but actions are like that
    not possible without a fallout of thought

they shout Malcolm X without certainty
they shot Kennedy likewise
Abraham Lincoln, etc

    just as certainly as myself
    when I grope and stumble from bed
    another morning breathe again
    have the eyes open begin to see
    and be out and about again doing
    without a thought
    as to where it's leading

only the pretence at that thought
an assumption of this making that
one and one are
what the teacher taught
    how not to divulge to yourself
    one thought
    too many
    they shot Malcolm X
    they shot Malcolm X

    after a while
    no meaning

    and that is consoling
    if only partly true

Response in Sheffield and Manchester

The Sheffield Student Union paper, *Darts*, on its front page for the issue of 4 March 1965, printed a photograph of Malcolm taken when he had addressed the students some three months previously, and noted that the Islamic Circle had held a condolence prayer meeting and issued a statement:

> Malcolm X was a sincere man; Muslim and non-Muslim admired his understanding. Let us thank God and our Union Secretary, Mr. Neil Rackham, who has truthfully and justifiably expressed his and our feelings of respect toward Malcolm X.

Neil Rackham is quoted as saying, 'Malcolm X was an extremist, but he had a sense of humour – his saving grace.' Kadim Mallallah, in a letter to the paper, described how, after he had heard Malcolm speak at Oxford and Sheffield, he realised how misleading the press reports had been: he had found Malcolm to be 'the leader of a just movement and a man with the ability to fight for the cause of his people'. Mallallah believed that the murderers were just as likely to have been the CIA, as Malcolm has 'gained a lot of support and popularity in Africa' and elsewhere, which made him a 'dangerous man'. In his letter Nigel Ings recalled Malcolm's visit: 'we in the Union heard him, and he simply appeared to be an intelligent man, angry and bitter, reacting in the most understandable way to an intolerable situation...By what right was Malcolm X condemned, when in the face of terrible violence he taught violent self-defence as a means of survival?'[7]

The Manchester Student Union paper, *The Independent*, ignored Malcolm' death as it had ignored his visit. The *Manchester Evening News* reported the assassination briefly on pages 10 and 9 of its 22 and 23 February issues.

Response in North Africa

The *Egyptian Gazette*, which headlined the murder (22/2/1965, pp.1, 5) felt no need to introduce or describe Malcolm to its readers. The account of the assassination was followed by daily reports of the investigation, and then of the funeral. *The Militant* in New York summarised some of the other North African press:

---

7 *Darts*, 4/3/1965, pp.1,2.

The *Le Peuple*, an Algerian daily headlined its issue of February 27: 'The weakness of the American authorities is at the root of the assassination of Malcolm X.'...*Jeune Afrique*, the weekly published in Tunis, carried an article by its New York correspondent Simon Malley, [which concluded with]: 'the murder took place in circumstances sufficiently strange to excite grave suspicions as to the role of the white law-enforcement authorities and security agents of the country.' The March 6 issue of the Algerian *Révolution Africaine* again devoted a big article to the death of Malcolm X: 'Malcolm X was no more nor less than a fearless nationalist and revolutionist, spokesman of an oppressed people whom he wanted to lead on the difficult road of liberation. That is why the American imperialists saw in him the champion of Afro-American liberation and a particularly dangerous enemy. In his struggle against American racism, Malcolm X did not hesitate to internationalise the question and seek the support of all the forces in the world opposed to US imperialism.'[8]

The *Voice of Ethiopia* and the *Ethiopian Herald*, as so many other papers, while reporting the murder on page 1, used the press release put out by the Reuters news agency. This was a fairly 'straight' report of the shooting at the Audobon. It had nothing positive to say about Malcolm. Both papers followed the evolving story, using agency reports.[9]

Response in East and South Africa

As the *East African Standard*, published in Nairobi, carried exactly the same article as the *Morning Post* on its editorial page (23/2/1965, p.8), we can perhaps conclude that the USIS or the US Embassies were distributing information and pressuring for its use.

Interestingly, the *East African Standard* also carried an account of the actual shooting on page 1 of the same issue, which is a 'straight' description. An adjacent column reports that in Dar-es-Salaam, 'freedom fighters, yesterday expressed shock, grief and dismay when they heard of the death...Many of them had met Malcolm during his recent visit to

---

8 'African Reactions to Malcolm X's Death', *The Militant*, 29/3/1965, p.6. The article begins with quotations from the 13/2/1965 issue of *Révolution Africain* which carried an article entitled 'Road to Liberty: Rev. Martin Luther King or Malcolm X?'

9 *Voice of Ethiopia*, 22/2/1965, pp.1,2,3; 24/2/1965, p.4; *Ethiopian Herald*, daily reports from 23/2/1965 to 27/1/1965, usually on page 1. Apart from Reuter, the *Herald* also used information put out by the AFP, another press agency, and the American government's USIS.

African states...A statement released by the African National Congress of South Africa said:

> The murder of Malcolm X...is the most shocking to all of us. Not all Africans nor Afro-Americans agreed with everything in which he believed or said, but all of us recognised in him a militant fighter for the recognition of the Black man as a man. [The ANC then criticizes the United States] for having the characteristics of a sick society that thrives on political gangsterism. [This is followed by a call] to decent Americans to root out the evil that caused Malcolm's death. [He] should never have found it necessary to spend his adult life fighting racialism.

By reporting the ANC's statement relatively fully, was the paper making an attempt to avoid US strictures? The *Standard* followed the evolving story with daily reports of events in New York.

Nairobi's *Daily Nation* (23/1/1965, p.1) also carried 'straight' reports, but called the assassination 'bizarre', and also carried a 'profile' of Malcolm. This was yet another copy of the *Standard* article, but now we learn that it emanated from 'AP & Reuter'.

The Nationalist in Dar also carried almost daily reports of events in New York but provided no commentary or analysis. It did not mention the freedom fighters resident there, but noted an anti-American demonstration in Jakarta by about 500 students who 'said the demonstration was over the assassination of the American nationalist leader, Malcolm X' (24/2/1965, p.5) Thus it seemed to be adopting the tactic of the *Standard* in order to alert readers to strong feelings elsewhere about the assassination.

Response in Nigeria

Reactions in Africa were not as muted as in Britain, but some of the media, under Western control/influence toed the 'establishment' line or followed the undoubted suggestions/requests from the US (and the British?) Embassy to play down the murder. One such was the federal government sponsored *Lagos Morning Post* (24/2/1965, p.8), which had not a positive word to say about Malcolm. Strangely, Azikiwe's *West African Pilot* carried no commentary, but did report the assassination on page 1 of its issue on 23 February.

Response in Ghana

In Ghana, where President Nkrumah was soon to be overthrown, the press was fulsome in its appreciation of Malcolm X. The *Daily Graphic*, which carried almost daily accounts of the murder and its aftermath, reported J.K. Tettegah, the Secretary-General of the All African Trade Union Federation, condemning 'the blatant, brazen and dastardly act' of the assassination. 'Once again', said Tettegah, 'the progressive forces of Africa and the world have been taken agog by another vicious blow of US imperialism on humanity.' He appealed for 'all progressive forces of Africa and the world to be vigilant against US imperialism which is desperately and persistently forcing its way into our continen,t through its main agencies with the view to enslaving us.' (23/2/1965, pp.1, 6-7) Nkrumah's condolences to Betty Shabazz are detailed, as is the ongoing drama in New York. The paper reports that the Association of Ghana Journalists and Writers held a memorial service at the Press Club on 24 February.

The African Student – University Socialist Review, in its 1965 (vol.3) issue, carried a cartoon of a White cowboy with two gun belts around his waist, standing in front of a tombstone with Malcolm's name on it. He is saying 'Lumumba, Evers, Malcolm and –'. Julian Mayfield wrote a moving tribute and political analysis in *African Review*, and also, in *The Ghanaian Times*, noted that, 'heads of state received him with great cordiality...He won friends of high and low station everywhere he went...'

The Spark, a socialist theoretical and analytic weekly, devoted almost the whole of the front page on 26 February to an article headed 'Who Killed Malcolm X?'. William Gardner Smith bracketed the murders of Malcolm and Lumumba and asked, 'who profits?'. Malcolm, he wrote, was 'the most dangerous man in the whole United States...the man who was going to make a contribution to the anti-capitalist revolution in the United States'. It had become difficult for America to preach freedom abroad, Smith argued, when there was such 'unfreedom' at home, and this unfreedom was being demonstrated by the Black Revolt. But equality cannot be achieved under a capitalist system, and Malcolm understood this. 'He did not believe in privileges for a chosen minority of the black population...And, as his political sense matured...he discovered and proclaimed the great dangerous truth. He cried: you cannot win if you fight according to their rules...you must join the world revolution against imperialism...

> Leaders of fascist imperialism who control the invisible government of the United States...saw Malcolm X for what he was – the most dangerous man, from their standpoint, in the whole of the United States...What they saw in Malcolm X...was the man who was going to make a contribution to the anti-capitalist revolution in the USA. The 22 million Afro-Americans hold the key to America's domestic future. They are America's catalyst...The overwhelming majority of Americans are relatively satisfied with the USA the way it is...But who rocks the boat? Who moves? Who organises, marches, riots, demonstrates, goes to jail, dies? The Afro-American.
> This movement threatens what Afro-Americans call the US 'power structure' – that is, American capitalism...Afro-Americans form an 'internal colony' in the United States. They constitute a vast reserve of cheap labour...They cushion the white working class...They are a handy instrument for dividing the US working class movement...
> Internal dissent was crushed bloodily till the African Revolution. Then it became hard to massacre black Americans and still remain on good terms with vital Africa. It became embarrassing to preach 'freedom' abroad with this blatant example of un-freedom at home. Civil rights agitation does not change this – Martin Luther King and Wilkins do not frighten the capitalist rulers of America.
> But Malcolm X was something else. He did not believe in the privileges of the chosen minority of the black population. He fought for all his people...And, as his political sense matured, Malcolm did something else – the thing that signed his death warrant. He discovered and proclaimed the great dangerous truth. He cried: you cannot win if you fight according to their rules, you cannot win under capitalism; you must join the world revolution against imperialism. 'Practice without thought is blind; thought without practice is empty' equals a great truth he had discovered...He took steps to link up the Afro-American struggle with the liberation movement in revolutionary Africa...His ultimate aim, roughly

speaking was to form an Afro-American equivalent of the Algerian National Liberation Front...America's invisible rulers knew this, because their agents had penetrated his organisation. So they condemned him to death.

The paper also printed a poem by Julia Wright, the daughter of Richard, who was then living in Ghana:

To Malcolm X

When we get down
To fight the fundamental fight,
We are alone.
When we strip away the fatty slogans
And dig deep down into the marrow
Of our purpose
We are exiled.

When we challenge the stupor of tradition
And bare the real earth
With our weed-stained fists,
We are assassinated
In flesh
But not in meaning.

Response in the Caribbean

The Progressive Youth Organization, the youth section of the People's Progressive Party in Guyana, issued a statement that Malcolm's assassination had 'come as a great shock'. Malcolm, the Youth claimed, had been a 'courageous, honest and dynamic leader, bitterly opposed by US big business and by ineffectual Negro-American moderates in the civil rights battle...His approach was unconventional, vigorous and revolutionary...Malcolm X was the victim of the violence on which racism survives in the United States...The dignity and determination he has given to his people have provide d a firm foundation for victory. Malcolm X has not died in vain.'[10] I could not find a report of this statement in the *Guiana Graphic*, which carried the daily reports released by Reuters. In its Sunday issue for March 7th, the paper reproduced an interview by Spellman which had appeared in the *New World* (volume 9), to serve as an obituary. It calls Malcolm a revolutionary, 'the most brilliant representative of the new

---
10 *The Militant*, 22/3/1965, p.6.

American who sees that the struggle cannot be confined to America, who see themselves as potentially an integral part of the world revolutionary movement to break down the old barriers and systems imposed by a decadent Europe...Malcolm was perhaps the forerunner of a new era.'

In Jamaica, the assassination was front page news in the conservative *Daily Gleaner*. It printed a Reuters release, which, *inter alia*, stated that Malcolm had 'often advocated violence as a means of settling racial problems...'. There were some details of his past politics, some more accurate than others, but, as no details of his current politics were given, readers would have been left confused. The paper carried two more AP releases, but made no comment of its own.

The news of the assassination was on page one of the weekly political paper, *Public Opinion*, but there was no commentary.

In Trinidad, the daily Reuters reports were printed in the *Guardian* throughout February. On February 23rd, an editorial stated that,

> Malcolm personified the feeling that there is still discrimination, prejudice and the denial of civil rights...In the USA the technique used is judicial; in Indonesia, Algeria it is force...Islam has proved itself oblivious to colour...The circumstances which bred a Malcolm X ideology have to be eliminated before his death can mean an end to this grave national dispute. It is poor comfort that the assassin was African American and not white.

In the words of that great son of Trinidad, C.L.R. James, 'Malcolm X, [was a] great fighter whose potentialities were growing so fast that his opponents had to get rid of him by plain murder'.[11]

At the United Nations

The Special Committee on Colonialism, whose members were mainly from the 'Afro-Asian bloc' at the UN, continued its campaigns, putting in front of the General Assembly many of the issues Malcolm had spoken about, such as the Portuguese 'owned' territories, and in 1965 the British military action in Aden against protestors. At the end of 1965 the 'bloc' succeeded in transforming the *Declaration* for the Elimination of All Forms of Racial Discrimination into a *Convention*, which has more power. And during the ongoing debates on the Congo late in 1965 the United States was heavily criticised for its policies there and at home.[12]

---

11 'Black Power', transcript of a talk given in London in 1967, in Anna Grimshaw (ed), *The C.L.R. James Reader*, Oxford: Blackwell, 1992, p.367.

12 See UN General Assembly, *Official Records*, 1964 - 1965.

Forty and More Years Later

That Malcolm X had a profound effect on many of the people he had met is amply demonstrated by the powerful recollections published decades after his death.

Some of the publications give us an indication of ongoing confusions about this remarkable man and the evolution of his attitudes, analyses, philosophies; some others are more insightful.

For example, the *London Times* published an article, 'Malcolm X's terrible legacy' on 13 November 1992, just before the release of the film on Malcolm by Spike Lee. It is a very confused article, conflating Malcolm's pronouncements over many years and thus unable to acknowledge that at least some people can rethink their ideology, their philosophy, their politics. For example, the article charges that Malcolm advocated 'racial intolerance', but admits that Malcolm had said, 'I have made sweeping indictments of all white people. I never will be guilty of that again.' A recent survey had apparently found that 84% of 'young American blacks regard Malcolm X as a "hero"'.

William Sales' book, *From Civil Rights to Black Liberation*, published in 1994, carried what I think are useful assessments of Malcolm's travels in Africa: 'the most useful aspect of Malcolm X in Africa was that he presented other views than what was propounded by the United States Information Service...only from Malcolm X did the militant leadership group receive a briefing on US racial situation in a language immediately recognizable to them.' (pp.104, 124) Sales then questions whether Malcolm was beginning to 'approve' socialism, as he had noted that many African leaders had moved from capitalism to socialism. (p.86)

A few years later, another British national newspaper, *The Independent* (8 March 2002), published an article by Diran Adebayo, entitled 'A hero who gave black people an enduring legacy'. Adebayo talks about the

> reason for his endurance as an icon...Malcolm X and his allies wrested control of black American politics – and therefore black politics throughout the Western diaspora – away from those who espoused the Christian-dominated softly-softly approach... He established the legitimacy of a more robust response to racial injustices...In the last year of his life he moved to an understanding that the lack of respect shown to blacks in America was part of a wider disrespect to people of colour throughout the world.

Cameron Duodu, who had met Malcolm in Ghana in 1964, had an article published in the *New African* (May 2005) a London-based paper which circulates in West Africa. Entitled 'Malcolm X when he came to Ghana', the article begins with,

> I cannot believe that it is already 40 years since Malcolm X, the African-American civil rights leader, died. But it is true – he was gunned down on 21 February 1965, as he addressed a meeting in the Audubon Ballroom in Manhattan, New York. He had attained worldwide fame at the time of his death. Yet he was only 39 years old. What could he have achieved had he been allowed to live longer? Personally, I am still traumatised by Malcolm's murder. For in May 1964 – a few months before he died – he had been my luncheon guest at my home in Accra, Ghana.

The article ends with:

> Whatever the truth about his murder, there is no doubt that, in death, Malcolm X has achieved almost as much as if he were alive, or probably more than he could have achieved. From baseball caps and T-shirts marked "X", worn by the 'cool' youngsters of America and the world, to films by Spike Lee and others, the Malcolm X brand is one that just keeps growing and growing, year after year. His explanation of why he called himself "X" – because he said his surname was an "unknown factor", taken not from his ancestors' names but from that of his ancestors' slave masters – still makes perfect sense to the youth of today.
>
> Would Condoleezza Rice or Colin Powell have gotten their positions in the American government if Malcolm X had never lived? We cannot know. What is indisputable is that, even though he lived in an age when there was neither CNN nor the internet, Malcolm X reached so many people with his simple message that we can only marvel at what he achieved.[13]

Mr. Duodo was also one of the many people who objected to an article in the *Guardian* (19/5/2005, G2) headed 'Malcolm X – gay black hero. On Malcolm X's 80th birthday, Peter Tatchell reveals the hidden gay past of the American nationalist leader.'[14] In his letter published two days later, Mr. Duodu pointed out that Malcolm X engaged in homosexual acts in his

---

13 Mr Duodo told me that he had written the article 'Mainly from memory. I wrote about what he said at Legon in a 1964 edition of the [Ghana] Drum Magazine'. (email 16/7/2008)

14 One can think of many reasons for the *Guardian* publishing such an article,: to increase its readership? To stir up controversy?. Whatever the reason, I agree with Akinti – it was a gross insult to commemorate Malcolm's birthday in such a way.

youth. 'But that would relate only to Malcolm Little, not Malcolm X. Once he converted to Islam in prison...he would have regarded homosexuality – rightly or wrongly – as a "sin".' (p.21) On the 26th, the paper published a long article by Peter Akinti, who was clearly as angered as the letter-writers had been: 'Malcolm X insulted. Last week Peter Tatchell outed Malcolm X. To mark the great man's 80th birthday in this way was an insult'. Akinti writes that,

> we don't know where Malcolm X's political, spiritual or moral journey would have ended...Malcolm X will always stand out among the greatest of men...Malcolm remains a serious political figure...We remember him always for occupying himself with one thing throughout his short political life. One thing steadfast and unquestionable: the liberation of blacks, all blacks, by any means... That's the beauty of Malcolm X. He pushed the acceptable limits of black political thought.[15]

The BBC also marked the fortieth anniversary of Malcolm's assassination in its 'On This Day 21 February 1965' program, quoting the original notice of the assassination of the 'controversial black leader... who once called for a 'blacks-only' state in the US'. *Q News*, a 'Muslim Magazine' devoted its February 2005 issue to Malcolm.

On Jan 23, 2005 Kharl Daley, a Jamaican now living in Canada, published an article entitled 'El Hajj Malik El Shabazz (Malcolm X)' on a website for expatriate Jamaicans.[16] He had seen a poster of an unknown Black man in a park in Kingston in 1962; intrigued by the face, he went to the library to find out more. His article concludes that,

> One can never under-mine the achievements of Malcolm X; a devout Muslim whose teachings were laden with references to the faith of Islam. A self educated man who after dropping out of school from grade seven, reformed himself while in prison to gain the respect of scholars, statesmen and leaders all over the world. He debated at some of the world's most prestigious learning institutions, Oxford University and Harvard Law Forum and travelled to Kenya and all over Africa and the Middle East to meet Kings and Dignitaries and fellow Comrades in the fight for Human Justice and Black Unity. *'To have been in prison is no big stick, to remain is'*, he would later tell a gathering. We must never forget that in 1984 the government of Iran issued a stamp commemorating Malcolm X on the Universal Day of the Struggle Against Race Discrimination. Today there are many

---

15 Peter Akinti, London-born of Nigerian parentage, is a law graduate, a journalist, the founder of the short-lived *Untold* magazine and a novelist (*Forest Gate*, published 2006).

16 www.jamaicans.com/articles/primecomments/malcolmx.shtml

books, movies and documentaries written about Malcolm X and we all owe it to ourselves to scatter this seed of our beloved plant and as Malcolm X once stated, *'Of all our studies history will best reward us for our research'*.

Also in 2005 the British *Socialist Worker* published a 'special Malcolm X supplement'. This consisted of a long summary of his life, a brief article by Cheryl Garvey, in which she explained that for her, 'as someone working in the contemporary world of race equality, Malcolm X continues to be an inspiration, a relevant and meaningful reference'. Then there is another long article 'Malcolm X: an inspiration to Muslims struggling for justice' by Dr. Adnan Siddiqui:

> Historically when Muslims strived for social justice and civil societies, their 'reward' was imprisonment or death. Yet they persisted. Malcolm's struggle personified this and is an inspiring example for us all. His role as a preacher who practised what he preached and did not fear authority stands in stark contrast to the 'scholars for dollars' that tend to populate our mosques, who read scripted sermons authorised and cleared by the government...First, he was a human with human failings...Malcolm left the Nation of Islam after performing his pilgrimage to Mecca and realising its reality. He was humble enough to accept his error, but brave enough to face the consequences of such a public withdrawal from the Nation...After Malcolm's withdrawal from the Nation, he became more inclusive to people and movements. This would have allowed a greater cooperation with Dr. King – which would have posed a real danger to the establishment...Both understood the struggle and paid with their lives...[17]

The British *Guardian,* in its 'This week in 1968' column on 3 April 2006, focuses on the murder of Martin Luther King, but ends with: 'You pass the corner of Seventh Avenue and 125th Street, where Malcolm X used to preach. Malcolm, dead Malcolm, is the only one they speak of now with the same respect they always accorded the live Martin.'

---

17 Dr Siddiqui is a neurosurgeon and very active political campaigner on many human rights issues.

CONCLUSION

So books and articles continue to appear and websites on Malcolm multiply. He has become an icon for the young, now wearing T-shirts embossed with his face.

Malcolm's long conversations with African and other leaders, with writers and intellectuals in Africa and in the African diaspora in Paris and Britain, with Muslim philosophers, with the many 'ordinary' people and students throughout Africa, in Beirut, in Paris and Britain, clearly had an enormous influence on him. His own influence is world-wide and lives on. As he said many times, his philosophy was evolving. We have to respect that and read his final words carefully. The BBC, quoted above, clearly does not.

Working on this fairly superficial account of Malcolm's travels, raises some political questions for me:

Are readers grappling with Malcolm's condemnation of 'dollarism', which can be interpreted both as 'consumerism' and also as the power of money to 'purchase' people and governments?[18] This is sometimes called international 'aid'.

Do the followers come to grips with Malcolm's growing analyses of the new forms of imperialism, today often labelled 'globalisation'?

Do they engage with his growing espousal of socialism as a way to overcome the racial and other ravages of capitalism?

How many in the world's conflicting and conflicted religions are debating what Malcolm had said about the role of religion: 'It's true we are Muslims and our religion is Islam but we don't mix our religion with our politics and our economics and our social and civic activities – not any more'.[19]

It seems to me that Malcolm's developing analyses are as pertinent – and possibly even more urgent – than they were forty and more years ago.

My 'shining prince' – thank you!

---

18 Among the recipients of this 'dollarism' must have been, I presume, the many who gave information on Malcolm to the FBI/CIA.

19 Quoted in Kevin Ovenden, *Malcolm X: Socialism and Black Nationalism*, London: Book Marks 1992, p.39.

BIBLIOGRAPHY*

* Only for publications from which quotations have been taken.

Hakim Adi & Marika Sherwood, *The 1945 Manchester Pan-African Congress Revisited*, London: New Beacon Books 1995

Abdul Alkalimat (ed), *Perspectives on Black Liberation and Social Revolution*, Chicago: Twenty-first Century Books 1990

Maya Angelou, *All God's Children Need Travelling Shoes*, London: Virago 1987

Tariq Ali, *Street Fighting Years* (1987), New York: Citadel Press 1991

William Attwood, *The Reds and the Blacks: a personal adventure*, New York: Harper & Row 1967

The Autobiography of Malcolm X, as told to Alex Haley, New York: Ballantine Books 1965

Nelson Blackstock, *Cointelpro*, New York: Vintage Books 1976

William Blum, *The CIA: a forgotten history*, London: Zed Books 1986

George Breitman (ed), *Malcolm X Speaks*, New York: Grove Press 1966

George Breitman (ed), *The Last Year of Malcolm X*, New York: Schocken Books 1968

George Breitman (ed), *By Any Means Necessary*, New York: Pathfinder Press 1970

Jimmy Booker, 'Real Malcolm X', *N.Y. Amsterdam News* 27/3/1965, p.11

Peter Calvocoressi, *World Politics Since 1945*, London: Longman (1968) 1991

Jan Carew, *Ghosts in Our Blood*, Chicago: Lawrence Hill Books 1994

Steve Clark (ed), *February 1965: The Final Speeches*, New York: Pathfinder 1992

John Henrik Clarke, *Malcolm X: the man and his times*, Toronto: Macmillan 1969

Harold Cruse, *The Crisis of the Negro Intellectual*, New York: William Morrow & Co. 1967

Ossie Davis & Roby Dee, *With Ossie and Ruby*, New York: William Morrow 1998

Larry Devlin, *Chief of Station, Congo*, New York: Public Affairs 2007

Archie Epps (ed), *The Speeches of Malcolm X at Harvard*, New York: William Morrow 1968

E.U. Essien-Udom, *Black Nationalism: the rise of the Black Muslims in the USA*, (1962 Harmondsworth: Penguin Books 1966

Karl Evanzz, *The Judas Factor*, New York: Thunder Mouth Press 1992

Michel Fabre, *the Unfinished Quest of Richard Wright*, Urbana: University of Illinois Press 1993

Michel Fabre & Robert E. Skinner, *Conversations with Chester Himes*, Jackson: University Press of Mississippi 1995

James Farmer, *Lay Bare the Heart: An Autobiography of the Civil Rights Movement*, New York: Arbor House 1985

Kevin K. Gaines, *American Africans in Ghana*, University of North Carolina Press 2006

David Gallen (ed), *Malcolm X As They Knew Him*, New York: Carroll & Graf 1992

Peter Goldman, *The Death and Life of Malcolm X* (1973) Urbana: University of Chicago Press 1979

David Goldsworthy, *Tom Mboya: the man Kenya wanted to forget*, Nairobi & London: Heinemann Educational 1982

Chester Himes, *My Life of Absurdity*, New York: Thunder's Mouth Press 1976

LeRoy Hodges, *Portrait of an Expatriate*, Westport: Greenwood Press 1985

Derek Humphrey & David Tindall, *False Messiah: the story of Michael X*, London: Hart-Davis 1977

R. L. Jenkins & M.D. Tryman, *The Malcolm X Encyclopaedia*, Westport: Greenwood Press 2002

Benjamin Karim, *Remembering Malcolm*, New York: Cassell & Graf 1992

Leslie Lacy, 'African Responses to Malcolm X', in L. Jones & L. Neal, *Black Fire*, New York: William Morrow & Co. 1968

Leslie Lacy, *The Rise and Fall of a Proper Negro*, New York: Macmillan 1970

John Lewis, *Walking with the Wind*, San Diego: Harvest Book 1998

Louis E. Lomax, *The Reluctant African*, New York: Harper & Bros. 1960

Louis E. Lomax, *To Kill a Black Man*, Los Angeles: Holloway House 1968

Hugh MacDiarmid, *The Company I've Kept*, London: Hutchinson 1966

Ras Makonnen (edited by Kenneth King), *Pan Africanism from Within*, Nairobi: OUP 1973

Malcolm X, 'We are All Blood Brothers', *Liberator*, July 1964, pp.4-6.

Malcolm X Talks to Young People, (1965) New York: Pathfinder 1992

Malcolm X, *The Final Speeches*, New York: Pathfinder 1992

Michael Abdul Malik, *From Michael de Freitas to Michael X*, London: Andre Deutsch 1968

Jay Mallin (ed), *Che Guevara on Revolution*, Coral Gables: University of Miami Press 1969

Carlos Moore, *Castro, the Blacks and Africa*, Los Angeles: UCLA 1988

Edward Margolies & Michel Fabre, *The Several Lives of Chester Himes*, Jackson: University Press of Mississippi 1997

Kofi Natambo, *The Life and Work of Malcolm X*, Indianapolis: Pearson Education 2002

Kwame Nkrumah, *Neo-Colonialism: the last state of imperialism*, New York: International Publishers 1965

Eric Norden, 'The Murder of Malcolm X', *The Realist*, #73, February 1967, pp.4-13

Oginga Odinga, *Not Yet Uhuru*, London: Heinemann 1967

Fred I.A. Omu, *Press and Politics in Nigeria 1880-1937*, Atlantic Highlands: Humanities Press 1978

Bruce Perry, *Malcolm*, Barrytown, NY: Station Hill 1991

Carol Polsgrove, *Divided Minds: Intellectuals and the Civil Rights Movement*, New York: W.W. Norton & Co. 2001.

Ramparts editors, 'The CIA as an Equal Opportunity Employer', *Ramparts*, vol. 17, #3, June 1969, pp. 24-33

William A. Sales, *From Civil Rights to Black Liberation*, Boston: South End Press 1994

Ed Smith, *Where to, Black Man?*, Chicago: Quadrangle Books 1967

Joe Wood (ed), *Malcolm X: In our own image*, New York: St. Martin's Press 1992

ACKNOWLEDGEMENTS

Without archivists historians could not do their work.

I am, as so often in the past, hugely indebted to Diana Lachatanere, André Elizée and the other archivists at the Schomburg Center's Manuscript Division. Also to Peter Filardo and his co-workers at the Tamiment Library Archives of New York University; and to Mandy Banton at the Public Record Office in London, for help with the fruitless search in British government files.

I must thank Dr. Walter Hill of the National Archives in Washington for sending me material from the State Department files. Jennifer Cuddeback of the Lyndon B. Johnson Library and Museum searched the holdings there for me. The staff at the British Library's newspaper division fetched endless material for me: thank you.

Thanks to Josef Keith, the Friends' Library, London; Pamela Ripley at ETSU; Kevin Gaines and Margaret Busby for help with tracing various people. And to Paul Lee, for his many helpful criticisms and forwarded material.

For information of Pio Gama Pinto, thanks to Cornel DaCosta and Shiraz Durrani.

Thanks to Samar Mikati Kaissi, Special Collections Librarian at the American University of Beirut, for the copy of the articles in the Beirut Daily Star.

Other helpers are thanked in the footnotes.

Last, because they are so crucial, my profound thanks to the people who granted me interviews or sent written recollections: Abdullah Abdur-Razzaq; Kojo Amoo-Gottfried, Lindsay Barrett, Jan Carew, Dylan Dalton, Cameron Duodu, Richard Gibson, Shirley Joshi, Avtar Jouhl, Preston King, Dr Robert Lee, Tom McGrath, Carlos Moore, Robert Moore, Gamal Nkrumah, Judith Okely, Ebrahimsa Mohamed, Hoossain Rajah, David Roussel-Milner, Peter Worsley and Yaki.

Without the hospitality provided by my friends Susan Hauser and Ulrike Bernhardt in New York and Alcione Amos in Washington I would not have been able to do this work.

Finally thanks to my son Craig Sherwood for all his help.

Thank you all.
Marika Sherwood

The photographs are from:

Hoossain Rajah; *Nairobi Sunday Post*, 15/11/1964; *Tanganyika Standard* 13/10/1964; *Magnet*; LSE's *Beaver*, 18/1/1965; University of Sheffield's *Darts*, 19/12/1964; William Strickland, *Malcolm X: Make It Plain*, New York: Penguin Books, 1994.

Thank you.

INDEX

A
Abdullah, Said 92
Abdur-Razzaq, Abdullah 15, 17
Abrahams, Eric Anthony 151
Abu Bakr El Sadiq Conference (Egypt) 91
Abu Bekr Sediz Campus (Egypt) 91
Accra (Ghana) 28, 30, 32-33, 36, 38, 42-43, 49, 50, 55, 57, 59-60, 63, 73, 88-89, 104, 116, 125-128, 130, 136, 224
Action Group (Nigeria) 26, 32, 150
Addis Ababa (Ethiopia) 9, 38, 73, 84, 94-95, 97, 105, 108, 113, 115, 118-119, 122, 136
Adebayo, Diran 223
Adebo, S.O. 26
Adi, Hakim 48, 184, 192, 209
African-Asian Solidarity Council (Egypt) 22
African Liberation Committee (of the OAU) 103
African National Congress 55, 190, 218
African Review (Ghana) 38, 39, 219
African Students Union (France) 144
African Student - University Socialist Review (Ghana) 219
African Union 40, 73
African Union of Journalists 40
Africa Unity House (London) 183, 192
Afro-American (Baltimore) 3, 6, 17, 20, 26, 29, 31, 38, 41-43, 47, 49, 52, 55, 57, 60-61, 70, 74-75, 78, 85, 89, 91, 107, 114-115, 119, 124, 128, 130, 145, 169, 170, 180, 184, 186-187, 189, 192, 210, 217, 220-221
Afro-Asian People's Solidarity Organisation 47
Afro-Shirazi Party (Zanzibar) 102
Ajala, Olabisi 119

Ajayi, Professor J.F. 27
Akinti, Peter 225
Alabama (USA) 190, 199-201
Al-Azhar University (Egypt) 90, 91
Alexandria (Egypt) 22-23, 88-90, 92
Algeria/Algiers 10-12, 25, 62-63, 73, 83, 108, 112, 116, 121, 133, 142, 157, 159, 183-184, 190, 222
Ali, Tariq 156-157, 229
All-African People's Conference (Ghana) 104, 110
All African Trade Union Federation 219
Allsop, Kenneth 162
Al-Sabban, Muhammad Surur 93
American Committee on Africa 59, 117
American Negro Leadership Conference 136
American Negro Leadership Conference (ANLC) 9, 10, 136-137
American Society for African Culture 10, 137, 174
American University 20
American University (Beirut) 20, 22, 233
Amoo-Gottfried, Kojo 12, 184, 192, 204, 209
Anderson, Ed 106, 107
Angelou, Maya 35, 37, 41, 45, 49, 56, 125, 127-229
Angola 42, 52, 75, 102, 190
Anim, Goodwin 119
Anim, G.T. 40
Anti-Apartheid Movement 152, 158
Arab League 18, 47, 93
Arab Observer (Cairo) 79, 87, 89
Arab Society (Manchester) 164
Arusha Declaration 103
Asian-African Peoples Solidarity Conference 22

Association of Ghanaian Journalists and Writers 42
Aswan (Egypt) 22-23, 93
Attwood, Ambassador William 112
Awad, Dr. 70
Awolowo, Obafemi 26
Azikiwe, Nnamdi (President, Nigeria) 26, 32, 123
Azzam, Abd al-Rahman 17, 18, 93
Azzam, Omar 18

B
Baako, Kofi 47
Babu, Abdulrahman Muhammad 87, 102, 104
Backlash (OAAU's paper) 91, 96
Baffoe, T.D. 40
Bailey, Kofi 127
Baldwin, James 211
Bamako 116
Bandung Conference 194, 207
Barrett, Carlton 144
Barry Gray Show (USA) 147
Bashir, Tahseen 12, 74
Basner, H.M. 57
Batsa, Kofi 40, 42
BBC (UK) 94, 140, 149, 153, 162, 199-200, 201-202, 225, 227
Beaver (LSE students' paper, London) 192, 195
Bechuanaland 94
Beirut (Lebanon) 15, 19-23, 83, 94, 99, 104, 227
Belafonte, Harry 58, 117, 132
Belgium 11, 79
Bella, Ahmed Ben (President, Algeria) 12
Bennett, US Consul (Lagos, Nigeria) 32
Bergus, Donald 82
Berkeley, Humphrey 152
Berlin (Germany) 25, 34, 98, 103
Bern (Switzerland) 187
Bethune, Lebert 143-144, 152, 189
Biafra (Nigeria) 26
Binagi, Lloyd A. 192
Birmingham (UK) 197, 199-202, 204
Blackstock, Nelson 68, 178
Boaten, F.E. 88
Bois, David Du 89
Booker, Jimmy 27, 37, 60
Borai, Zaki 74
Boswell (US Embassy, Cairo) 80-81
Boutiba, Mahmoud 12
Boutorra, Tewfik 12, 177
Brazzaville (Republic of Congo) 185
Brennan, Dan 158, 164
Britain/UK 3, 6, 10, 13, 19, 22, 25-26, 34, 41, 48, 51, 58, 62, 70, 79, 86, 93, 98, 100, 102-103, 107, 139, 149-150, 152, 156-159, 161, 163, 166, 170-171, 183, 185-186, 190-192, 194, 196-197, 201-202, 205, 211-212, 214, 218, 227
British National Party (BNP)/British Fascists 200
Britz, Daniel A. 59
By Any Means Necessary 6, 96, 189

C
Cairo (Egypt) 6, 15-18, 22-24, 26, 48, 63, 69, 71-74, 77, 79, 81-82, 84, 87-96, 102, 104-105, 111-112, 117, 133-134, 139-140, 147, 174, 184
Cairo (US Embassy) 77, 80, 82
Cambridge Student Union 152
Cape Blanca 62
Cardinale, Claudia 162
Carew, Jan 85, 86, 137, 157, 179, 191, 204, 207
Carney, Art 118
Casablanca Group 123
Casablanca (Morocco) 62-63, 73, 123, 131
Cassandra 200
Cassandra (columnist, UK) 200, 214
Castro, Fidel (President, Cuba) 11, 143
Chad 148
Chester, Lewis 203
Chicago Tribune (USA) 69, 70
'Chicken comes home to roost' 161
China 10, 23, 55, 58, 90, 93, 99, 103-105, 129, 140, 174
Chinese Ambassador (Ghana) 52, 55
Chinese News Agency (Ghana) 126
Chorlton-on-Medlock (UK) 158
CIA (Secret Service, USA) 9-10, 24, 31, 52, 71, 80-82, 85, 107, 111, 114, 128, 134-137, 142-144, 148, 171, 174, 188, 208, 216, 227
Civil Rights Bill/Act 70, 72, 76, 88, 101, 115-116, 122, 125, 127, 130, 148, 180, 202
Clarke, John Henrik 38, 55, 75, 89, 143, 181
Clark, Pauline 88

Clay, Cassius 9, 26-27, 109, 125, 135
Coker, H.T.O. 123
Coker, Increase 123
Cold War 10, 22-23, 25, 34-35, 83, 88, 103, 134
Collins, Ella 85
Columbia Daily Spectator (Columbia University, New York) 173
Columbia University (New York) 178, 207
Committee of African Organisations (CAO - UK) 183
Commonwealth Prime Ministers Conference 71
Commonwealth Prime Ministers Conference (UK) 71
Conakry (Guinea) 32, 61, 116, 131, 132
Conference of Non-Aligned States 95
Congo 2, 11, 39, 55, 58, 63, 76, 78-79, 86, 89, 95, 99, 103-104, 106, 126, 132, 144, 147-148, 152, 164-165, 173-178, 181, 185-186, 188, 193-194, 214, 222
Congress of Azania (South Africa) 55
Congress of Racial Equality (CORE - USA) 9, 135, 136
Conservative Parliamentary West Africa Committee (UK) 152
Constitutional Conference (Kenya) 98
Convention People's Party (CPP) 126
Convention People's Party (CPP - Ghana) 34, 59, 126
Cooper, Sam Paine 131
Corriere della Somalia 42, 52
Cuba 11-12, 35, 39, 58, 142-144, 156, 178, 186

D
DaCosta, Dr. Cornel 196
Dakar (Senegal) 25, 62-63, 116, 133
Daley, Kharl 225
Dalton, Dylan 191-192
Darden, Helen 39, 119
Dar-es-Salaam 70
Dar-es-Salaam (Tanzania) 70, 77, 80-81, 103, 105-108, 112-113, 115, 217
Darts (student newspaper, Sheffield, UK) 166, 168-170, 216
'Dateline' (ITV, UK) 153
Dathorne, O.R. 29
Davidson, Basil 183, 185
Davis, Bill 118
Davis, Chuck 144

Davis, Dr. Asa 90
Davis, Ossie 7, 67, 68
Debater, The (student newspaper, Sheffield, UK) 166
DeBerry, Clifton 68
Declaration for the Elimination of All Forms of Racial Discrimination (UN) 74, 222
Dee, Ruby 68
de Freitas, Michael 192, 196-197, 203, 204
Demerdash, Homeed 94
Denzer, La Ray 43
Detroit (USA) 5, 23, 31, 85, 86, 88
Diggs, Charles C. (Congressman, USA) 82
Diop, Alioune 88, 135, 139, 142
Diran Adebayo 223
Du Bois, David 77, 89
Du Bois, Shirley Graham 49, 127
Du Bois, W.E.B. 52
Duodu, Cameron 40-41, 44-45, 47-48, 126, 224

E
East African Standard (Kenya) 116
Economic Commission for Africa (UN) 95
Economist, The (UK) 213
Egypt 11-12, 15-16, 18, 22-23, 54, 70, 73-74, 81, 90-93, 108, 134, 160, 164, 168
Egyptian Gazette 237
Ein Champs University (Egypt) 92
El-Shubban Al-Muslimeed 90
Entralgo, Armando 39
Equator Club (Kenya) 99
Erveida, Dr Mohammed Teufie 91
Essien-Udom, Professor E.U. 26
Ethiopia 73, 93-95, 102, 105, 108, 117-119, 136, 217
Ethiopian Herald 217
European Common Market 189
Evers, Medgar 33

F
Faisal, Prince (Saudi Arabia) 18
Fanon, Frantz 63, 142
Farmer, James 9, 135-136
Farouk, King (Egypt) 22
Fattby, Muhammad 73
FBI (USA) 6, 9, 12, 15-16, 23, 28-29, 38, 49, 55, 59, 61, 66-67, 73, 83, 85, 90, 92, 94-95, 107-108, 113, 116, 122, 132,

140, 153, 171, 173, 175, 177, 187, 208, 227
Federation of African Students (France) 187
Federation of Islamic Students 202
Federation of Islamic Students Societies (FOSIS - UK) 167
Federation of Mohammedan Students' Societies (London) 140
Feinberg, Professor Ben 22
Final Speeches 194, 200-201, 211
Flamingo (UK) 211-212
Ford, Anna 163
France 3, 6, 10, 19, 22, 41, 51, 62, 63, 127, 131, 139, 140, 143, 182, 187-190, 205
Freedomways (USA) 149
Front Libération Nationale (FLN - Algeria) 63

G

Gabin, Sheikh Omar 72
Gaines, Kevin 36-37, 43, 49, 123
Galamison, Milton 175, 176
Gambia 137
Gardiner, Robert 95
Garvey, Cheryl 226
Garveyism 37
Geneva (Switzerland) 16, 121, 133, 134, 159, 160, 187
Ghana 10-12, 16, 25, 34-38, 40-45, 48-49, 51, 53, 55-60, 63-64, 68, 70, 72-73, 76, 88, 94, 103, 110, 116, 119, 121-124, 126-128, 130-131, 135, 137, 139, 148, 179, 181, 183-185, 190, 192, 194, 205, 219, 221, 224
Ghana (Parliament) 50
Gibson, Richard 50, 142, 189-190, 205
Goldman, Peter 2, 12, 16, 36, 96, 121, 136,
Goldwater, Barry 151
Gonzales, Armando Entralgo (Cuban Ambassador) 39
Goodman, George 84, 86, 87
Graham, Dr. Billy 170
Grant, Earl 15, 181
Gray, Jesse 175
Griffiths, Peter 197, 200-201
Guevara, Che 76, 127, 176-178
Guinea 11-12, 56, 58, 61, 73, 111-112, 117, 121, 122, 131-132, 148, 181, 185
Guyana 86, 221

H

Ha, Huang (Chinese Ambassador, Ghana) 52
Hajj 3, 8, 12, 15, 17, 19, 27, 47, 66, 78-79, 225
Handler, M.S. 69, 83, 86, 177, 181
Hansberry, Lorraine 68
Hansberry, William Leo 122
Harkan, Sheikh Muhammad 16
Harlem (New York) 5-6, 7, 9, 11-12, 31, 39, 48, 62, 64-65, 68, 74, 79, 87, 93, 104, 127, 142-143, 174-176
Harris, Donald 58
HARYOU 174
Hassoun, Shaykh Ahmed 93, 175
Havana (Cuba) 157, 177
Henry, Milton 80, 85
Himes, Chester 142, 144, 187-189
Hinds, Donald 200, 213
Hitler, Adolf (Chancellor, Germany) 110, 199
Holocaust (Jewish) 44-45
Homecoming Rally 94, 106, 109-110, 133, 147
Home Office (UK) 140, 152, 201
Hoover, J. Edgar 58, 153
Hotel Theresa (Harlem) 11, 39, 64, 143, 189
Howard University (USA) 123, 145
Humphry, Derek 192, 203
Hunton, Alphaeus 68

I

Ibadan (Nigeria) 26-27, 29-30, 38, 42, 90, 123
Iffeora, Joseph 31, 123
Igbo (Nigeria) 26, 123
Ige, Bola 32
Indian Workers' Association (IWA - UK) 197, 199
Ings, Nigel 216
Iran 225
Iraq 10, 18, 23, 54
Isis (Nile river boat, Egypt) 74, 80, 85, 88
Isis (student newspaper, Oxford) 150, 153
Islamic Circle (UK) 167, 169, 170, 216
Islamic Cultural Centre (UK) 160, 170, 196
Islamic University (Medina) 93
Israel 10, 19, 22, 37, 123, 164

J

Jamaica 222
James, C.L.R. 178, 222
Jedda (Saudi Arabia) 16-19, 93
Jeune Afrique (Tunis) 217
Johnson, Lyndon B. 147
Johnson, Lyndon B. (President, USA) 55, 59, 78, 128-129, 137, 148, 165
Joint Action Committee Against Racial Intolerance (UK) 150
Jones, Clarence 67
Jones, Claudia 68, 149-150, 183, 186, 191, 197, 213
Jordan, Colin 200
Joshi, Jagmohan 197

K

Kaid, Taher 53
Kaissi, Samar Mikati 233
Kambone, Oscar (Otimi) 107
Kano (Nigeria) 26, 36
Karefa-Smart, Francis 62
Karume, Abeid 102
Kaunda, Kenneth (President, Zambia) 106, 136
Kazeem, Dr. Mohammed 92
Kempton, Murray 214
Kennedy, John F. (President, USA) 2, 6, 42, 109, 131, 161, 169-170, 208, 215
Kenya 10, 88, 93, 97-102, 104, 106, 108, 109-117, 119, 122, 171, 178, 186, 225
Kenyatta, Jomo 112
Kenyatta, Jomo (President, Kenya) 57, 88, 98, 106, 110-112
Khalifa, Algerian Ambassador (in UK) 183
Khartoum (Sudan) 94
Khrushchev, Nikita (Premier, USSR) 23
Kikuyu (Kenya) 88, 98, 99
King, Delphine 125
King, Dr. Martin Luther 20-21, 116, 122, 154, 156, 159, 165, 170, 195, 202-203, 213, 217, 220, 226
King, Preston 39, 41-42, 57, 125, 233
Koinange, Mbiyu 104
Komtona, Phillipe 118
Korea 10, 35, 44
Ku Klux Klan 141, 199
Kunene, Raymond 183
Kuwait 93-94, 108
Kwabena 36, 47

Kwame Nkrumah Ideological Institute 144-145

L

Labour Party (UK) 198, 201, 214
Lacy, Leslie 37, 42, 48, 50-51, 57, 124, 126, 127
Lagos Morning Post 121, 188, 218
Lagos (Nigeria) 26-27, 31-33, 38, 57, 63, 70, 71, 74, 103, 116, 119, 121-123, 136, 188, 218
Land and Freedom Army/Mau-Mau (Kenya) 10, 98, 100
Latin America 176, 181, 210
League of Nations 103
Lebanon 19
Lee, Dr. Robert 39, 49, 128
Lee, Paul 12, 74, 86, 90, 92-93, 106, 109, 127, 168, 187, 191, 196
Lee, Spike 223
Legon 42
Legon (University of Ghana) 12, 34, 37, 42-45, 48-49, 51, 57, 60, 124, 184, 224
Leonard, Graham 21
Lewis, Claude 13, 31
Lewis, John 58, 111, 117, 126
Liberator (magazine, USA) 20, 37, 39, 50, 122, 124
Liberia 62, 73, 121-122, 130-131, 134, 185
Logan Act (USA) 83, 116
London 8, 10,-1, 32, 48, 60, 63, 69-71, 73, 79, 81, 84-86, 88, 94, 98, 99, 104-105, 110-114, 119, 123, 134-135, 139, 142-143, 150-151, 153, 155, 157-160, 162, 168, 170-171, 174, 177, 183-184, 187-192, 194, 196-197, 200-201, 204-205, 207, 209-213, 215, 222-225, 227, 229-231, 233
London School of Economics (LSE) 157, 191-192, 200, 205, 212, 215
Lumumba, Patrice (Prime Minister, Republic of Congo) 2, 11, 39, 52, 60, 63, 78-79, 99, 126, 144, 159, 175, 194, 207, 210, 212, 219
Luo (Kenya) 98
Lutterodt, William 186
Luxor (Egypt) 93

M

Maa'moun, Hassan 92
MacDiarmid, Hugh 151

Maduekwe, Ebele 166
Magliozzi, Francis N. 52
Magnet (magazine, UK) 189, 191, 199, 211
Mahmoud, Khalil 89
Mahoney, William (US Ambassador, Ghana) 35-36, 59, 128
Makonnen, Ras T 48, 125, 139
Malaysian Islamic Study Group (UK) 170
Mali 47, 56, 70, 73, 131, 181, 185
Mallallah, Kadim 216
Malley, Simon 217
Manchanda 191
Manchester (UK) 48, 157-166, 168, 212-213, 216
Mandela, Nelson 52, 154, 190, 202
Mao Tze-Tung (Head of State, China) 55
Marshall Street (Smethwick, UK) 198-199, 201
Martin, Abram V. 30
Marxism/Marxist 37, 42, 46, 57, 59, 64, 105, 112, 129, 131, 166, 179
Marxist Forum (Ghana) 46, 57, 59
Masai (Kenya) 98
Masha, Alhaji A.F. 31
Masha, H.E. 70
Mauritania 54
Mayfield, Julian 38, 39, 40, 48, 57, 88, 125, 143, 181, 205, 219
Mboya, Tom 88, 100, 109-111, 114
McGrath, Tom 195-196, 215
McHardy, Miss Cecil 48
Meagher, John (US Consul, Nigeria) 27-29
Mecca (Saudi Arabia) 3, 6, 12, 15-17, 19, 21, 66, 70, 79, 91, 93-94, 140, 175, 226
Medina (Saudi Arabia) 70, 93
Metropolitan Police (UK) 71, 139-140, 153, 186, 201, 204
MI5 (Secret Service, UK) 71, 109, 139, 204
Militant, The (USA) 3, 11, 19, 33, 64-65, 68, 75, 114, 144, 148, 153, 176, 177-180, 211, 216-217, 221
Mississippi Freedom Democratic Party 176
Mississippi (USA) 86, 101, 142, 176, 177, 181
Mogadiscio (Somalia) 52
Mohamed, Ebrahimsa 159, 166, 170, 192
Mombasa (Kenya) 109, 196
Monrovia (Liberia) 25, 62, 130

Monthly Review (New York) 140
Moore, Carlos 39, 50, 142-144, 176-178, 187, 189, 211
Moore, Dr. Robert 202
Morocco 25, 54, 62, 63, 73
Mosley, Sir Oswald 158
Movement for Colonial Freedom (UK) 104
Mozambique 102, 106, 190
Mphahlele, Ezekiel 84, 86
Muhammad, Elijah 1-2, 5-6, 15, 26-27, 170, 213
Muhammad Speaks 6, 15
Mungai, Dr. Njoroge 111
Muslim Youth Association 90
Muslim Brotherhood (Egypt) 48, 134, 160
Muslim Mosque Inc. (USA) 17, 68, 72, 92, 141, 150, 178, 180
Muslim World League 93, 160
Muthu, Eliud 97

N
NAACP (USA) 136
Nairobi (Kenya) 10, 48, 57, 81, 94, 98-102, 105-110, 112-117, 119, 121, 131, 136, 217-218
Nasr-al-Din, M. Fathi 89
Nasser, Gamal Abdel (President, Egypt) 11, 127
Natambo, Kofi 63, 231
National Council of Nigeria and Cameroons (NCNC) 30
Nationalist, The (Tanzania) 102, 107-108, 112, 218
National Liberation Front (NLF, Algeria) 11, 221
Nation of Islam (NOI) 1-2, 5-6, 11, 15-17, 33, 38, 64, 68, 74, 79, 125, 141, 157, 164, 168, 178, 208, 226
Neguib, General Mohamed (President, Egypt) 22
Nehru, Jawaharlal (Prime Minister, India) 100
New African (Ghana) 40-41, 45, 48, 181, 224
Newsweek (USA) 23, 33, 104, 106
Nigeria 16, 24-26, 28, 30, 32-33, 36, 60, 66, 72-73, 86, 89-90, 118-119, 121-124, 134, 136, 192-193, 218
Nketsia, Nana Kobina 67
Nkrumah, Kwame (President, Ghana) 11,

34-36, 38, 49-53, 57, 59-60, 128-129, 131, 145, 219
Norden, Eric 24, 85, 188
Notting Hill (UK) 177, 196
N.Y. Amsterdam News (USA) 27, 37, 39, 175, 229
Nyerere, Julius (President, Tanzania) 76, 84, 102-103, 105-106, 109, 115, 136
Nye, Victoria 39

O
OAAU, Information Bureau 55, 89, 124
OAAU (Organization of Afro-American Unity) 3, 6, 15, 17, 33, 38, 47, 55, 61, 65-67, 72, 74-76, 80, 88-89, 91, 96, 104, 106, 110, 122, 124, 144-145, 147-148, 150, 165, 168, 173-181, 186, 202-205, 210, 212, 214
OAU (Organisation of African Unity) 6, 9, 17, 47, 55, 66-67, 69, 72-73, 76-77, 79-82, 84, 86, 88-89, 91, 96, 103-104, 107, 111, 113, 118-119, 127-128, 131, 134, 148
OAU's Liberation Committee 107, 134
Obote, Milton (President, Uganda) 106, 109
Observer, The (UK) 88, 212
Odinga, Oginga (Vice-President, Kenya) 98-100, 110, 231
Odongo, Okello 178
Okely, Judith 155, 233
Omayad, Mr (Ghana Embassy, New York) 36
Orubu, Ben 32
Osman, Omar 16
Oxford (UK) 7, 11, 72, 150-154, 156-157, 159, 161, 171, 213, 216, 222, 225

P
Padmore, George 48, 76, 104
Pakistan 11, 23, 52, 100, 158, 167
Pakistan Welfare and Information Centre (UK) 158
Palestine 21-22, 164
Pan-African/Pan-Africanism 28-29, 36, 37, 40, 48-50, 99, 144, 148, 158, 186, 229
Pan-African Student Union (USA) 148
Pan-African Union of Journalists 40
Pan-African World Pioneers (UK) 186

Paris (France) 13, 50, 59, 63, 121, 127, 133-135, 139-140, 142-145, 152, 174, 183, 185, 187-191, 201, 211, 227
Parker, Clarence 131
Parker, Mark 33
Parkinson, Michael 160
Peace Corps 29, 32, 64, 94, 174, 193
Peace News (UK) 186, 195, 213
Peking (China) 99, 104
Pinto, Pio Gama 233
Pittsburgh Courier (USA) 84, 202
Poitier, Sidney 67
Port Said (Egypt) 90, 92
Portugal 51-52, 102
Powell, Colin 224
'Power in Defense of Freedom is Greater than Power in Behalf of Tyranny' 179
Présence Africaine (France) 88, 134-135, 142
Press Club (Ghana) 40, 42, 52, 56, 124, 126, 219
Progressive Youth Organization (Guyana) 221
Public Opinion (Jamaica) 222

Q
Qidwai, Dr. Ahmed 202
Q News (UK) 225
Quaison-Sackey, Alex 11-12, 148

R
Racial Preservation Society (UK) 199
Rackham, Neil 168, 216
Rajah, Hoossain 159, 161-162, 164, 166, 233-234
Ramadan, Dr. Said 134, 159, 160
Randolph, A. Phillip 67
Realist, The (USA) 24, 188, 231
Redbrick (Birmingham student paper, UK) 202
Reisel, Victor 82
Révolution Africaine (France) 217
Rice, Condoleezza 224
Ring, Harry 180
Robeson, Paul 152
Robinson, Basil 186
Rome (Italy) 73, 143
Roper, Professor Hugh Trevor 149
Roussel-Milner, David 191
Rusk, Dean 83, 128, 190

S

Sadat, Anwar (Vice-President, Egypt) 15
Sales, William 12, 223
Salle de la Mutualité (Paris) 144, 189
Saturday Evening Post (Kenya) 116
Saudi Arabia 18, 93-94, 108, 134, 180
Schechter, Dan 137
Scholefield, Alan 190
Seidman, Anne 76
Selassie, Emperor Haile (Ethiopia) 73, 95, 123, 136
Senegal 62, 73
Senghor, Léopold (President, Senegal) 73
Shabazz, Betty 118, 184, 210, 219
Shahey, Salah 167
Shawarbi, Dr. Mahmoud Youssef 12
Shawarbi, M. 26
Sheffield (UK) 159, 166-169, 216, 234
Shubban Al-Muslimeed 90
Siddiqui, Dr. Ghayasuddin U. 167
Sierra Leone 48, 62, 123
Simmons Jr., Jake 'Oklahoma' 122
Slave Trade/Slaves 142
Smethwick (UK) 151, 166, 197-203, 214
Smith, Ian (Prime Minister, Southern Rhodesia) 70, 107, 194
Smith, William Gardner 127, 219
Sobukane 52
Socialist Leader, The (UK) 213
Socialist Workers Party (SWP - USA) 39, 68, 178
Socialist Worker (UK) 226
South Africa 27, 36, 41-42, 48, 51-52, 55, 71, 75, 82, 84, 86, 88, 99, 102, 124, 149, 181, 183, 188, 190, 217-218
Southern Rhodesia 70, 107
Soviet...see USSR/Soviet Union/Russia 23
Spark, The (Ghana) 40, 130, 194, 219
Spear 124
Spectator, The (UK) 214
Spellman, A.B. 140
Stallibrass, Chloe 155
Stanleyville (Democratic Republic of the Congo) 177
Stevenson, Adlai (US Ambassador to the UN) 29
St. Lucia 191
Stonham, Lord 152
Strickland, William 175
Stubenbord, Dr and Mrs John George (Ship Hope) 133
Student Nonviolent Coordinating Committee (SNCC - USA) 58, 111, 117-118, 126, 132, 213
Students' Union of Poland 185
Sudan 16, 90, 175
Sudanese Cultural Center (Beirut) 20
Suez Canal 10, 22, 92
Suez Canal Authority Club 92
Sunday Express (Nigeria) 32-33, 71
Sunday Mirror (Ghana) 116
Sunday Post (Kenya) 116
Sunni Islam 6, 79, 161
Supreme Council for Islamic Unity (Cairo) 72
Supreme Council on Islamic Affairs (Egypt) 91
Switzerland 48, 134, 142
Syria 19, 23, 134, 164

T

Tafawa, Abubakar 26
Tanganyika Standard 70, 107, 108, 234
Tangi (Mr & Mrs) 123
Tanzania 77, 102-107, 110, 136, 175, 177
Tatchell, Peter 224
Telli, Diallo 12, 55, 73, 89, 111, 118, 132
Tema (Ghana) 126
Tettegah, John K. 88
Till, Emmett 33
Tolbert, William (Vice-President, Liberia) 131
Touré, Sékou 11, 58, 111-112, 117, 131-133
Trades Union Council (UK) 198
Trenchard Hall (Ibadan University) 29
Tribune (UK) 215
Tshombe, Moise (Prime Minister, Congo) 78, 81, 95, 123, 147-148, 152, 165, 174, 185-186
Tsiboe (Tzibo), Nancy 70
Tubman, William (President, Liberia) 131
Tunis/Tunisia 62, 217
Twi (Ghana) 56

U

Uddin, Nazir 161
Uganda 89, 97, 106, 109-110, 112, 113, 115

Uganda Argus 109, 112, 113, 115
Umma Party (Zanzibar) 87, 102
Umra (Pilgrimage) 93
Union of African Students in Europe 211
United Arab Republic/UAR 12, 23, 48, 73, 79, 87, 89, 126
United Nations Association 152
United Nations Commission on Human Rights 75
United Nations/UN 11-12, 16, 21-23, 26, 30-31, 36, 39, 41, 47, 48, 51, 58, 62, 64, 67-69, 70-77, 82-86, 89, 92, 95, 100, 102-103, 106, 115, 121, 127, 130, 132, 134, 141, 148, 152, 165, 173, 176-177, 181, 194, 222
United Republic of Tanganyika and Zanzibar (URTZ) 102, 107, 108
United States Information Service (USIS) 29, 64, 81, 110, 122, 135, 148, 217, 223
Universal Day of the Struggle Against Race Discrimination 225
Universal Declaration of Human Rights 74
University College of Addis Ababa 119
University of Cairo 12, 16
University of Ghana 37, 42, 44, 59, 124, 126, 192
University of Ibadan 26, 90
USA/United States 1, 3, 7-13, 15-16, 19-28, 31-36, 41-43, 49-52, 55, 57, 59-60, 62, 64-65, 68-72, 74-76, 78-86, 88-89, 93-95, 99-100, 102-103, 105-107, 110, 117, 119, 122-123, 127-128, 130, 134-137, 140-141, 147-148, 153, 165, 169-170, 173-174, 176-178, 180-181, 184, 186, 192-194, 197, 201, 203, 210, 214, 218-223
US Nazi Party 164
USSR/Soviet Union/Russia 10, 23, 25, 34-35, 83, 93, 99, 103, 111, 117, 137
Uwechwe, George 192

V
Verwoerd, Hendrik (Prime Minister, South Africa) 41
Vexhüll, Baron Jakob von 213
Vietnam 10, 44, 58, 156-157, 181, 188, 194, 214
Voice of Ethiopia 95, 105, 217

W
Wachuku, Jaja 30, 123
Wade, Aida 135
Wali, Alhaji Isa 52
Washington (USA) 23, 26, 32, 41, 53, 81, 85, 95, 105, 123, 128, 132, 145, 157, 174, 181
Welbeck, N.A. 126
West Indian Gazette (UK) 185-186, 191
West Indians in Britain 149, 158, 184, 194, 200, 204, 212
West Indians in Ghana 48
West Indian Standing Conference (UK) 200
'white devils' 1, 154
Wilford, Hugh 136
Wilkins, Roy 68
Willard, Ned 134
Williams, John Bell (Congressman, USA) 82
Wilson, Harold (Prime Minister, UK) 198
Windom, Alice 35, 38-39, 50, 56, 94, 118
Winneba/Winneba Ideological Institute 51
Wood, Victor 36
World Assembly of Youth 185
World Islamic League (Saudi Arabia) 134
World War I 19
World War II 44, 149, 157
Worsley, Professor Peter 162
Wright, Julia 41, 76, 88, 221
Wright, Richard 41, 59, 134, 142, 194, 230

Y
Yemen 12
Yoruba 26-27, 32, 66
Young Men's Muslim Association (Egypt) 90
Young Socialist Alliance (USA) 179
Young Socialist (USA) 6, 54, 179
Young, Whitney 67
'Your success is our success' 51

Z
Zanzibar 81, 87, 97, 102-105, 108-109, 112-113, 117
Zionism/Zionist 37, 164

www.ingramcontent.com/pod-product-compliance
Lightning Source LLC
Chambersburg PA
CBHW071707160426
43195CB00012B/1606